TRADING VOICES

TRADING VOICES

THE EUROPEAN UNION IN INTERNATIONAL COMMERCIAL NEGOTIATIONS

Sophie Meunier

PRINCETON UNIVERSITY PRESS

PRINCETON AND OXFORD

Library of Congress Cataloging-in-Publication Data

Meunier, Sophie.
Trading voices : the European Union in international commercial negotiations /
Sophie Meunier.
p. cm.
Includes bibliographical references and index.
ISBN-13: 978-0-691-12115-4 (cl. : alk. paper)
ISBN-10: 0-691-12115-X (cl. : alk. paper)
1. European Union countries—Commerce. 2. European Union countries—
Foreign economic relations. 3 Negotiation—European Union. I. Title.
HF3496.5.M48 2005
382′.91—dc22   2004058459

British Cataloging-in-Publication Data is available

This book has been composed in Sabon

Printed on acid-free paper.∞

pup.princeton.edu

Printed in the United States of America

10   9   8   7   6   5   4   3   2   1

To Yacine, Idir and Ines

Contents

List of Tables and Figures

Preface

THIS BOOK is about the external consequences of combining forces with others. It shows that the requirement for the members of the European Union (EU) to have a common trade policy and defend it on the world stage with a single voice has affected the outcomes of international commercial negotiations. It finds, however, that the level of institutional unity in Europe is not positively correlated with its external bargaining power. Ironically, this is not at all why I designed this research project in the first place. As an enthusiastic Europhile college student in France in the run-up to "Europe 1992" and the completion of the single European market, I set out to study the external effects of European integration from the other side of the Atlantic. What I had hoped to prove was that the stronger the institutional ties within Europe, the stronger Europe's collective voice, and therefore the more member states would want to reinforce Europe's institutional ties. After a few years of research on this topic for my Ph.D. dissertation at the Massachusetts Institute of Technology, I had to abandon my "militant" stance and instead settle for a different, more nuanced conclusion.

At MIT my dissertation advisor was Suzanne Berger. I do not even know where to start to acknowledge the profound influence that she has had on me, from both a scholarly and a personal perspective. A mentor and a model, she taught me so much, from how to construct an argument to how to pick a research topic, from emphasizing the role of domestic factors on international politics to trusting that the study of Europe was still interesting, that I feel deeply indebted to her. I am trying to repay some of that debt by, willingly or not, working on research that increasingly bears her mark. As a counterbalance to the strong pull of comparative politics over the project, Kenneth Oye offered many suggestions as to how to ground the topic into the international relations literature and provided invaluable comments on my dissertation, as well as many useful insights into the profession. Finally, I was lucky enough to count Stanley Hoffmann as one of my advisors, which was an immense privilege and honor, especially for a French scholar.

I took the familiar advice that one should let the dissertation rest for a little while before turning it into a book a little too literally. Indeed, I quickly moved onto a different research topic (the study of globalization) and wrote my second book before I wrote my first—*The French Challenge: Adapting to Globalization*. Fortunately, by the time I came back to the study of the external impact of Europe's move toward institutional unity, the EU was still negotiating trade agreements with one voice; deepening and widening were making the issue even more difficult than before; and no one else had published a book on the subject! Even as the present book goes to press, it is clear that the topic is not about to become irrelevant, as the difficult negotiations in the Doha Development Round of the World Trade Organization, the contentious debates surrounding the ratification of the EU Constitution, and the elusive creation of a real common foreign policy seem to demonstrate.

I am grateful to John Keeler, Alberta Sbragia, and two anonymous reviewers for reading the entire manuscript and offering helpful suggestions, as well as to Jean-Francois Brakeland of the EU Commission for his thorough, legalistic, and quick-as-lightning yet very detailed comments on the whole book. I also thank Christina Davis, Jeffry Frieden, Maria Green Cowles, Andrew Moravcsik, Pascal Riché, and Martin Staniland for their comments on specific chapters. I am particularly indebted to two friends and colleagues who have shared their enthusiasm for the EU over the years as well as their enthusiasm for France, food, and family. Karen Alter, whom I met on our first day at MIT, was the co-author of the first article I ever wrote and presented at an academic conference. Not surprisingly, she was also the first reader of this manuscript. For this, as well as our friendship, I am very thankful. Kalypso Nicolaïdis has also played a big role in the development of my thinking on EU trade policy. We co-authored many pieces on this topic (after five, we stopped counting) and challenged each other into understanding the politics of complex, often unintelligible legal distinctions with respect to European trade competence. I am grateful for this collaboration, which, judging by the numerous projects in which we recently agreed to participate, is far from over. I also thank the many U.S. and EU officials whom I interviewed over the years, including former Commission president Jacques Delors and former EU Trade Commissioner Pascal Lamy. As is customary, all remaining errors are, of course, mine alone. Finally, I thank Duncan Alford, the EU librarian at Princeton University, as well as the librarians at the John F. Kennedy Presidential Library, who helped me navigate some of the archives of the Kennedy Round of GATT.

The various stages of this book were completed in different places, and I am grateful to the institutions and individuals who made this possible. The MIT political science department was a wonderfully challenging yet nurturing place to be introduced to political science, and my gratitude goes to my teachers as well as to my fellow students. The Minda de Gunzburg Center for European Studies at Harvard University was an exciting institution to be part of, but so much was constantly going on there that it proved hard to get any work done! The Program on International Politics, Economics and Security, in particular Charles Lipson, welcomed me at the University of Chicago, which enabled me to complete my dissertation. And Princeton University has been a wonderful home ever since, thanks in large part to the defunct Center of International Studies and its director Michael Doyle; to its successor the Princeton Institute of International and Regional Studies and its director Miguel Centeno; to the Woodrow Wilson School and its dean Anne-Marie Slaughter; and to all my engaging colleagues and dynamic students. Finally, I wish to acknowledge the European Union Studies Association (EUSA), an association dedicated to the study of European integration worldwide. Thanks to its many grants, conferences, and publications, I was able to find an echo for my work and meet devoted colleagues and friends.

Most importantly, my deepest, most loving thanks go to my husband Yacine Ait-Sahalia, who makes academia in particular and life in general seem so easy, and to our children, Idir and Ines, who do not know much about European commercial policy but have taught me a lot about trades and bargaining. It is to them that I dedicate this book.

TRADING VOICES

Introduction ────────────────────────────────

Let's unite. And the world will listen to us.

— Pro-European ad campaign, September 1992

THE EUROPEAN UNION (EU), the world's largest trader and a heavyweight in the international political economy, is not an easy bargainer to deal with. The complex, unusual, often unintelligible nature of the European "beast" has left many foreign negotiators perplexed: if the EU speaks with one voice in trade, does it hold the final say over international trade agreements? Once concluded by EU negotiators, can agreements be overturned by recalcitrant EU member states? When is it appropriate to negotiate with the EU or with the member states directly? Over time, both the requirement to present a common front and the complexity of the EU's institutional structure have served the EU well in international trade negotiations.

Just take the negotiation of the landmark free trade agreement with South Africa as an illustration. In 1995 the EU and South Africa started negotiating a sweeping trade-liberalizing deal supposed to free 90 percent of the trade between them. After four years of intense, sometimes tense negotiations—in particular over the issue of the labeling of South Africa's fortified wines as "port" and "sherry," which it eventually agreed to phase out—EU and South African negotiators finally concluded a deal in 1999, due to enter into force in January 2000. To the dismay of other EU member states, at the last minute Italy refused to ratify the agreement, unless South Africa dropped the use of the words "grappa" for its minuscule annual production of 30,000 bottles of the similar alcoholic drink, and Greece decided to block ratification as well, unless South Africa dropped forever the use of the name "ouzo" (which, embarrassed EU negotiators later realized, was not produced at all in South Africa).[1] South African negotiators were astonished by these new demands and by the inability of the EU to overcome its internal disputes. South African President Thabo Mbeki lashed out at the EU for showing bad faith in raising objections after the signature of the accord, and the South African Trade Minister Alec Erwin lamented that it was impossible to negotiate with the EU if it was incapable of raising itself above peripheral concerns, but their

[1] Victor Mallet, "Attempts to Rescue EU-SA Pact," *Financial Times*, January 19, 2000; Nicol Degli Innocenti, "Brussels Wins Pyrrhic Victory on Spirits Labeling," *Financial Times*, February 17, 2000.

protests were to no avail.[2] South Africa eventually caved in and agreed to end the controversy over the names of spirits, and the landmark EU-South Africa free trade deal was finally implemented.

As many trade negotiators around the world have come to realize, it is not easy to bargain with the European Union. With its complex institutional procedures and multiple masters, more often than once its trade partners have been forced to give in to a EU speaking with a single voice, but a single voice reached through an unclear division of competences. Nor is the United States an easy bargainer, for that matter. Between checks and balances among the various branches of government and the easy capture of Congress by special trade interests, American trade negotiators have often used their institutional constraints as bargaining advantages. Willingly or not, the EU has come to rival the United States in this domain. It has become a mighty actor in world trade policy because its member states have pooled sovereignty and external representation in trade, thereby making the collective whole greater than the sum of its parts. But part of this might has come from the incomplete integration of European trade policy, leaving room for involvement by the member states, and from the constant political battles over trade competence between national and supranational actors.

The fact that the EU speaks with a "single voice" in trade has enabled it to affect the distributional outcomes of international trade negotiations and shape the global political economy. Indeed, the EU has exerted a particularly liberalizing influence on the international trading of services and has actively contributed to the development of institutional rules within the World Trade Organization (WTO) designed to prevent unilateralism. In this case, international bargaining power has been a positive externality of the pooling of the diverse European national positions on trade under a single institutional umbrella. By contrast, cacophony is costly, or so it seems: only when the European Union speaks with a single voice has it been able to convey its structural weight into international negotiating leverage.

This book aims to answer many of the questions raised by the process of "trading voices" in the European Union. By which mechanisms does a single internal voice translate into external bargaining power? What are the distributional outcomes of trading individual voices for a single one in an international negotiation? Does the EU's influence lie merely in the combined weight of each of the member states, or does it depend on individual states' preferences or the rules through which these preferences are aggregated into a single voice? When the member states have diverse

<hr/>

[2] Charlotte Denny, "Trading Names: EU and South Africa's War of Words," *The Guardian*, February 15, 2000.

positions, how does this diversity translate into the outcomes that the collective entity is able to extract in the international negotiation? In particular, which combination of institutional rules and individual preferences makes member states winners or losers from the single voice arrangement? Finally, what are the trade-offs between the advantages of scale in terms of international influence and the internal political costs of having to override heterogeneous preferences?

This book is about the politics of international trade bargaining. It analyzes the determinants of EU bargaining power in international trade negotiations, with a detailed study of four cases of transatlantic trade disputes. The central argument is that the EU's complex institutional structure and the obligation to negotiate international agreements with a "single voice" have an important, sometimes decisive, impact on international trade negotiations—but a different one than is commonly believed. Most claim that the EU has little influence or that it strengthens the European voice in such disputes; instead, I show that the requirement to present a common front in international trade negotiations can strengthen or weaken the EU's bargaining leverage, predictably so, depending on the type of voting rules employed, the distribution of preferences, and the specifics of the issue. Specifically, I find that unanimity voting strengthens the hand of EU negotiators to resist demands for policy changes but weakens their ability to advocate policy changes. Adding to the growing literature on both rational and historical institutionalism, this book aims to specify the conditions under which institutions matter and transform outcomes in a way not predicted by preferences and power alone. A related argument is that, far from having a negative impact on the collective bargaining power, the diversity of European positions might, in some circumstances, act as an influence multiplier and therefore become an asset.

This book is also about the EU as a global actor. In spite of its reputation as an economic giant but a political dwarf, the EU has developed into a highly active, though unorthodox, global actor with a multifaceted set of foreign policies. These policies are far more ambitious than those of any other regional economic organization. From trade to global aid, from sustainable development to democratic consolidation, the EU has become implicated in world affairs and has developed an international presence not captured by a focus on military and diplomatic capacities alone. The EU is the single biggest market for imports from developing countries, and it exports more than twice the amount to developing countries than the United States, Japan, and Canada put together.[3] The EU is the world's largest aid donor, providing more than 50 percent of global

---

[3] Eurostat, in "The European Community's Development Policy," communication from the Commission to the Council and the European Parliament, April 26, 2000.

aid, and it has long offered trade preferences to the least developed countries. Yet the EU still lacks a comprehensive external policy encompassing trade, development, diplomatic action, security, and defense. By analyzing the one area in which the EU is an uncontested world power, this book sheds light on some misunderstood determinants of its international influence and offers a glimpse at the EU's potential as an international actor—potential not yet realized in areas of international activity other than trade.

This book is also about transatlantic relations, which are becoming more complex and more contested in the twenty-first century. Trade being the only forum in which the EU speaks to the United States with an equal voice, an analysis of the EU as a global trader and trade negotiator can provide an understanding of the dynamics of the sometimes stormy transatlantic trade relationship. The EU is currently the world's largest trader and one of the main players involved in negotiating trade agreements as part of the ongoing Doha Development Round under the WTO. This provides opportunities for further transatlantic trade conflicts, as do the numerous EU-U.S. disputes under consideration at the WTO, such as those on Genetically Modified Organisms and on tax breaks on exports ("Foreign Sales Corporation").

Finally, this book can be read as a primer about the history and making of trade policy in the European Union. Trade is the EU's oldest, and most successfully integrated, common policy.[4] Over the past two decades, trade policy has spilled out of the restricted confines of customs duties and tariffs. It now links commercial flows and the collective preferences of societies on issues such as health, the environment, culture, and social rights. This book traces the evolution of the rules for making trade policy in Europe from the 1957 Treaty of Rome to the 2003 draft Constitution, from De Gaulle's 1965 empty chair policy to the 1994 judicial challenge to the EU's competence over trade in services. By focusing on the political trade-offs associated with the pooling of external representation, this book presents the first systematic evidence of why the current battle over trade is located partly in the battle over institutions, as antiglobalization activists have realized. The institutional battle is particularly acute in the EU because of its complex multilevel structure and the ambitious constitutional exercise in which its members have engaged ahead of its enlargement to the east. The results of this battle seem of prime importance for the rest of the world since the EU is the world's largest trader.

---

[4] In a table summarizing issue areas and levels of authority in Europe, "commercial negotiations" is the only issue out of twenty-eight to be coded as having all policy decisions taken at the EC level. The table was originally designed by Lindberg and Scheingold (1970) and was updated and reproduced in Donahue and Pollack (2001).

Trading Voices: The Pooling of International Representation

From its very beginning in 1958 with six participating member states, the European Economic Community (EEC) became a single actor in trade policy. The requirement of pooling external representation in international trade negotiations was enshrined in the emerging European institutional structure. Why did national governments transfer part of their trade policymaking authority to the supranational level with relatively little hesitation? The main reason was legal and practical: the only way the EEC could legally exist under the General Agreement on Tariffs and Trade (GATT) was to be a customs union, and the only practical way to manage the external relations of such a union was by adopting a single voice in trade. The EEC's founding fathers also believed that the benefits of "trading voices" far outweighed the costs. As in the United States, where negotiating authority is often transferred temporarily to the executive branch, the delegation of competence could provide greater insulation from domestic pressures and therefore ensure economic liberalization.[5] A final motivation was the assumption that unity brings strength, and therefore that a unified voice would reinforce Europe's international bargaining power.

---

[5] Petersmann (1991: 288–289) enumerates the traditional arguments in favor of the delegation of foreign policy to the executive branch. If trade policy is conceived as part of foreign policy, then some of these arguments could justify the delegation of trade policy to the most centralized level of government.

A first argument (e.g., by Locke) is that foreign policy decisions have to react to foreign events and often result from international bargaining processes, in which the national bargaining position may be weakened by openness and internal disunity, and which may be conducted best in secrecy by "professionals" who know the adversary and know how to bargain. National parliaments have little influence on these international bargaining processes, and parliamentary debates "will normally involve only retrospective examination of the consequences of irrevocable decisions already implemented." Hence, the sovereign right of parliament to change such an agreement or to stop its implementation is, in fact, mainly theoretical because of the costs that such actions might entail.

A second argument traditionally invoked in support of the incompatibility hypothesis is that foreign policy questions involve the nation's security and integrity and that these "supreme interests" are too important to be left to democratic politics, which often tends to avoid unpleasant choices (e.g., military expenditures) and may lead to irrational foreign policy decisions.

A third line of argument is that the implications of foreign policy questions for the individual citizen are often remote, indirect, and obscure, so that most people and also parliamentarians tend to give little attention to foreign policy issues and leave them to "the experts."

Legal Obligation and Efficiency of the Negotiating Process

The Common Commercial Policy was created, above all, by an exogenous legal obligation. The single voice in trade was indeed necessary for the European Community to be allowed under the existing GATT rules. European regional integration represented an exception to the principle of multilateralism on which the GATT was based, but according to its article XXIV, the rule of the most favored nation could be circumvented by the creation of a free-trade zone or a customs union, in the hope that such zones would eventually encourage comprehensive global trade liberalization.

The objective of the 1957 Treaty of Rome was to create a customs union among Belgium, France, Italy, Luxembourg, the Netherlands, and West Germany in which there would be no barriers to trade and a common external tariff would be applied to imports from third countries. The EEC's founding fathers chose to build a customs union for both economic and political reasons.[6] Economically, it did not seem to make sense to keep separate tariffs with third countries while abolishing customs duties among member states who were geographically contiguous. If external tariffs were kept separate, imports from third countries would flock to the member state with the lowest tariffs and then circulate freely within the zone, thereby rendering national tariffs obsolete. Moreover, contemporary customs union theory argued that the dismantling of tariffs and quotas, as well as the establishment of a common external tariff, would force a more efficient use of factors of production.[7] Politically, the creation of a customs union, which entailed some sharing of sovereignty with respect to the conduct of trade policy, meant closer cooperation and relationships between former enemies.

Because a customs union is a community of nations that liberalize trade internally while erecting common external barriers, it does require a common policy toward third countries. In particular, a mechanism was needed to harmonize the national rules governing the entry of products from third countries into each of the EEC's member states, in order to avoid diversion of trade, misallocation of factors of production, and distortion of competition stemming from the free movement of goods within the boundaries of the Common Market. The creation of a customs union therefore meant the establishment of a common external tariff (CET)—

---

[6] See, for instance, the "Spaak report," "Rapport des chefs de délégation aux ministres des affaires étrangères," Bruxelles, April 21, 1956, Mae 120 f/56.

[7] See, e.g., Viner (1950).

that is, a tariff rate uniformly applied to imports of goods and services from countries outside the EEC, irrespective of the member state of destination. Originally the CET was the arithmetic average of the national tariffs applied in 1957 by the member states. It was subsequently negotiated down in successive rounds of multilateral trade negotiations under GATT. The newly created European Commission was granted the authority to negotiate for the collectivity in order to allow the internal market to function as a unit.

The delegation of negotiating competence to the collective entity was expected to increase the efficiency of the process. Indeed, trade policymaking has always been a long and complex process. In the United States, the passage of the American Smoot-Hawley Tariff Act of 1930 had been a "truly Sisyphean labor," according to Schnattschneider, who counted eleven thousand pages of testimony and briefs collected over forty-three days.[8] Concentrating the power to negotiate into the hands of a small number of executive agents could maximize the gains obtained in the external negotiation and accelerate the attainment of these gains since it likely speeds up the negotiating process.[9] Increased efficiency is indeed a traditional argument used in principal/agent analysis to justify the delegation of competence from a principal to an agent.

As in the United States, efficiency was, and still is, one of the main arguments used in Europe to justify the delegation of trade negotiating competence to the supranational level. Commission negotiators are better equipped than national negotiators to bargain internationally with successful results because they avoid long domestic debates about the details of the issues being negotiated. Moreover, if EU negotiators are given sufficient but restricted competence, they can credibly conclude agreements that the other party knows will be approved internally. The efficiency argument was succinctly summarized by former EU Trade Commissioner Sir Leon Brittan, who argued that wider powers for the Commission and an end to the unanimity rule would "speed up negotiations, simplify decision-making and increase the EU's trade policy influence in relation to the U.S. and Japan."[10]

---

[8] Schnattschneider (1935), quoted in Bailey, Goldstein, and Weingast (1997: 312).

[9] Some scholars of U.S. trade policy have recently expressed doubts about the validity of the "efficiency" rationale. While it is true that the concentration of negotiating authority into the hands of the executive reduces inefficiencies, recent work argues that there are other ways to streamline the process than by delegating to the president. The legislators could have chosen instead to use differently existing organizations, to create new committees and commissions, and to establish new rules. See Bailey, Goldstein, and Weingast (1997).

[10] Lionel Barber, "Brussels Strives to Call the Tune on Trade," *Financial Times*, March 12, 1997, p. 6.

Trade Liberalization through "Insulation"

European policymakers also chose to centralize trade policymaking in order to insulate the process from protectionist pressures and, as a result, promote trade liberalization. Drawing on their familiarity with the American system and their admiration of the Interstate Commerce Clause, the founding fathers of Europe, Jean Monnet and Paul-Henri Spaak above all, planned to replicate the system in the European Community.[11]

The political economy canon has long been that the politics of trade are characterized, almost universally, by collective action problems and a bias toward protectionism. The benefits from protection are concentrated, whereas its costs are dispersed.[12] Therefore, it is easier for import-competing industries than for consumers to act collectively, because they form a much smaller group in relative terms.[13] As many scholars of political economy have observed over the years, the political system is thus structurally biased in favor of protectionism.[14]

The delegation of trade policy-making authority to the most unitary level of government facilitates the insulation of the process from domestic pressures and, as a result, promotes trade liberalization. This is because different decision-makers have different constituencies, and local politicians are more susceptible to special interests than the president, whose constituency is national. Looking at the U.S. experience illuminates the dilemmas faced by policymakers in trying to achieve collective policy in the midst of special interest pressure. A standard view among studies of the American trade policymaking process is that Congress delegated trade authority to the president to insulate its members from protectionist domestic pressures and to promote a more liberal international political economy.[15] Because each representative can become hostage to a handful of special interests, the congressional policymaking process leads either to policy impasse or to logrolling and inefficiently high levels of protectionism, such as the 1930 Smoot-Hawley Tariff Act.[16] With a national rather than parochial constituency, the president is expected to have more

[11] Interview with Paul Boel, May 2004.

[12] This was first noticed by Schattschneider (1935: 127–128).

[13] On collective action problems, see the seminal work of Olson (1982).

[14] See, for instance, Olson (1982); Goldstein (1988); Magee, Brock, and Young (1989); Goldstein (1993); O'Halloran (1994); Destler (1996); Gilligan (1997); Hiscox (2002).

[15] See, for instance, Bauer, Pool, and Dexter (1963); Destler (1996). There are some disagreements in the recent literature over the primary motivations for the delegation of trade policy, as well as the nature of the delegation itself. See O'Halloran (1994) and Bailey, Goldstein, and Weingast (1997) for dissenting views.

[16] See O'Halloran (1994: 7).

liberal preferences on trade policy than members of Congress. Therefore, delegation facilitates liberalization.[17]

The delegation of trade authority to the executive branch has enabled congressional representatives to pursue the goal of an open world economy. The hope of the legislators who initiated the institutional change in the United States in 1934, and later of those who signed the 1962 Trade Expansion Act, was to embed liberalism into the institutional process. The Democratic legislators designed institutions that would lower tariffs and outlive their partisan control over Congress.[18] At the same time that it created free trade, the delegation of trade authority to the executive enabled U.S. legislators to avoid being blamed for the domestic consequences of these liberal policy decisions. They delegated decision making, but they retained their right to criticize foreign countries and the administration on behalf of disaffected constituents. O'Halloran summarizes the "blame shirking" argument: "This decision-making process allows the United States to pursue liberal trade policies without holding members of Congress directly accountable to constituents injured by import competition. Legislators can thereby claim credit as a champion of the disaffected without having to deliver on their threats."[19]

Coming in the postwar era, with the memory of the international consequences of American protectionism still fresh in their minds, the decision of the founding member states of the European Community to delegate trade negotiating authority to the supranational level can similarly be explained by this willingness to insulate international trade agreements from protectionist pressures. The newly designed Council of Ministers, where the national interests of the European member states are represented, could also be prone, like the U.S. Congress, to protectionist tendencies. European policymakers even have to face an additional level of lobbying, as special interests can be of a national, regional, or sectoral nature. Letting international trade negotiations be conducted by supranational agents and trade policy decisions be taken by a majority of member states was expected to prevent the disproportionate capture of trade policy by protectionist interests.[20]

[17] See Destler (1996); O'Halloran (1994).

[18] The central argument of Bailey, Goldstein, and Weingast (1997: 316) is that the RTAA was passed in 1934 not so much because Congress abdicated control or sought to deflect political pressure, but because "the Democratic leadership wanted lower tariffs that would pass an increasingly skeptical Congress and would be able to outlive Democratic control of Congress. The institutions they designed met this goal."

[19] O'Halloran (1994: 17–18). These arguments were originally made by Bauer, Pool, and Dexter (1963) and Mayhew (1974).

[20] One main difference from the American institutional structure, however, is that the protectionist or liberal tendencies of the EU trade policy process are less easy to predict because of the blurring of the executive and the legislative branches into the Council of Ministers

A Single Voice as Instrument of International Power

A third rationale for delegating the trade negotiating authority from the national to the supranational level rested on the traditional assumption that internal unity brings external strength, and therefore that the pooling of international representation would enhance the external voice of the European Community. This assumption has been prevalent in the rhetoric of pro-integrationist politicians and permeates the literature on European integration.

The initial motivations of European policymakers for fostering unity in Western Europe and setting up the EC institutions were primarily economic (to improve standards of living and create a large market) and security-related (to act as a bulwark against the progression of communism and prevent the return of a nationalist Germany).[21] One of the less avowed goals of integration was to restore Europe's past might and transform it into a force equal to that of the United States.[22] The phrase "United States of Europe," given worldwide fame by Winston Churchill's 1946 speech and later popularized by Jean Monnet in his "Action Committee for the United States of Europe," is in itself a testimony to this goal.

Integration arose from the loss of influence of Europe, sanctioned by the Second World War, and coincided with the demise of the European colonial empires. Europe relayed dreams of grandeur for some politicians, who pledged to use European unification to bring back international strength. Many proponents of European integration feared the growing dependence of Europe on the United States as a consequence of the Marshall Plan and envisioned European integration as a means to assert the

---

and the European Commission, as argued by Petersmann (1991: 167): "The lack of separation of legislative and executive governmental powers in the EEC, especially in the field of the common agricultural and commercial policies, has born out this liberal concern that the combination of discretionary legislative and executive powers, unconstrained by substantive constitutional principles and effective judicial control, risks to be abused for the sake of coalitions of various organized interests and to lead to the abandonment of liberal principles in favor of discriminatory measures benefiting the various 'distributive coalitions' (e.g. agricultural, textiles, and steel lobbies in the EEC). The increasing number of bilateral and sectoral special arrangements for trade in agricultural products, textiles, apparel, steel, shipbuilding, synthetic fibres, automobiles, etc., first negotiated with domestic industry lobbies and subsequently on the intergovernmental level, reflect an increasing prevalence of special interests over the general public interest."

[21] See Dinan (1994) for an introduction to the history and origins of the European Community. See Monnet (1978) and Milward (1984) for analyses of the relationship between European integration and the U. S. global power.

[22] Some American actors of this period deny that this was ever an underlying motivation, but there is plenty of evidence to the contrary, starting with Jean Monnet's own writings and testimonies.

continent's independence.[23] As the French newspaper *Le Monde* wrote in 1957, "Is the lack of enthusiasm [of the United States for the creation of the EEC] prompted by the thought that, were the Common Market to succeed, Europe would need less American aid and would become more independent?"[24] Even Jean Monnet, the pro-American "founding father" of the European Community, envisioned building a European bloc equal to the United States in economic and political strength. He aimed to realize an equal partnership between the United States and Europe.[25]

The "third force" mythology was omnipresent in the public debate in Europe in the postwar years. German and Italian policymakers assumed that European unity would bring strength in order to mobilize political forces longing for a new form of national identity.[26] The French were particularly intent on resisting the United States to demonstrate Europe's new strength and independence. This motivation for furthering European integration culminated in the Gaullist period. Although De Gaulle's suspicions of regional integration were deep for the transfer of sovereignty it seemed to imply, he also foresaw its potential for interposing Europe as a third force in the world, where France alone could not have succeeded.[27] According to this Gaullist rhetoric, the movement toward European integration was an important step toward independence from the American tutelage.

The reasoning that applied to political relations also applied, with even more vigor and persuasion, to trade relations. The European and American press commonly assumed since the early days of European integration that being united would give the Europeans greater bargaining leverage vis-à-vis the United States. The issue was already raised in 1943, when the U.S. State Department analyzed the policy opportunities and dangers of the afterwar period. According to economist Jacob Viner, a member of the Special Subcommittee on Problems of European Organization, Euro-

---

[23] Dinan (1994: 18).

[24] *Le Monde*, editorial, January 20, 1957.

[25] In "Jean Monnet's Methods," François Duchêne, a Monnet collaborator, writes: "Few contemporaries beyond a restricted circle of like-minded reformers ever fully grasped the paradox, in traditional, national terms, of Monnet's refusal to be a European nationalist, and yet his determination that a uniting Europe should achieve 'equality' with the United States. It is ironic that Gaullists saw Monnet as a pawn of the Americans (thus jettisoning Monnet's cherished goal of association in equality); while Kissinger, in the *Years of Upheaval* (ch. V) viewed him as a subtler kind of European Gaullist proposing to obtain from America by stealth what de Gaulle hoped to snatch by defiance (thus jettisoning the stress on interdependence and cooperation)" (in Brinkley and Hackett 1991: 204).

[26] In Italy, this argument was particularly popular with the anti-American right wing, but it was widely used and supported by all major political parties. I am grateful to Federico Romero for bringing this point to my attention.

[27] Dinan (1994: chap. 2).

pean economic unification would increase the area's bargaining power, as it had in its time increased the power of the United States and the Zollverein, and this bargaining power would be directed primarily against the United States.[28] This did not prevent successive U.S. administrations from strongly supporting the establishment of the European Community and thereby the strengthening of a trade rival because of the overriding priority of strengthening Europe as a security partner.

The spillover logic was expected to be at work in the domain of external relations: "speaking with one voice" in trade affairs would lead to increased international power of the EC, which ultimately translated into common foreign and security policy. American policymakers were well aware of the "third force" dangers associated with the creation of the European Economic Community. In 1961, in regard to the implementation of a regional trade bloc in Europe, the *New York Times* indeed warned of "the possibility that a united Western Europe might break from the United States and take its stand as the balancing power between East and West."[29] Therefore, not surprisingly, the "third force" rhetoric and the potential consequences of the Common External Tariff on transatlantic power relations were at the heart of the preliminary Kennedy Round discussions, which debuted in 1962.

The subsequent advances toward broader and deeper European integration led to even higher expectations that the EC was going to use its reinforced leverage to assert a new world leadership role in trade policy. This assumption was particularly prevalent in the early days of the Uruguay Round negotiations, which took place amidst the relaunching of European integration with the Single European Act and widespread academic and political discussions of the decline of U.S. hegemony. The progress of economic and political integration and the strengthening of the Commission's supranational powers suggested that the EC's negotiating effectiveness would increase.[30] Indeed, the Single European Act, which transformed the decision-making procedures in the EC and committed to complete the European internal market by 1992, provoked the fear of American negotiators. The United States worried, first, that the EC would retreat behind fortresslike walls, and second, that it could now stand up

[28] See Devuyst (1998) for an analysis of the intellectual debate in the United States during the creation of the European Community and references to the Special Subcommittee on Problems of European Organization, which can be consulted at the U.S. National Archives, General Records of the U.S. Department of State, Records of Harley Notter, 1939–1945, Records of the Advisory Committee on Postwar Foreign Policy.

[29] Richard Mooney, "Common Market: Effect on the US," *New York Times*, international edition, November 13, 1961.

[30] Claim made, for instance, by Steve Dryden, "Trade Warriors," *Europe* (May 1990): 15–16.

to the United States in bilateral and multilateral negotiations.[31] Once the renewed efforts toward integration became publicized around 1987–1988, a common view was that "the rest of the world is feeling at worst considerable apprehension and at best a great deal of anxious uncertainty about what the effects of 1992 might be for their trade and economic relations with this looming economic superpower."[32]

Most of the official U.S. response to the Single European Act emphasized the potential trade consequences of complete economic unity in Europe. American policymakers did not much discuss the institutional transformations toward increased supranationalism, which the act entailed. Once again, the assumption was that an institutionally stronger EC would produce yet a tougher EC bargaining stance in the GATT negotiations. The link between integration and political influence was made more apparent during the debate on the 1992 Maastricht Treaty on European Union, which provided steps toward further monetary and political integration. The argument that deeper supranational ties would strengthen the EC's position in trade, and possibly foreign policy, negotiations was used again during the 1997 and 2000 Inter-Governmental Conferences leading to the redrafting of the treaty, including the articles governing trade policy. In the discussions of the Constitutional Convention (2002–2004), especially those that took place in the wake of the transatlantic debacle over Iraq, the argument that pooling sovereignty over external representation would enhance Europe's international power was heard once again.

Arguments, Evidence, and Findings

What are the expected effects of transferring trade policy sovereignty to the supranational level and pooling external representation? Despite the theoretical and practical salience of this question, the literature on European integration has neither asked nor answered it.[33] The lack of prior

---

[31] As Joseph Greenwald stated: "The return of self-confidence engendered by the Europe 1992 process has led the EC to be more contentious in disputes with its trading partners. European Commission officials say privately that, while the United States can push weak countries around, the Community can now stand up and slug it out with an aggressively protectionist United States" (quoted in Hufbauer 1990: 346).

[32] Golt (1988).

[33] One of the most systematic studies to date is Frieden (2004). Scholars in the Deutschian and, more recently, constructivist traditions have suggested in passing some relationship between the EU's internal features and external influence, as have some contributors to the neofunctionalist literature, but none has formulated testable hypotheses on this possible linkage. See, for instance, Deutsch et al. (1957); Schmitter (1969); Lindberg and Scheingold (1970); Wendt (1994); Mercer (1995).

research on the subject may stem from the fact that European integration was long believed to be an experiment in the making—and an experiment likely to fail. As a result, scholars initially addressed issues such as how the EEC was created, where it was going, and through which process.[34] When European integration proved resilient and the EEC expanded and deepened, the next wave of scholarship started to study the internal effects of European integration: how does it affect domestic politics and democratic legitimacy?[35] What is the impact of integration on national policies?[36] This is the focus of most of the current literature on European integration. Since the European Union has withstood forty years of progress, crises, and enlargement, however, it is time finally to ask how the process of integration affected outsiders and the EU's own position in the world political and economic system.

Another explanation for the lack of scholarly focus on the question of the EU's external impact is the widespread assumption, both in political rhetoric and in the political science literature, that internal unity creates external strength. The belief that economic and political unity would put Europe on an equal basis with the United States in the conduct of world affairs, including in the formulation of world trading rules, has long been anchored in politicians' rhetoric in Europe and, to some extent, in the United States. Yet does "trading voices"—the transfer of negotiating authority to the supranational level—represent the best means for European states to secure a meaningful international voice in trade? This book analyzes whether the EU has indeed become increasingly effective in international trade negotiations as it has integrated and consolidated internally.

Finally, the absence of systematic study of the linkage between internal unity and external strength may have been influenced by the realist assumption that the EU acts merely as a messenger, relaying the preferences of the member states from one forum to another without altering them. The common European position, which is reached internally through an intergovernmental bargain, can only reflect the preferences of the more powerful member states. As Grieco wrote during the Uruguay Round, "the arguments presented by the EC Commission in the context of the GATT, as in other international forums, are based on and driven by the

[34] This is the classic neofunctionalism vs. intergovernmentalism debate exemplified by Haas (1958) and later Sandholtz and Zysman (1989) and Moravcsik (1991). See Caporaso and Keeler (1995) for an overview of the evolution of the scholarship on European integration.

[35] On the rich controversy over the issue of the "democratic deficit," see, among others, Williams (1991); Wallace (1993); Majone (1996); Weiler (1997); Banchoff and Smith (1999); Scharpf (1999); Cederman (2000); Schmitter (2000); Moravcsik (2001); Siedentop (2001).

[36] See, for instance, Cowles, Caporaso, and Risse (2001).

interests and preferences of the individual EC member states and especially the EC's core countries, Britain, Germany, and France."[37] Therefore, institutional developments inside the EU appear to have an effect on international negotiations only insofar as the big member states change their strategic assessment of what is desirable in the international arena.

Recent scholarship on European integration has attempted to analyze the EU as an actor able to enjoy some autonomy from its constituent member states. Inspired by rational-choice theory and focusing on the autonomous behavior of goal-oriented supranational actors through the lens of the principal-agent theories of delegation, this literature tries to specify the conditions under which institutions matter and how causal mechanisms operate.[38] In internal negotiations over EU policy, supranational actors derive their autonomy primarily from the cleavages among member states' preferences, from their own role as agenda-setters, and from the loopholes in the oversight mechanisms established by the member states to control them, which vary by issue area.[39] The result is an independent causal role attributed to the EU.

In external settings, the EU derives some of its autonomy from the multilevel nature of the international negotiating process, which requires agreements to be reached at the domestic, supranational, and international levels. The two-level games highlighted by Robert Putnam imply that negotiators are able to increase their influence on the final outcome of a negotiation by using their relay position to manipulate both their domestic constituency and negotiating opponents.[40] Applied to the three levels of bargaining faced by EU representatives when they engage in international negotiations, this argument suggests that the EU's external bargaining impact is determined by the ambitions of its institutional agents.[41] As a result of their partial autonomy and ability to manipulate their various constituencies, the supranational negotiators can exert a definite impact on the final international agreement, which is likely to be tilted in favor of their own pro-integrationist (or proliberalizing) views.

This rational supranationalist hypothesis about the EU as an autonomous actor in a multilevel setting rests on the fundamental assumption

[37] Grieco (1990: 21).

[38] On rational choice institutionalism, see Riker (1980); Moe (1984); Weingast and Marshall (1988); Shepsle (1989); North (1990). On historical institutionalism, see March and Olsen (1984); Steinmo et al. (1992); Pierson (1996, 2000); Thelen (1999). For the insights of institutionalist analysis applied to the study of the EU, see, for instance, Tsebelis (1994); Garrett (1995); Garrett and Tsebelis (1996); Nicolaïdis (1998); Jupille and Caporaso (1999); Keohane and Martin (1999); Dowding (2000); Aspinwall and Schneider (2001); Pollack (2003).

[39] Pollack (1997).

[40] Putnam (1988); Evans, Jacobson, and Putnam (1993).

[41] See Patterson (1997) on the three-level games in the EU.

that supranational negotiators are purposive actors with preferences distinct from those of the constituencies they have been created to serve. The independent causal effects of the EU on external bargaining stem from their drive to maximize their autonomy. Therefore, the EU is in a strong international position when its negotiating agents have enough leeway to promote their own agenda. Yet, in practice, EU negotiators are often forced to defend internationally a Community position that goes against their own preferences, but they seek to conclude the agreements for which they have been mandated anyhow.

This book builds on the insights provided by rational supranationalism but focuses on specific institutional features in addition to the autonomy of supranational actors and specifies how third countries can exploit these supranational preferences to their advantage. By examining variation in institutional rules within the EU for making trade policy, I try to answer the question not only of how the EU matters, but more precisely of how internal EU rules affect external outcomes. I develop a model of the bargaining power of the European Union in international trade negotiations, defining bargaining power as the ability of a negotiating actor to obtain the best possible deal in the negotiation—that is, to obtain the most from its opponent while conceding the least, *ceteris paribus*. Since it is problematic to define the "collective" interest of the EU as a whole other than by looking at the common position the member states selected as a result of the voting rule in use, I will observe the EU's collective bargaining power from the point of view of its negotiating opponent.

To explain variations in EU international bargaining power, I examine the procedures (formal and informal) through which the national positions of the member states on trade are aggregated into a single voice at the European level, and the procedures through which this single voice is relayed at the international level. Who represents the voice of the EU in international trade negotiations, and how do the member states agree on what to say? Based on the concepts and methodology of new institutionalist theory, my central argument is that the EU is not merely a forum in which the European states exchange concessions. Rather, it is primarily an institutional framework that has been designed by, but can become constraining for, the member states. Indeed, the main finding of this book is that the EU's institutional structure exerts an independent causal effect on the process and outcome of international negotiations, given an exogenous distribution of national preferences.

In the chapters that follow, I consider the impact of the pooling of external representation on international negotiations. Chapter 1 offers a historical account of the transfer of the authority to negotiate international trade agreements to the supranational level in the EC (and later the EU), explaining the legal and political battles over national sovereignty and supranational autonomy, which rose to the forefront of the institutional debate in Europe in the 1990s. This chapter also attempts to shed light on the complexities of the trade policymaking process in the EU, in particular the making of the "single voice" in trade. In chapter 2, I develop an institutionalist model about the strategic implications of being forced to negotiate externally as a single entity. This model is based on two central variables, which will be explained in chapter 2: (1) the degree of supranational competence (including the internal voting rules in the EU—unanimity vs. qualified majority voting—and the nature of the delegation by the member states to their negotiating agent—restrictive vs. extensive); and (2) the negotiating context relative to the status quo. Differentiating between a "conservative" and a "reformist" negotiating context, I argue that the EU supranational competence determines both the probability that the negotiating parties will conclude an international agreement and the substantive outcome of the negotiations. The main finding of this model is that the institutional design of the EU has a clear impact on those international trade negotiations designed to change the European policy status quo. In this "conservative" case, unanimity and restrictive delegation make the EU a tough bargainer: the negotiating opponent cannot obtain more than what the most conservative EU state is willing to concede. By contrast, qualified majority and extensive delegation produce a more favorable agreement for the EU's negotiating opponent. Thus, in the "reformist" case where the EU seeks a change in the policy status quo of its opponent, I find that the institutional design of the EU plays a lesser role in the determination of the final outcome of international negotiations. If the negotiation has to reach a conclusion for outside reasons, however, I find that majority voting strengthens the influence of the EU over unanimity voting.

Contrary to the conventional assumption that the EU's cumbersome decision-making procedures have negative effects on its external bargaining potential, in certain circumstances the EU can indeed use its institutional constraints strategically in order to reach its negotiating objectives. In these specific cases, I show that being "divided but united" (that is, having divergent preferences but being forced to present a single face to the outside world) can give the EU an edge in international bargaining, as was originally foreshadowed by Schelling.[42] Conversely, when the EU does not have exclusive negotiating competence and the third country aims to change the status quo, each member state, acting as free agent, can try to resist external attempts at changing the status quo but has no control over the fallout of its neighbors' own international agreements. When some member states wish to change the international status quo,

[42] Schelling (1960).

one member state alone does not have sufficient weight to successfully launch an offensive against a third country without the support of a collective bargaining unit.

Pointing to the strategic implications of "trading voices" does not imply, however, that the EU uses its institutional structure consciously as a bargaining constraint to extract concessions from its opponents. As the book will show, the EU's institutional peculiarities may force its negotiating opponents to accept a hard bargain, but this may be in spite of the preferences of a majority of EU member states who would have preferred a different common bargaining position from the lowest common denominator. Nevertheless, whether the EU uses its institutional peculiarities as negotiating tricks or is constrained by them in its negotiating margin of maneuver, the end result is the same: the EU's internal rules have an external outcome, willingly or not.

To explore the predictions that key institutional features of the EU's internal trade policymaking process affect the outcomes of international trade negotiations, I study four cases of conflictual trade negotiations between the EU and the United States. I selected the United States because it has been the EU's main trading partner since its creation, because it has enjoyed a fairly balanced trade relationship with the EU, and because it is almost structurally equal to the EU—whether in terms of economic output, population, level of development, or standard of living. The particular cases presented offer different combinations of the independent variables to illustrate the argument that negotiating as a single bloc can strengthen or handicap the bargaining position of the EU as a whole, depending on a determined set of conditions.

1. *The EC-U.S. agricultural negotiations in the Kennedy Round (1964–1967)* are an example of "conservative" negotiation in which supranational autonomy was nonexistent and the mode of decision making in the EC was unanimity. The United States capitulated to an inflexible Common Market, and the final deal reflected the EC's lowest common denominator position.

2. *The EC-U.S. agricultural negotiations in the Uruguay Round (1986–1993)* provide an interesting variation in the independent variables, since in this "conservative" negotiation informal changes in the decision-making process and greater autonomy seized by European negotiators enabled an EC-U.S. agreement to be reached, only to be renegotiated when some member states reaffirmed their veto right and curbed the "free hands" of the Commission. As a result, the final agreement was less satisfactory for the United States and for the majority of member states than the original one.

3. *The EC-U.S. negotiations on public procurement (1990–1994)* illustrate the rather successful "reformist" attempt by the Community to open up the American public procurement market, thanks to the majority requirement and in spite of U.S. attempts to introduce a "Trojan Horse" in the EC by concluding a forbidden bilateral deal with one of the member states.

4. *The transatlantic "open skies" agreements on international aviation (1992–2003)* represent a "control" case since negotiating competence initially belonged to the individual member states before being partly turned over to the supranational level in 1996. From a legal perspective, transportation is not subject to the usual rules of trade policy (neither in the EU nor at the WTO), but from a political perspective it falls under the general heading of trade. In the "open skies" case, the United States was able to exploit the absence of European discipline by concluding a series of bilateral agreements with several small member states, without being held up by the three big states that initially opposed this U.S.-led liberalization. This case illustrates how third countries can strike better deals when member states are free agents in the external sphere than they would have when dealing with a unified EU.

These cases all point to the fact that, given exogenous member states' preferences and depending on the conservative/reformist negotiating context, the degree to which member states were willing to let go of their sovereignty affected the process and outcome of the final international trade agreement. The main conclusion is that member states do not benefit equally from being forced to share their external trade powers with others. States with conservative preferences can improve their bargaining power over acting on their own on the international scene by negotiating with a "single voice" while retaining their power to veto the deal and control the negotiators' moves. Member states with median preferences, especially if they are small, are better off inside a Community governed by majority rule. Of course the alignment of member states' preferences varies by issue, but member states cannot opt in and out of the EU on an issue-by-issue basis. The model presented in this book should help predict how ongoing institutional changes will affect the EU's future external bargaining capabilities, the process of European integration, and the nature of the pressure (liberal or protectionist) exerted by the EU on the world political economy.

This study of the bargaining effects of combining negotiating forces with others has theoretical implications. First, it may be useful for explaining the bargaining effectiveness of institutionalized coalitions in settings other than the EU (e.g., NAFTA, federal systems) and in international negotiations over issues other than trade (e.g., monetary policy, environment, foreign policy).[43] Second, this study confirms that the EU exerts an independent causal effect on world politics. The mere fact of belonging to the EU transforms a state's chances of shaping the outside world. The realization that small states may exert a disproportionate influence on world affairs through the EU's institutional design should be seriously considered as the EU has recently expanded its membership to more small states and is simultaneously taking on new roles in foreign affairs. Moreover, because the EU now initiates international policy changes rather than reacts to them, it has an increasingly proactive role in the world's political economy. The argument developed in the present book suggests that the EU's capacity at setting the agenda in key areas of the international economy depends heavily on its own institutional features.

Even though this book focuses primarily on the implications of institutional rules on external bargaining power, efficiency and influence are not the only concerns when politicians design and alter the rules for making trade policy. Increasingly, political leaders are struggling to find a politically acceptable balance between efficiency and legitimacy. As the famous demonstrations in Seattle and subsequent antiglobalization protests have shown, the issue of the political legitimacy of trade policymaking institutions can no longer be taken lightly. The grievances regarding the undemocratic nature of trade policy have the potential to be particularly acute in the European Union, where the global economy is increasingly important in determining the daily lives of citizens because of the extensive trade openness of EU members, and where trade policy is affecting Europeans in a more direct manner than ever before, as the nature of what is now considered as "trade" and therefore up for international bargaining and deregulation has changed dramatically in the past few years.

---

[43] On the potential application of the institutionalist argument to monetary policy, see McNamara and Meunier (2002). On the environment, see Jupille (2000); Sbragia (1997).

1

A Single European Voice in Trade

Europe's external trade policy has been perhaps the finest advertisement for the pooling of national sovereignty since the European Community came into being. It has made Europe a powerful force for open markets across the world, giving her the lead in trade liberalization, securing access for European firms abroad and preventing the worst excesses of predatory trading by our partners. It has converted the single European market into a vast negotiating lever to win global access for European exports and investment by challenging our partners to be as open as we are to them.

— Sir Leon Brittan, vice-president of the European Commission, 1996

FOR MANY practical purposes, the European Union today resembles a single, albeit diverse, state when it comes to negotiating international trade agreements.[1] At least this is how third countries have long viewed the role of the EU in the GATT, which for the negotiating phase of trade agreements treated the European entity as one of its contracting parties, and today still view it in the WTO.[2] The trade policy-making process in the EU is a unique blend of intergovernmental and supranational features, which makes it challenging to comprehend even to the participants involved, let alone the foreign countries with which the EU negotiate. Therefore, understanding the trade policymaking process is vital to understanding the institutionalization of the EU. Trade policy can serve both as a barometer of acceptable institutional designs and transfers of sovereignty and as a template for further European integration in other policy areas.

Trade policy in the EU involves two levels of delegation.[3] First, the 1957 Treaty of Rome formally transferred the competence to negotiate and conclude international agreements on trade[4] from the individual member states to the collective entity—often referred to as "exclusive

---

[1] For instance, Costa Tavares (2003) has shown that the EU is acting like a single country, instead of a collection of countries, when setting the Common Customs Tariff.

[2] On the particular status of the EC in GATT, see Bourgeois (1995); Denza (1996); and Meunier and Nicolaïdis (1999).

[3] Meunier and Nicolaïdis (1999).

[4] At that time limited, in practical terms, to trade in goods.

competence," "Community competence," or "supranational competence." The second level of delegation is the practical transfer of competence from the Council of Ministers, composed of representatives of the
member statesin charge of defending their national interest, to the European Commission, composed of EU bureaucrats in charge of defending
the collective interest.

Even though the common commercial policy is always hailed as a success and the single voice in trade as a model of cooperation to be imitated
in other policy areas, this two-step delegation has proven quite complex
and quite contested in practice. This chapter analyzes in turn these two
levels of delegation. The first section investigates the history of the legal
and political battles about the transfer of competence from the member
states to the supranational level, particularly acute over the past ten years
because of the changing nature of trade itself. The second section examines the practical transfer of competence from the Council of Ministers
to the Commission and the inner workings of the EU's "trading voice" in
international commercial negotiations.

The Supranational Trade Competence Battles

As the nascent European Community's raison d'être, trade policy immediately came under supranational competence.[5] In the field of trade, the
1957 Treaty of Rome was a revolutionary document. Not only did it
contain unusually broad injunctions for achieving free trade internally,
it also granted the new supranational entity an external personality.[6] In
particular, it delegated the competence to elaborate, negotiate, and implement trade policy to the European level through its article 113.[7] This

---

[5] This section is based on Nicolaïdis and Meunier (2002).

[6] The 1951 Treaty of Paris started from the principle that the powers of the member
states in commercial policy should not be affected by the integration of their coal and steel
sectors, and therefore the European Coal and Steel Community did not have external powers. See *Trade Policy Review: The European Communities, 1991*, vol. 1 (Geneva: GATT,
1991).

[7] Article 113 of the EEC Treaty amended by the Treaty on European Union states:

1. The common commercial policy shall be based on uniform principles, particularly
in regard to changes in tariff rates, the conclusion of tariff and trade agreements, the
achievement of uniformity in measures of liberalization, export policy and measures to
protect trade such as those to be taken in the event of dumping and subsidies.

2. The Commission shall submit proposals to the Council for implementing the common commercial policy.

3. Where agreements with one or more states or international organizations need to
be negotiated, the Commission shall make recommendations to the Council, which
shall authorize the Commission to open the necessary negotiations.

transfer of competence manifests itself both during the actual trade negotiation stage (where EU negotiators speak on behalf of their constituent
members) and at the ratification stage (where individual member states
no longer have the power to formally ratify international engagements
but instead delegate this power to the collective Council of Ministers).

The pooling of external representation in international trade negotiations, cornerstone of the Common Commercial Policy, placed the need for
international bargaining efficiency above the desire to preserve national
sovereignty. Member states often contested this transfer of negotiating
power to the supranational authority when it did not serve their immediate national interests. This resulted in intra-European crises and confusion for the negotiating partners. Nevertheless, the core principle of the
single voice was never questioned until the 1990s. The changing nature
of trade started, however, to heighten this fundamental tension between
national sovereignty and international bargaining efficiency. From the end
of the Uruguay Round in 1994 to the conclusion of the Nice Treaty in
2000 and the draft constitution in 2003, member states engaged in a spir-
ited legal and political battle to regain some of the supranational autonomy that they had delegated earlier to the Community, leading to a formal
reassessment of the EU's external trade competences.[8]

The Uruguay Round Challenge to EU Trade Competence

During the two decades following the Treaty of Rome, the European
Community successfully negotiated on behalf of its members two major
trade rounds under the GATT, as well as a host of bilateral trade
agreements. However, the emergence of services onto the international
trade agenda in the mid-1980s started to question the clear foundations of
the Community's trade competence. Issues such as aviation and product
standards had been discussed already at the close of the GATT Tokyo
Round in 1979, but most EC member states considered these too domestically sensitive to leave entirely to the supranational Commission to han-
dle. The subsequent expansion of the world trade agenda onto policies
traditionally not "at the border" (e.g., tariffs and quotas) but "inside the

---

The Commission shall conduct these negotiations in consultation with a special committee appointed by the Council to assist the Commission in this task and within the
framework of such directives as the Council may issue to it.

The relevant provisions of Article 228 shall apply.

4. In exercising the powers conferred upon it by this Article, the Council shall act by
qualified majority.

[8] For a detailed analysis of the competence debate and the Court's Opinion 1/94, see
Meunier and Nicolaïdis (1999).

state" (e.g., national laws and regulations) forced an explicit European debate on the issue of competence.

In addition to dealing with unfinished business (including agriculture), the Uruguay Round of GATT launched in 1986 was designed to introduce "new issues," such as intellectual property and trade-related investment measures and services, onto the global trade agenda. Services in particular, ranging from telecommunication infrastructure to professional accreditation and banking, concerned areas that had traditionally fallen under domestic jurisdiction and where concerns about externalities, consumer protection, and the public goods were generally more acute than for trade in goods.

These "new issues" challenged the delegation of trade competence from national to supranational authorities included in the Treaty of Rome. Who, of the Commission or the member states, was responsible for negotiating these new issues was a matter of interpretation, since the founding treaty neither explicitly included services as an area covered by supranational competence nor explicitly excluded them. A political compromise proved necessary in order for the negotiations to proceed: the Ministerial Declaration launching the Uruguay Round at Punta del Este in 1986 was approved both by the Council, on behalf of the European Community, and by the member governments, individually, postponing the question of competence to the end of the round.[9] Whatever the final settlement on the formal competence front, there would be unity of representation throughout the negotiations, but this delegation of competence was to be only temporary.

Serious transformations occurred in Europe during the course of the Uruguay Round negotiations, above all the fall of the Berlin Wall in 1989 and the signing of the Maastricht Treaty in 1992, which formally replaced the European Community with the European Union. Maastricht was supposed to foster closer European integration and further transfers of sovereignty, including in the monetary domain with the eventual creation of a common currency.[10] Yet the spirit of Maastricht apparently did not reach European trade policymakers. As soon as the Uruguay Round negotiations were over, EU member states engaged in a heated debate over whether they should each sign the Final Act of the Round individually or let the Commission and/or the Council do it on their behalf. They finally came up with a typical EU compromise whereby Greece, the Council president, and External Trade Commissioner Leon Brittan signed the act on April 15, 1994, on behalf of the EU, while representatives of each member

---

[9] Arnull (1996).

[10] The Maastricht Treaty deleted and added some text to article 113 but did not modify its substance. See Devuyst (1992) and Maresceau (1993) for a description and analysis of the changes to commercial policy brought about by the treaty.

state signed in the name of their respective governments. In a halfway house between mixed and exclusive competence, individual member states asserted their competence symbolically, but without requiring parliamentary ratification (although some states chose to undergo such ratification).

The Legal Battle over Trade Competence

One of the Uruguay Round's outcomes was the formal placement of the GATT under the umbrella of the new World Trade Organization. The question of membership constituted an unavoidable legal challenge for the EU, even though the rest of the world left it up to the Europeans to decide how this would be settled. The EU had never formally substituted the member states in the GATT, whose creation preceded that of the Community. Since the GATT was only an "agreement" with signatories but no members, the question of Community membership had never formally arisen.[11] For all practical purposes, therefore, the EU—represented by the Commission—had been accepted by the other GATT partners as one of them. Moreover, formally replacing the member states by the EU could have a cost, since the individual voting rights of member states in the GATT would give way to a single vote.[12]

The creation of the WTO, with a broader trade agenda than the GATT, forced the issue of EU trade competence to the fore.[13] Several member states, reluctant to give up forever sovereignty over entire new sectors of their trade policy, insisted on being granted their own competences with respect to the new issues, arguing that these were not covered under the original Treaty of Rome. The Commission suggested in 1994 that the member states become contracting parties in the WTO provided that they would accept the principle of the EU's unitary representation. The Commission even proposed that the WTO agreement be agreed to by a unanimous Council and approved by the European Parliament, when neither was required by law. In effect, the Commission was willing to give up some authority (in granting member states and even the European Parlia-

[11] Denza (1996).

[12] In practice, the cost may not be so high since the WTO has so far always made decisions by consensus and not formal vote. Moreover, there is also a reverse, financial cost of maintaining the member states as WTO members: since the contributions to the WTO are national, the combined contributions of all fifteen EU member states account for 42 percent of the total WTO budget, whereas they would be only 20 percent if the EU were consolidated (and intra-EU trade were not taken into account in these calculations). I am grateful to Jean-Francois Brakeland for his remarks on the real costs of WTO membership.

[13] Devuyst (1995).

ment formal veto power) to retain the principle of exclusive competence in all trade matters. Many in the Commission felt that the restrictions imposed by member states were seriously hindering their effectiveness on the external front.

To solve the competence dispute, the Commission decided to bring the issue to a head. If member states were not going to compromise politically, perhaps their objection could be overruled legally. In April 1994 the Commission asked the European Court of Justice for an "advisory opinion" on the issue of competence. There was actually little doubt inside the Commission that the Court would back its stance and confirm that the scope of exclusive competence extended to new issues. This was going to be a test case of the Court's approach to European external relations, and more generally European integration, in the post-Maastricht era.

The Council and eight member states opposed the Commission's reasoning. France was at the helm of the "sovereignty" camp mostly for ideological reasons, with new concerns over national sovereignty in the wake of the almost disastrous referendum on the ratification of Maastricht in 1992 and a growing mistrust vis-à-vis the Commission.[14] The United Kingdom, traditionally one of the most proliberalization states in the EU, was also opposing the formal expansion of Community competence to the new issues in trade out of a traditional ideological bias against any expansion of supranational authority. Germany also resisted transfers of sovereignty on ideological grounds, mostly because German regulators were highly protective of their powers. It can also be argued that Germany was less secure about its competitive position regarding services than France and Britain and therefore less supportive of the liberal stance taken by the Commission. Finally, countries motivated by sectoral concerns, such as Greece (shipping) and Portugal (textiles), preferred to keep their sovereignty over the new trade issues. On the other side of the spectrum, irrespectively of their economic competitiveness in services, countries with traditionally pro-integrationist stances—e.g. Italy, Belgium, and Ireland—strongly backed the Commission. These countries, especially the small ones, recognized that without the collective negotiating umbrella they would always be at the mercy of the EU's big trade partners.

In their November 1994 opinion, the European judges confirmed that the EU had sole competence to conclude international agreements on trade in goods.[15] In a controversial move, however, they also held that the member states and the EU shared competence in dealing with trade in the new issues. The Court's Opinion 1/94 shocked the Commission and its

[14] In part as a result of the Uruguay Round's Blair House episode, which will be discussed at length in chapter 4.
[15] Including goods falling under the European Coal and Steel Community and Euratom agreements, thereby solving a long-standing dispute. See Court of Justice of the European Communities, Opinion 1/94, November 15, 1994, I-123.

supporters, first by framing the debate over new trade issues as one of "expanding" instead of "updating" the scope of competence, and second by limiting such expansion. The European Court of Justice refrained from (re)establishing exclusive competence for new trade issues because of a change in its assessment of the weight given by some member states to sovereignty concerns in this area—one more piece of evidence that the ECJ's rulings reflect calculations over political acceptability.[16] The recapture of formal power by the member states was also part of a more general trend in the EU. In the aftermath of the Maastricht ratification debates and increased scrutiny and skepticism on the part of national public opinions, it had become clear that most European governments were now increasingly wary of further devolution of sovereignty to the supranational level.

The Court did not, however, ignore the concerns of the advocates for a single voice. To allow for the evolutionary nature of trade, the language of the Court was imprecise, leaving room for interpretation when future conflicts on new issues would arise. In effect, the Court sent the ball back to the politicians. To avoid future competence disputes, they would have to amend the treaty either by following the Court's opinion and enshrining this new sharing of sovereignty in the texts or by explicitly "expanding" supranational trade competence to include new issues.

The Court felt that its restrictive interpretation would not significantly detract from the effectiveness of the EU as an international negotiator. That this would be the case was one of the Commission's central claims. By negotiating with a single voice, the Commission argued, European countries would have more clout in international bargaining. By contrast, exposing the internal divisions between member states would become a bargaining handicap. Although the judges rejected this efficiency argument by stating that the division of competence could not be determined by practical difficulties, they nevertheless directed the Commission and the member states to cooperate closely for the negotiation of WTO agreements, even referring to the "requirement of unity in the international representation of the Community"—crucial since in trade disputes third countries may use retaliation against the Community or the member states, even when their proper competences are not involved.[17] The Court did not immerse itself, however, in the details of how to work out an acceptable practical compromise.[18] Heeding the judges' advice, the presidency drew up in the months that followed an informal "Code of Conduct" spelling out the respective roles of the Commission and the member states.

---

[16] On this debate, see, for instance, Rasmussen (1986); Weiler (1991); Burley and Mattli (1993); Alter and Meunier (1994); Alter (1998, 2000).

[17] Denza (1996).

[18] Arnull (1996).

28   CHAPTER 1

The Political Battle over Trade Competence:
The Amsterdam Compromise

The 1996 Inter-Governmental Conference (IGC) was originally called for
in the Maastricht Treaty to amend its foreign policy provisions. Subsequently the IGC took on board a host of new tasks on human rights and
citizen-related issues, as well as the design of an institutional reform that
would enable the Union to function with twenty-five members in the next
millennium. The revision of article 113 on trade policy was tacked onto
this broad and ambitious agenda. The actual negotiations lasted more
than a year, accelerating in the spring of 1997 in the run-up to the June
Amsterdam summit.

Given the unfavorable legal and political context, the Commission approached the trade competence battle very cautiously. It explicitly stated
that it was not necessary to extend article 113 to the new areas of "trade
and the environment" and "trade and social standards." The Commission
insisted, however, on being granted the exclusive authority to negotiate
trade agreements on all types of services and intellectual property on
grounds of efficiency. With the increasing globalization of the world economy and the growing complexity of trade negotiations, the Commission
argued it was becoming practically impossible to disentangle matters falling under exclusive supranational competence from matters falling under
shared competence since they may all be negotiated as part of the same
package deal. Having to move back and forth between two authority
regimes could only hinder the EU's bargaining strength in international
negotiations. In the words of then External Trade Commissioner Sir Leon
Brittan, wider powers for the Commission and an end to the unanimity
rule in new issues would "speed up negotiations, simplify decision making, and increase the EU's trade policy influence in relation to the U.S.
and Japan."[19]

The national positions taken in the run-up to Amsterdam had evolved
significantly in the two years following the Court's judgment. The "sovereignty" camp shrunk from a majority to a minority, consisting of France,
Britain, Denmark, Portugal, and Spain. France remained staunchly opposed to any further transfer of competence to the EU level. In Britain, the
tension between the ideologically motivated interests and the underlying
economic interests became increasingly apparent. The British position on
the competence issue became less radical and more open to compromise.
By contrast, the "expansionist" camp gained considerable support with

[19] Lionel Barber, "Brussels Strives to Call the Tune on Trade," *Financial Times*, March
12, 1997.

the reversal of Germany's position a few months before the summit. It seemed to have become clear to the trade authorities that Germany had more to lose in keeping future agreements captive to the protectionist demands of Portugal or Spain. Greece and the Netherlands had also changed sides. In addition, the three new member states that joined the EU in 1995 (Austria, Sweden, and Finland) were all firmly with the expansionists. Despite their growing numbers, however, the expansionists failed to create any sort of operational alliance as they sought to retain power over other institutional issues during the Amsterdam conference, and the revision of article 113 was not their top priority. Moreover, it appeared unrealistic to waste political capital on an issue where France and Britain were decidedly on the other side.

After a series of failed compromises and last-minute disagreements, the member states eventually agreed to a simple and short amendment to article 113—renumbered 133—allowing for future expansion of exclusive competence to the excluded sectors through a unanimous vote of the Council.[20] The Amsterdam outcome was, at a minimum, a statement that extension of supranational competence should be the result of case-by-case political decisions rather than some uncontrollable spillover.[21] Supranational competence could now be extended to new issues without having to go through a formal revision of the treaty. This was a significant gain for the parties concerned with efficiency, such as the Commission. This new provision also gave greater flexibility to the Council, allowing it to revisit past decisions if necessary. Arguably, the very possibility of such flexibility—or the "reversibility of delegation"—made it more acceptable to delegate powers to the Commission in the first place.[22]

The Political Battle Settled: The Nice Compromise

Not surprisingly, it quickly became clear that the hard-fought Amsterdam compromise was not sustainable and would need to be revisited. The first reason was the significant increase in trade in services that had taken place since 1997. To capitalize on such growth, Commission trade officials,

---

[20] The new article 113 (5) as finally adopted in Amsterdam reads as follows: "The Council, acting unanimously on a proposal from the Commission and after consulting the European Parliament, may extend the application of paragraphs 1 to 4 to international negotiations and agreements on services and intellectual property insofar as they are not covered by these paragraphs."

[21] It represents one among several examples of "hybrid" decision-making procedures introduced at Amsterdam falling between classical Community delegation and pure intergovernmental approaches. See Moravcsik and Nicolaïdis (1998).

[22] Coglianese and Nicolaïdis (1998, 2001).

under the helm of Frenchman Pascal Lamy since September 1999, insisted that trade in services be transferred under exclusive EU competence for reasons of efficiency, especially in view of the upcoming "Millenium round" of multilateral trade negotiations expected to be launched in Seattle. "United we stand, divided we fall" became the motto of the Commission's trade directorate.

Second, trade had suddenly become a hot political issue, as globalization gave rise to a new brand of well-organized activists worldwide. The defeat of the OECD-based Multilateral Agreement on Investment in 1998, followed by the "Bové incident" in France in July 1999 and, most prominently, the Seattle debacle in December 1999, both reflected and further contributed to the increasingly contentious character of trade.[23] Specifically, antiglobalization activists focused their attention on issues such as trade in cultural, educational, and social services—issues that had been left open to further transfer of competence by the Amsterdam compromise.

Third, the prospect of imminent enlargement of the EU also contributed to calls for revisiting the trade competence issue. Widening membership in the EU to many more countries, with disparate and even contradictory interests, lent a double sense of urgency. On the one hand, external representation—like other policy areas—risked increased inefficiency at best, stalemate at worse. An arrangement originally designed for six members would likely no longer be adequate when the single voice had to represent twenty-five different countries. On the other hand, the current members may have had an interest in locking in their preferred institutional design before the widening to new members. The prospect of new entrants eager to use their veto power to block trade liberalization in some sectors or, on the contrary, eager to favor liberalization in other areas where existing members would prefer protection may have proven enough of an incentive for the existing members of the EU to settle the institutional question in Nice.

Finally, the streamlining of voting procedures on trade fell right within the basic premises of the new Inter-Governmental Conference to be concluded in Nice, France, in 2000—above all, the extension of qualified majority, as put on the agenda by the Portuguese presidency.

In the negotiations preceding the Nice battle, France proved again the most vocal opponent of exclusive Community competence. As French politicians catered obligingly to the antiglobalization rhetoric very popular with a vast majority of public opinion, especially in its cultural dimension, they could not afford to appear to be surrendering the country's cultural heritage to the neoliberal logic of Brussels' bureaucrats—espe-

---

[23] On the Bové incident, see Meunier (2000b).

cially not during a period of "cohabitation" (divided government), which made French politicians even more susceptible to a complete obsession with unanimity on culture.[24] Therefore, France requested a veto on cultural services, masking these demands under other demands for unanimity in equally sensitive services, such as human health and education, which ought not to fall prey to pure market logic. The French did not trust the Commission's capacity to defend Europe's Maginot line against Hollywood.

Unsurprisingly, in Nice as in Amsterdam, the Commission was the strongest advocate of "communitarization"—ironically through the voice of its French trade commissioner, Pascal Lamy, who argued for an extension of majority voting on trade:

> We have to ensure that negotiations on services, intellectual property and investment are handled the same way as negotiations on trade in goods, by qualified majority voting. . . . Crucially, it would enhance European negotiating leverage vis-à-vis third countries. If we want to punch our weight (20% of world trade), that's the key point. Ask any other major trading power, such as Japan or the US. At least in private, they regret our proposed reform, because it would reduce their chances of manoeuvring Member States into blocking an EU position in trade negotiations. And it would thereby reduce the risk of our policy, on crucial parts of the new trade agenda, collapsing to the lowest common denominator. Our leverage in trade negotiations comes from being the world's largest single trading entity. We must take all steps to preserve that, if we are to use trade policy to help bring people out of poverty and to harness globalization.[25]

The Commission proposed to switch all trade issues over to majority voting, while retaining the member states' veto right when basic societal values could be affected. This proposal was supported by Finland, Sweden, Italy, and the Benelux, and more quietly by Germany, Denmark, and Great Britain. Over the course of the IGC, it became clear that a compromise between the maximalist option, which would communitarize all trade in services and intellectual property, and the minimalist option, which would retain the "mixed competence" status quo except for the issues included in a list, could be achieved only by distinguishing between two separate components of the negotiations: (1) whether to communitarize competence, and (2) to the extent that (some or all) competence would be transferred to the Community level, whether to preserve unanimity voting. The introduction of this distinction was the crucial move that opened up the possibility for a compromise.

---

[24] On France and globalization, see Gordon and Meunier (2001).

[25] Pascal Lamy, "Trade Is Changing—So Must Europe," *Financial Times*, December 5, 2000.

The final agreement reflects the bargaining dynamics of the overall negotiation in Nice. There was a general momentum to expand qualified majority voting, and article 133 was to be no exception. Since the implementation of the treaty in February 2003, the general rule for trade in services is now exclusive supranational competence (133.5). At the same time, the compromise included clearly stated exceptions to exclusive competence in order to satisfy residual national sensitivities. First and foremost, the concept of "mixed competence" developed by the Court in its 1994 jurisprudence is now enshrined in the treaty as a new legal category. Particularly noteworthy therefore is the explicit inclusion of the "cultural exception" clause in Community law, with cultural and audiovisual services falling under mixed competence alongside education, social services, and human health services. In addition, transport remains under a separate legal basis (title V and article 300), also subject to mixed competence.

The main result of Nice with respect to trade authority has been to clarify the sharing of competence. This final result proved quite satisfactory for most member states: for France (which was adamant about cultural exception), for Great Britain (which cared more about the linkage with taxation), for Germany (which was happy about the result for air transport, and whose Länder are content with shared competence on culture), and for the pro-integration countries who could claim that the original spirit of the Treaty of Rome has been, at least to some extent, restored.

Trade Competence in the EU Constitution

The Doha Round of multilateral trade negotiations, launched in 2001, is providing the first test of the functioning of the new EU institutional arrangement agreed to in Nice. The true test, however, will be how well this arrangement withstands the new challenges and pressures brought about by enlargement. It remains to be seen how twenty-five, if not more, countries will be able to reach a single voice on matters of trade and abide by the results of international agreements negotiated on their behalf, even against their interests.

The debate over competence in trade policy was not closed with the Nice Treaty, however. When a European Convention on the Future of Europe was convened in the spring of 2002 to draft a constitution for Europe, many voices demanded a greater role for the European Parliament in trade. Indeed, these demands increased as the reach of trade policy expanded to politically sensitive issues that used to be the exclusive domain of domestic regulation, such as food safety and culture. A group of EU parliamentarians filed a constitutional amendment that would give

the Parliament unprecedented powers in shaping EU trade policy, including the establishment of a right to a vote of assent in the Parliament for
any significant bilateral and multilateral trade deals entered into by the
EU. The Commission also strongly pushed for a greater role for the Parliament in trade policy—especially through the voice of Trade Commissioner Pascal Lamy.

In response to these multiple demands, the convention introduced in
its 2003 draft several important institutional changes with respect to trade
policy. First, the constitution project opens up great avenues for parliamentary control. If the constitution is ratified, trade-related legislation,
such as antidumping rules, will now be adopted jointly by the Council
and the Parliament (the so-called codecision procedure). The Commission
is in charge of the implementation of these rules. The Parliament will be
kept informed of the progress of trade negotiations and will get to approve the conclusion of trade agreements. Overall, it will mean equal
power of the Council and the Parliament over trade policy. If adopted,
these institutional changes would make the European trade policy regime
more similar to that of the United States, where Congress has the right to
grant negotiating authority to the president and to veto multilateral and
bilateral trade deals. In the European case, however, the Parliament does
not participate in the elaboration of the negotiating mandate.

The second institutional problem currently faced by the EU is how to
keep an efficient decision-making system in an enlarged Europe. The convention has introduced rules to simplify the complex policymaking apparatus in trade. The proposed constitution clarifies that trade policy is an
exclusive supranational competence, whether in goods, services, intellectual property, or foreign direct investment. This goes further than what
the 2000 Nice Treaty had established. Moreover, the use of qualified majority voting is broadened, with only a few exceptions remaining in matters of trade in cultural and audiovisual services, at the insistence of
France, supported by a majority of member states, including Belgium,
Germany, and Poland. The text actually reverses the burden of proof,
stating that the Council uses unanimity for agreements in trade in cultural
and audiovisual services when it can jeopardize the cultural and linguistic
diversity of the EU. In other cases, majority voting will apply.

From the Council to the Commission: The Single Voice in Practice

The common trade policy entails a second level of delegation—the practical transfer of the competence for negotiating international trade
agreements from the Council (representing national interests) to the Com-

mission (representing supranational interests).[26] This delegation is complex in practice since the Commission negotiates on behalf of the member states, but they retain full political control through the granting of a mandate to begin negotiations and an agreement to approve the results.[27]

The Negotiating Mandate

The European Commission has the power to propose legislation, act as the guardian of EU treaties, and ensure that EU legislation is implemented by all members. The Commission's role in the EU institutional edifice is to act in support of the collective goals and needs, independently of instructions from national governments. Therefore it is up to the Commission to elaborate proposals for the initiation and content of international trade negotiations. The initial proposals are made by staffers in the Trade Directorate (DG Trade), based in Brussels. DG Trade assists, and answers to, the EU trade commissioner, nominated by the member states along with the nineteen other commissioners for a five-year term (between 1999 and 2004, Pascal Lamy; Peter Mandelson since 2004).

Once DG Trade has elaborated proposals for trade negotiations, the key policy discussions take place in a special advisory committee, the Committee 133, named after article 133 on trade policy. It plays a key role in helping member states influence EU trade policy, even though its role is formally consultative only.[28] The agenda of the Committee 133 is set by the Commission, in collaboration with the six-month rotating presidency of the EU. The Committee 133 meets weekly at either the senior level or the level of deputies. The senior members ("titulaires"), senior civil servants from the member states' national ministries as well as the director general of DG Trade, meet once a month in Brussels. In addition they meet in Geneva whenever there are WTO plenary sessions. These senior members serve on the committee for extended periods of time and have a good sense of what actions are politically acceptable within their state of origin. They deal only with politically sensitive problems. The Committee 133 also meets three Fridays a month at the level of deputies, who are drawn from the member states' permanent representations in Brussels, sometimes from the national ministries, in addition

[26] For a general overview of the principal characteristics of the Common Commercial Policy, see Hayes (1993); Smith (1994); Collinson (1999); Meunier and Nicolaïdis (1999); Woolcock (2000); Young (2000); Nicolaïdis and Meunier (2002); and GATT, *Trade Policy Review, 1991*.

[27] For an overview of trade policymaking in the EU, see Meunier and Nicolaïdis (1999); Johnson (1998).

[28] See Ahearn (2002).

to the director of the WTO unit within DG Trade and special experts. The deputies deal with more technical issues. Additionally, there are also subcommittees of a sectoral nature (such as 133 textiles, 133 services, 133 steel), which prepare the work for the Committee 133. Matters are typically discussed until a consensus emerges, and no formal votes are recorded.[29]

The Commission almost always follows the advice of the Committee 133, since its members reflect the wishes of the ministers who ultimately can refuse to conclude the agreement negotiated by the Commission.[30] Once the Committee has amended Commission proposals, they are transmitted to the Committee of Permanent Representatives (COREPER), a key group based in Brussels and composed of the member state officials who are national ambassadors to the EU, their deputies, and staff. COREPER then transmits the negotiating proposal to the Council of Ministers, which has the power to establish objectives for trade negotiations (known as the "negotiating mandate"). Composed of ministers from each government, the Council represents the national interests of the member states. The composition of the Council varies, depending on the subject matter under discussion. With respect to trade policy, the issues are often tackled by the Council of Foreign Ministers, although sometimes it is composed exclusively of trade ministers.

The Council then agrees on a negotiating mandate to hand out the Commission. The mandate is actually made out of "negotiating directives" that are not legally constraining: the negotiator can depart from those directives but then takes the risk of having to sell the negotiating package to the Council at the end of the negotiation. Court jurisprudence and treaty articles spell out the cases in which policy decisions are made according to majority or unanimity. According to the 1957 Treaty of Rome, unanimity should have been used for external trade only until January 1966, the end of the transitional period. Majority voting would have been automatically instituted after this date, had France's Charles de Gaulle not paralyzed the functioning of Community institutions with the "empty chair" crisis during the Kennedy Round. The crisis resulted in the Luxembourg Compromise, an agreement according to which an individual member state could veto a decision otherwise taken according to qualified majority if it deemed that vital national interests were at stake.[31] The

---

[29] The deliberations of the Committee 133 are not published, which is a complaint often raised by antiglobalization groups like ATTAC. But with twenty-six delegations around the table, secrecy can go only so far.

[30] See Hayes-Renshaw and Wallace (1997: 88).

[31] See Garrett (1995) on the Luxembourg Compromise and the various legislative procedures today. See chapter 3 of this book for an analysis of the historical relation between the Luxembourg Compromise and the Kennedy Round.

subsequent addition of new member states increased the divergence of interests within the EC and rendered even more difficult the task of reaching a common bargaining position for international trade negotiations. The 1987 Single European Act attempted to establish the primacy of majority voting. With the exception of sensitive areas such as taxes, employee rights, and the free movement of persons, the member states agreed to use majority voting to legislate on all economic matters.[32] Since then, at least on paper, the Council agrees on a common external bargaining position for international trade negotiations on "traditional" trade issues (exclusive of services and intellectual property) according to a "qualified majority" system. This is a procedure under which member states are assigned different voting weights, based approximately on the size of their population, and roughly two-thirds of the votes are needed in order for a proposal to be accepted.[33] Nevertheless, in reaching a common bargaining position for international trade negotiations, as in reaching most other policy decisions in the Community, member states have most often attempted to find a general consensus around a given issue without resorting to a formal vote.[34]

The competence over external trade negotiations is therefore fairly centralized at the Commission and Council levels. Unlike in other fields of external agreements, such as the association agreements, the European Parliament has no formal say in the process. Subsequent treaty modifica-

[32] See Moravcsik (1991) on the issue of voting in the Single European Act.

[33] From 1995 to 2003, Germany, France, Italy, and the United Kingdom each had 10 votes; Spain, 8; Belgium, Greece, the Netherlands, and Portugal, 5; Austria and Sweden, 4; Ireland, Denmark, and Finland, 3; and Luxembourg, 2. At least 62 votes out of a total of 87 votes needed to be cast in its favor for a Commission proposal to be adopted. In other cases, the qualified majority remained the same, but the 62 votes had to be cast by at least 10 member states. The qualified majority requirements were changed by the 2004 Accession Treaty. A qualified majority will be obtained if the decision receives at least a specified number of votes and the decision is approved by a majority of member states. The weighting of the votes was also changed. See http://www.europa.eu.int/comm/igc2000/dialogue/info/offdoc/guidecitoyen_en.pdf for a table of the new voting weights, including those of the candidate countries.

[34] In 1994 only 14 percent of the legislation adopted by the Council was formally put to a vote and subject to negative votes and abstentions (The Council, *Guide to EU institutions*, EUROPA web server). Moreover, while in theory the consultation procedure (under which Commission proposals can be amended by the Council only unanimously) applies, in practice the Commission alters its proposal several times following the deliberations of the 133 Committee to ensure adoption by the Council. (Garrett and Tsebelis [1997] argue that the consultation procedure gives the agenda-setting Commission the possibility to act strategically in presenting its proposals to the Council.) Even during the height of the crisis created by French demands for a renegotiation of the Uruguay Round agricultural agreement between the EU and the United States in 1993, member states insisted that the tradition of consensus be not broken. See also Devuyst (1995); Paemen and Bensch (1995); and Woolcock and Hodges (1996) on the EC negotiating process during the Uruguay Round.

tions, such as the 1987 Single European Act, the 1992 Maastricht Treaty, the 1997 Amsterdam Treaty, and the 2000 Nice Treaty, have not increased the role of the Parliament in the trade policymaking process. In practice, the Commission and the Council inform the Parliament of the conduct of international trade negotiations on an informal basis and may request the Parliament's approval before the formal ratification of an international agreement. Nevertheless, while it cannot veto trade legislation (unlike legislation in social policy, agriculture, and the internal market), the Parliament can hold hearings and issue reports on trade issues, thereby influencing indirectly the course of trade negotiations. Lately it has tried to exert greater clout over trade, especially those issues with a heavy regulatory component that have divided the EU and the United States.[35] The European Parliament was indeed the driving force behind the EU ban on aircraft engine hushkits to meet noise standards, data protection issues that affect U.S. firms, and broadcast and motion picture quotas. Perhaps this will change with the adoption of the EU Constitution.

The Negotiations

Following the adoption of the negotiating mandate by the Council, the actual conduct of international trade negotiations for the EU is carried out by members of the Commission, acting under the authority of the trade commissioner. In principle, as long as they remain within the limits set by the mandate, Commission negotiators are free to conduct bargaining with third countries as they wish. In practice the negotiators' latitude and flexibility vary case by case, depending on the member states' willingness to retain control over the issue being negotiated, as will be discussed in chapter 2. Moreover, the form of the actual mandate also varies depending on the negotiation: in some cases the mandate takes the form of one or several directives, while in other cases the mandate is only a vague document.[36]

International trade negotiations all include formal, semiformal, and informal phases. In each of these, the role of the Commission and the member states is distinct. In large, formal meetings such as the WTO plenary sessions, member states' representatives are allowed to observe, but only Commission negotiators speak, even on issues involving mixed competences. In semiformal, technical meetings, member states' representatives are not always present in the room. In domains of exclusive competence

[35] See Ahearn (2002).
[36] On the formal vs. informal shapes of the negotiating mandate in trade policy, see Kerremans (2003).

(such as goods and public procurement), the member states are not present at all during the negotiation. They can sit in on a session in the background but not take part in negotiations relating to issues of services, intellectual property, and investment. After each of these technical sessions, the Commission does a debriefing for the member states—including potential difficulties in the negotiation and the need for overstepping the mandate, but not necessarily the actual text agreed to at the end of the day. If during these sessions a member state manifests its opposition, it is up to the Commission's chief negotiator to decide to move forward or to go back on the concessions made to the negotiating partner, arguing that the EU's hands are tied, or to contact the member state directly to bypass the perceived dogmatic position of one of its representatives. Finally, in informal sessions between chief negotiators, few witnesses are present, and the details of the negotiation are not always reported back to the member states.

Ratification

At the conclusion of the negotiations, the trade agreement must be ratified. In cases of agreements falling entirely under EU competence (such as on textiles and steel), the Council approves or rejects the final text according to qualified majority voting—with the exception of some services and intellectual property negotiations where unanimity is the rule. In most cases, however, the ratification process is complicated by the mixed nature of many of the big, packaged trade agreements, which must be approved both by the EU as a whole and by the individual member states. EU ratification occurs through adoption in the Council (concretely, meaning a vote on a one-page decision followed by a thousand pages of annexes). Member states ratify the trade agreement according to their own internal procedures, such as a vote in parliament.

In practice, the Council always decides on the temporary implementation of the EU-only part of the agreement. The rest, subject to national ratification, is implemented later—often years later. Hence, there is no room for big surprises at the ratification stage of the negotiation, since member states have had ample time to manifest their reservations during the course of the international negotiations.

A DELICATE balance between the national and supranational levels therefore characterizes trade policy in the EU, and in particular the negotiation of external trade agreements. The member states retain their power to make the ultimate decisions, but they delegate the day-to-day operation of trade policy to their agent, the Commission. Although based on simple rules for a two-step delegation, the practice of European trade policy has proven quite complex and confusing for the EU's negotiating partners. This is especially the case with the discrepancy between formal and informal rules for making policy decisions. More often than once have the formal voting rules been bent, within certain limits, to satisfy a discontented member state. This institutional uncertainty may make third countries more reticent to conduct negotiations and make concessions to EU representatives. The Uruguay Round triggered questions about the legitimacy of the Commission's representation not only inside but also outside the EU, leading some of its negotiating partners to question the credibility of the Commission if it "cannot deliver on the outcome of a negotiation."[37] Since then, there have been other instances of deals negotiated with a single voice by the Commission on behalf of the whole Community, only to be reneged on later by the member states.[38] Because negotiations are an iterated game, the growing uncertainty that the concluded deal will hold may weaken the long-term credibility of the Commission and render its negotiating task more difficult in the future. Moreover, U.S. negotiators have already started to exploit the EU's institutional uncertainties as bargaining leverage in their favor, for instance by contesting the legality of the negotiators' competence when the proposals are not in the United States's favor.[39] How this complexity has impacted the EU's international bargaining leverage is the subject of the next chapter.

[37] The Uruguay Round will be discussed in chapter 4. See Peter Cook, Australian trade minister, quoted in "US Position on Uruguay Round Talks Needs to Be Less Rigid, French Official Says," *Bureau of National Affairs*, October 21, 1993.

[38] In 1997 the Council attacked deals with Mexico and Jordan, leading to vocal criticisms about the way EU trade policy was being conducted. "Trade Deal Debacles Bring Criticism of Union Mandate," *European Voice*, July 10–16, 1997.

[39] Interview with DGI official, April 1997.

2

EU Institutions and International Trade Negotiations

> In the area of trade policy, negotiations between the member states can sometimes be far more grueling than negotiations with third countries. Inevitably, proposals intended to reflect the collective position—i.e., the Community interest—are amended to take account of the disparate national views until, in many cases, all that is left is the "lowest common denominator." During the Uruguay Round negotiations, this fundamental institutional flaw was cruelly exposed from time to time by the lackluster performance of the European Community.
>
> — Hugo Paemen, principal EU negotiator, 1995

IN SPITE OF its complexities, the pooling of external representation in the EU is generally expected to strengthen the European entity in international trade negotiations. The common expectation is indeed that a united Europe is greater than the sum of its parts. Whether one believes that the distributional outcomes of negotiations are determined by power, preferences, or other ad hoc variables, the common assumption is that the more integrated the EU is, the stronger the bargaining leverage it can exert. Yet, as this chapter will show, the requirement to present a common front in international trade negotiations can strengthen or weaken the EU's bargaining leverage, predictably so, depending on the type of voting rules employed and the specifics of the issue. Specifically, I find that unanimity voting strengthens the hand of EU negotiators to resist demands for policy changes but weaken their ability to advocate policy changes. This chapter develops an institutionalist model of the bargaining leverage of the European Union in international trade negotiations.[1] It aims to specify the

[1] I define bargaining leverage as the ability of a negotiator to obtain the best possible deal in the negotiation—that is, to obtain the most from its opponent while conceding the least, *ceteris paribus*. Since it is problematic to define the "collective" interest of the EU as a whole other than by looking at the common position the member states selected as a result of the voting rule in use, I will observe the EU's collective bargaining leverage from the point of view of its negotiating opponent. The common bargaining position adopted by the member states sets the limits of the mandate given to Commission representatives in international negotiations. Although some or even most member states may not benefit from this common position, once it has been adopted it becomes the official position that EU negotiators defend with a single voice in international settings. Therefore it is possible to talk about an EU

conditions under which institutions matter and transform outcomes in a way not predicted by preferences and power alone. A related argument is that, far from having a negative impact on the collective bargaining leverage, the diversity of European positions might, in some circumstances, act as an influence multiplier and therefore become an asset. Indeed, the EU can sometimes use its institutional constraints strategically in order to reach its negotiating objectives.

Determinants of Trade Bargaining Leverage

Trade negotiations are designed to achieve market liberalization. Despite the expectation of reciprocal gains, however, the negotiating parties often wish to reduce other countries' trade barriers while retaining their own. Bargaining leverage is the ability to maximize one's relative gains in a negotiation. The literature on international political economy usually attributes the highest bargaining leverage in a trade negotiation to the most structurally powerful party, or to the one with the highest intensity of preferences. Indeed, most of the distributional outcomes witnessed in trade negotiations can usually be explained by a combination of power and preferences, while the remainder are usually attributed to ad hoc variables, such as the nature of the issue or the personality of the negotiators. All these explanations assume that the more integrated the EU is, the stronger the bargaining leverage it can exert. Indeed, since its creation in 1957, the European Community has been the sole interlocutor of the member states' trading partners and one of the most influential players in international trade negotiations. What has determined the bargaining leverage of the EC/EU in international trade negotiations? Can power and preferences suffice to explain the performance of Europe in international, especially transatlantic, trade negotiations since its creation more than forty years ago?

Power

Analyses of bargaining leverage in international trade negotiations have traditionally focused on power: the stronger one country's structural position, the more likely it is to get its way in international negotiations. The

"collective interest," equated with the common position. I considered that it was less ambiguous to define the EU's collective bargaining by default: if the U.S. bargaining leverage is enhanced, then the EU collective bargaining leverage is reduced, and vice-versa. On the controversies surrounding the definition of bargaining power, see Clark, Duchesne, and Meunier (2000).

structural determinants of bargaining power are mainly of two kinds: security-related and market-related. Structural theorists expect the configuration of capabilities in the international security environment to affect bargaining power. The larger one's military might and the smaller one's security dependency on the other, the higher the bargaining power in bilateral negotiations. Power determines an actor's bargaining leverage because it gives the capability to threaten and to offer side-payments.

The configuration of market capabilities is also a predictor of bargaining leverage. Negotiating strength can be derived from the size of one's market and by one's dependency on the economy of the negotiating opponent. The larger one's own internal market and the smaller the dependency on the other, the greater the bargaining power in bilateral negotiations. From a power perspective, the creation of a larger, unified internal market enhances the external bargaining strength of the region because the stakes are higher: whoever gets access to its market can now get access to a more desirable, larger market. As Hirschman argued in 1945, the bigger one's own market, and the greater the government's discretion in opening it up or closing it off, the greater one's potential economic power.[2] The offer to open up one's own huge market to other exporters, in return for concessions, can thus be an effective means of influence. This puts third countries in a position of *demandeur* and should therefore improve the EU's international bargaining position. Suddenly European countries have more to offer to the outside world, and they can expect some equal concessions in return.

Customs union theory suggests that, by its very nature, a customs union protected by a common external tariff discriminates against outsiders.[3] Countries inside the union enjoy preferential treatment at the expense of third countries. Thus the integrating region derives some bargaining advantage from being in the position of making concessions while the outside country is automatically placed in a position of *demandeur* since it cannot belong to the "club." Since article XXIV of the General Agreement on Tariffs and Trade exempted customs unions from the most-favored nation clause, which would otherwise oblige them to grant the same preferential treatment to outside members, this discriminatory effect could play in favor of the EU in international trade negotiations.

Competitiveness is another economic determinant of power through which internal integration can affect the EU's bargaining leverage. Liberal

---

[2] On the relationship between foreign trade and national power, see the groundbreaking work of Albert Hirschman (1945).

[3] See, for instance, Viner (1950). The discrimination effects against outsiders are more or less accentuated depending on the degree of trade diversion or creation engendered by economic integration, as was first argued by Viner and has since become a standard argument among economists (e.g., de Melo and Panagariya 1993).

economic theory, which has been underlying the process of European integration from the outset, argues that market integration has the effect of increasing competitiveness—through economies of scale in production, heightened competition, higher investment, and greater research and innovation. This enhanced competitiveness in turn increases the combativity of the EU, because of its new economic might and the argument that the Single European Market, the largest market in the world, can be self-sufficient. Becoming more independent from outside economies, the EU could therefore afford to refuse concessions and thereby increase its own influence on world trading rules. This assumption can explain the attitude of the EU in the late 1980s, which gave rise to third countries' suspicions of a "Fortress Europe."

Applied to the study of trade negotiations between the United States and the European Union, the power hypothesis predicts that EU members wield more international bargaining power when negotiating as one than they would if negotiating individually. It also predicts that U.S. negotiators should have fared better than their European counterparts when the EU market was still made up of a small number of countries, when EU competence applied to a limited number of policy areas, and when Europe felt that it needed the U.S. defense umbrella for its protection. On the other hand, the EU should have obtained better results in trade negotiations with the United States, with a membership of fifteen, with sectors in which EU economies are very productive under discussion in multilateral trade talks, and after the end of the Cold War. The transatlantic balance should tip even further in the direction of the EU once it boasts a membership of twenty-five countries.

Structural analyses of bargaining power, however, do not seem sufficient to explain the distributional outcomes of international trade negotiations. Indeed, the world is strewn with counterintuitive cases where the party that is believed to be weaker, measured through military and other classical structural factors, had the upper hand in an international encounter or at least did not fare worse than its opponent.[4] The Vietnam War and the Soviet-Afghan conflict are well-known examples of foreign affairs outcomes where the structurally weaker party ended up winning. Similar paradoxical results exist in international trade negotiations. For instance, the United States was more successful when negotiating with the European Community regarding its decision to elevate trade barriers on U.S. feedgrains after Portugal and Spain joined the EU in 1986 than it was when dealing with Brazil when the Latin American country introduced a national program designed to promote its national computer industry.[5]

[4] See Keohane (1971); Wriggins (1987); Zartman (1987); Habeeb (1988); Paul (1994).
[5] Odell (1993).

Clearly, any classical aggregate measure of power would assign greater power to the European Community than it would to Brazil. Hence, aggregate power could be an inadequate predictor of trade negotiation outcomes when it is not used in conjunction with other explanatory factors. Similarly, power cannot solely explain bargaining leverage in the U.S. use of the retaliatory trade tool known as Section (Super) 301.[6] A reliance on trade dependence as the sole predictor of bargaining leverage is often misleading. For example, the United States has obtained various degrees of success with "small" as well as "large" economic powers, and various amount of success with the same country on different issues. Moreover, the success rate for Section 301 has increased over time, especially for cases involving the EU, thus casting some serious doubts on a purely power-based analysis of bargaining power.[7]

Preferences

Alternatively, the literature on international political economy has also highlighted the configuration of preferences of the bargaining parties as a main determinant of the distributional outcomes of international trade negotiations. In this view, the willingness of states to make concessions in a negotiation depends on the nature and relative intensity of the actors' preferences—and so does the bargaining outcome.[8]

Preferences can be determined by security imperatives. As many scholars have shown, international trade parallels the logic of security alliances. Trade is more likely to occur between allies than between adversaries, in part because trade creates security externalities.[9] Parties to a negotiation may make efforts to find mutually agreeable solutions or may be ready to compromise and make concessions when the other negotiating parties are allies.

Preferences can also be determined by market position. The particular stance adopted by an actor in an international trade negotiation derives from the configuration of its domestic economic interests. Market structure creates incentives for both openness and closure. One can expect countries to push for trade liberalization in sectors in which they are competitive and ready to confront international competition. Con-

---

[6] Bayard and Elliott (1994); Clark and Duchesne (1997).

[7] From Bayard and Elliott's study of ninety-one cases of the use of Section (Super) 301 between 1974 and 1994 (1994: 65).

[8] See Moravcsik (1997) for a description of this view.

[9] See, for instance, Gowa (1994).

versely, countries will reject liberalization when it would threaten fragile domestic industries, until then sheltered from international competition by protection.

A major challenge in assessing the impact of preferences on international bargaining outcomes, however, is that different actors often hold conflictual preferences. Preferences are, therefore, also a function of domestic politics. An extensive literature has analyzed how politics within national borders determine patterns of interstate trade.[10] The traditional pressure group model of politics suggests that variations in the level of trade protection are explained by the pressures that sectors, firms, and workers exert on politicians.[11] A country will resist trade liberalization if free trade inflicts losses to groups with a disproportionate amount of political power. Political institutions become captive to those special interest groups who are especially powerful for a variety of reasons, including financial support, historical relationship, or potential for disruption (e.g., French farmers' and truck drivers' lengthy and violent protests). As a result, both the international negotiating position and the bargaining strength of a country can be directly traced to the domestic power of certain pressure groups.

To some extent, one could expect these conflictual preferences to be attenuated over time and gradually replaced by collective preferences. Many scholars have indeed speculated that European integration may have an indelible effect on its participants. They see the EU as a social laboratory that transforms national identities into a collective identity distinct from the sum of its constituent parts. Early studies of the emerging process of European integration posited that belonging to the Community would transform the preferences of its participants, and therefore alter the external environment. Karl Deutsch and his "communitarian" followers argued that successive stages of integration could be expected to gradually build a sense of community in the region, at the expense of outsiders.[12] By becoming socialized as "Europeans," EC policymakers, negotiators, and technical experts would develop ways of working that would increasingly isolate those who do not belong to this network. Therefore, the stronger the sense of European solidarity, the harder the EC would defend its position externally. Hence, in the spirit of this communitarian approach, giving the EC a single voice in international trade negotiations would contribute to strengthening its bargaining position. This theory of political communities finds resonance in today's constructivist approach

[10] See, for instance, Gourevitch (1986); Frieden (1988); Magee, Brock, and Young (1989); and Rogowski (1989).
[11] See, for instance, Gourevitch (1986); Rogowski (1987); and Magee and Young (1987).
[12] Deutsch et al. (1957).

to international relations. Alexander Wendt's focus on the transformation of state identities suggests that the creation of a European entity has altered national interests and implies that the Community's constituent members will identify collectively in the face of external pressure.[13] Similarly, constructivist scholars of the EU, such as Jeffrey Checkel, argue that "learning" and "persuasion" are an integral part of the process of European integration.[14] Therefore, the nature of collective preferences may differ from the sum of the individual preferences of the member states.

According to the preferences hypothesis, many crucial elements of an international trade negotiation are determined by preferences, such as the "win-set" (the overlap of what is acceptable by all parties) and the relative opportunity cost of forgoing an agreement. A major challenge in understanding the impact of preferences for explaining the EU as an international trade bargainer is the additional political level introduced by the supranationalization of trade policy. References to national preferences alone cannot explain why the EU agrees to trade liberalization, or rejects it in a given negotiation. Empirical observations of the discussions leading to the adoption of a common position reveal the strength of national preferences and thereby weaken (but do not reject completely) the constructivist claim that integration fosters the emergence of collective preferences. Since national preferences are still highly differentiated, we need to know how the diverse national preferences are aggregated into a single position. Combining power and preferences is not a sufficient explanation either: one could argue that the preferences of the most powerful EU members systematically become the preferences of the whole EU, but historically this has not been the case either, especially when the large member states disagree.

Ad hoc Variables

Additionally, analysts have focused on a variety of alternative and complementary factors specific to the negotiations in question to explain distributional outcomes. One argument that is sometimes used to account for differences in bargaining outcomes is that the nature of the issues at stake influences the final result. These outcomes can always be explained with reference to the "specificity" of the issue-area addressed in the negotiation. In other words, it is not possible to compare apples with oranges—or agriculture with aviation or public procurement.

[13] Wendt (1994).
[14] Checkel (2003).

Another common argument is the leadership and entrepreneurship role played by the negotiators themselves.[15] According to this view, the process and outcomes of negotiations can be explained, at least partly, by the skills, personal experience, values, and ideology of individual negotiators and decision-makers.[16] While these skills and values may indeed play some role in the negotiating process, they can only explain marginal outcomes. There is only so much a negotiator can do when he or she is constrained in their every move by strict negotiating instructions emanating from their home governments. The firmness, friendliness, and creativity that individual negotiators might display at the international table are allowed to exist only within the limits set by their principals.

Institutions

If power, preferences, and remedial ad hoc variables cannot explain fully international negotiating outcomes, what other variables account for the paradoxical "wins" of the structurally weaker over the structurally stronger parties in international negotiations, and for the decision of the EU to pursue liberalization or protection against the will of some of its member states? The central argument of this book is that the EU's complex institutional structure and the requirement to negotiate international trade agreements with a single voice have an important, sometimes decisive, impact on international trade negotiations. Joining the growing literature that examines the interrelation of domestic and international levels of analysis in the study of international political economy, this book argues that an understanding of the EU's role as a trade negotiator requires an understanding of the ways in which "domestic" institutions shape the bargaining behavior of international actors—"domestic," in the case of the EU, meaning at the national level. In the absence of fundamental structural asymmetries between two trade partners, it may be the evolution of their domestic and international institutional contexts that determines their respective bargaining power, and ultimately their level of success, in international trade negotiations.

Why and how has the EU been able to capitalize on its institutional requirement for unity in order to extract concessions from its negotiating opponents?[17] Is there a positive correlation between the depth of institu-

[15] See Moravcsik (1999) for an extensive critique of this argument.

[16] Not surprisingly, the various individuals whom I interviewed for this book all emphasized the crucial role played by individual negotiators in striking deals and concluding negotiations.

[17] For reasons of convenience, I mainly use the designation "European Union" (EU) throughout this chapter. While the broader European institution was renamed European

tional integration and the external bargaining power of the collective entity? If structural factors determine the ability of parties to a negotiation to obtain satisfactory outcomes, how can we explain variations in the distributional outcomes of simultaneous negotiations involving the same cast of players?

When the EU enters into trade negotiations with third countries, its member states have to reach a common position at the European level before it can be defended at the international level with a single voice. Throughout the history of European integration, member states have used several different rules to aggregate their divergent interests into this single voice, as was shown in the previous chapter. For instance, they can agree that they will each hold veto power over the common position adopted, or they can decide instead according to majority rule. They can also agree to grant their common negotiators leeway in the bargaining process, or they can keep their negotiators under tight rein. The institutional rules through which the divergent preferences of the member states are aggregated into one common position are open to change and strategic manipulation—often during times of grand bargaining, such as a treaty renegotiation, but sometimes even during the course of a negotiation.

How does this "single voice" obligation affect the likelihood of an international agreement, the content of the agreement, and the individual countries' chances at influencing the final agreement? It is easy to comprehend why countries strengthen their individual voices by combining forces with others when their interests converge on a given issue. But what is the effect of being forced to negotiate as part of a single whole when the interests of the constituent parties are divergent? More generally, what are the bargaining effects of combining negotiating forces with others? The remainder of this chapter will attempt to answer all of these questions by using a simple spatial model combining voting rules and nature of the negotiating context. Even though it is a clear simplification of the complex reality of international trade negotiations, it should provide some elements of answer.

Internal Constraints and External Strength

The standard assumption is that the EU is handicapped internationally by the complexity of its institutions and the limitations on the competence of its negotiators. Hugo Paemen, who was chief EC negotiator during the

---

Union by the 1993 implementation of the Maastricht Treaty, the EC is still the official designation of the EU's "first pillar," which is in charge of economic and trade policy.

TABLE 1
Determinants of EU International Bargaining Leverage: Independent Variables

Independent Variables	EU Bargaining Leverage		
	Mechanisms of Bargaining Impact	Role of EU	External Bargaining Impact
Power	Security environment Market position	Larger, more competitive market	Enhances collective bargaining leverage
Preferences	Security alliances Economic interests Domestic politics Collective identity	Transforms preferences	Enhances collective bargaining leverage
Ad hoc variables	Nature of issues Skills and personalities of negotiators	Supranational negotiators provide leadership	Enhances likelihood of pro-integrationist final agreement
Institutions	Institutional framework (decision-making rules, delegation rules)	Aggregates divergent preferences	Depends on specific institutional conditions

Uruguay Round, identified three "fundamental institutional flaws" in his own account of the negotiations.[18] First, the lowest common denominator position prevents the EU from making innovative proposals and therefore from having a lot to offer to its negotiating opponent in order to extract concessions of a similar nature. Second, the institutional design of the EU deprives negotiators of one crucial bargaining element: uncertainty. Because member states reveal their position during the Council meetings, which set the limits within which Commission negotiators are allowed to proceed, the EU cannot hide its bottom line. Finally, as a result of the sharing of power between the Commission and the member states, the EU is ill-equipped to act swiftly in the final hours of a negotiation, when agreements are always hammered out. This view of the institutional framework as constraint has been mostly propagated by the EU negotiators themselves, who have relentlessly asked member states for increased competence over trade issues. Yet is it always the case that the complex institutional structure of the EU and the need for member states to speak with a single voice weaken the capacity of the EU as an international negotiator?

[18] Paemen and Bensch (1996: 95).

The Schelling Conjecture

Negotiation theory indeed suggests that, in certain conditions, we could expect the EU to use some of its institutional flaws strategically to gain concessions from, or avoid making concessions to, its negotiating opponent. As Schelling noted in *The Strategy of Conflict*, having one's hands tied internally can be useful for extracting concessions externally. The "power to bind oneself," for instance through inflexible negotiating instructions and divisions highly visible to the opposite party, can confer strength in negotiations.

> The well-known principle that one should pick good negotiators to represent him and then give them complete flexibility and authority—a principle commonly voiced by negotiators themselves—is by no means as self-evident as its proponents suggest; *the power of a negotiator often rests on a manifest inability to make concessions and to meet demands.*[19]

This paradoxical idea that bargaining strength can, under certain conditions, derive from an apparent position of weakness has become known in the political science literature as the "Schelling conjecture."[20] In his "Essay on Bargaining," Schelling noted that an actor operating under certain constraints might be able to better accomplish his goals in a negotiation than a similarly situated, but unconstrained, actor. In particular, a domestic ratification constraint provides a negotiator with a bargaining advantage. U.S. negotiators have often employed this tactic, obtaining bargaining leverage by reminding their opponents of the likelihood of a rejection by Congress of the agreement under negotiation.

"Ordinary" bargaining, Schelling writes, occurs when the bargainers do not know each other's true reservation price and thus go through a process by which they attempt to misrepresent their own reservation price while discovering that of their counterparts. In this context, bargaining is the strategic use of information—one party wants to manipulate what the other party believes to be its reservation price. This transmission of information is the function served by the often dramatic posturing that occurs during real-life bargaining situations. However, since each actor knows that its counterpart has strategic incentives to obscure his own reservation price, this posturing is likely to convey little information that can be taken at face value. Since it is impossible for the seller to observe the buyer's preferences directly, and the merely verbal revelations of his

---

[19] Schelling (1960: 19); emphasis added.
[20] See, for instance, Milner (1997); Milner and Rosendorff (1997); Clark, Duchesne, and Meunier (2000); Tarar (2001).

preferences will be discounted by the seller, the buyer's efforts will be directed toward showing how he could not choose to spend more than his reservation price even if he wanted to. The seller's efforts, in contrast, are directed at determining whether or not the buyer's statements regarding these constraints are true. It is in this sense that Schelling asserts that "the process of discovery and revelation quickly becomes merged with the process of creating and discovering commitments."[21]

The existence of constraints can help a negotiating party accomplish the goal of minimizing the cost of the good by making it more difficult (or, better still, impossible) to retreat from a particular offer to something close to his or her true reservation price. In the case of U.S. government strategy in trade negotiations, Schelling points out that "If the executive branch is free to negotiate the best arrangement it can, it may be unable to make any position stick and may end by conceding controversial points because its partners know, or believe obstinately, that the United States would rather concede than terminate the negotiations."[22]

Two-level Games and the Schelling Conjecture Revisited

In a seminal article published in 1988, Robert Putnam elaborated on Schelling's argument and thereby triggered a scholarly debate on the strategic interaction between domestic and international variables in international negotiations. Putnam used an extended metaphor in which international negotiators are simultaneously seated at two tables—each corresponding to a different level of analysis. At level one, the international level, negotiators interact with their foreign counterparts. At level two, the world of domestic politics, negotiators interact with their domestic principals. Putnam describes the logic of the two-level game in the following way: "At the national level, domestic groups pursue their interests by pressuring the government to adopt favorable policies, and politicians seek power by constructing coalitions among those groups. At the international level, national governments seek to maximize their own ability to satisfy domestic pressures, while minimizing the adverse consequences of foreign developments."[23]

Since each of the actors possesses an effective veto over any agreement that would displace the status quo, Putnam's model implies that an agreement must lie at the intersection of each of the actors' "win sets"— that is, the set of alternatives that each actor prefers to a no agreement

---

[21] Schelling (1960: 27).
[22] Ibid., p. 28.
[23] Putnam (1988: 432).

outcome. The location of the actor's reservation point determines the size of his or her win set. It is important to point out that the international negotiator can be constrained by the domestic veto player only if the latter's win set is smaller than the former's.

How does the existence of a domestic veto player with a smaller win set than its international agent affect the distribution of the gains from cooperation?[24] Without delving into technical issues, suffice it to say that if the expected agreement in both of these cases is something like the midpoint of the interval in each case, and the probability of reaching an agreement is independent of the existence of a veto player, then an agreement in the presence of such a domestic veto player will be closer to the ideal point of the country A actors (and further from the ideal point of the country B actors) than it would be in the absence of such a domestic veto player. Furthermore, the distributional consequences of having a veto player can be expected to be an increasing function of the difference between the size of the domestic and international veto player's win set. It is the size of the domestic win set—not the difference in preferences between domestic principals and their negotiators—that drives the distribution of the gains in the outcome. In fact, if the domestic win set is smaller than the international win set, then the outcome is likely to be independent of the latter. Conversely, when the international negotiator has a smaller win set than the domestic veto player, then it is the former's reservation price that will set the bargaining parameters.

While the presence of a domestic veto player can constrain the international negotiator in a way that produces a better outcome for country A, this is not, under complete information, the result of the sort of strategic behavior—the bluffing and fooling—that Schelling was most interested in. If bargaining is about "the ability to set the best price for yourself and fool the other man into thinking this was your maximum offer," then the essence of two-level bargaining would be the attempt to misrepresent the reservation price of the actor that your foreign counterpart is least informed about—your domestic veto player. Thus, the heart of the "Schelling conjecture" is the attempt by the international negotiator of country A to convince country B's negotiators that the domestic veto player in country A has a lower reservation price than it actually does. If it can do so, then country A may be able to appropriate a bigger share of the gains from cooperation than it might be "objectively" entitled to.

Studies of two-level games, initiated by Putnam's article, have attempted to confirm Schelling's intuition that the constraints imposed by domestic institutions could prove a bargaining asset in international nego-

---

[24] See Clark, Duchesne, and Meunier (2000) for an extensive discussion of this issue.

tiations.[25] Putnam raised the possibility that international negotiators might be able to use domestic constraints to their advantage at the international negotiating table. Subsequent attempts to analyze the conditions under which such a strategy will be effective have led to conflicting views. Mayer modeled the conditions under which division can be an asset or liability in international negotiations.[26] Contributors to the 1993 *Double-Edged Diplomacy* volume, who attempted to test empirically the interactions between domestic politics and international bargaining, concluded that although potentially beneficial, the strategy of the divided bargainer has not been used much in practice.[27] Similarly, Milner and Rosendorff argued in 1997 that the conditions under which behavior consistent with the "Schelling conjecture" occurs were quite limited.[28] By contrast, Clark and Duchesne found evidence of Schelling-type behavior at work in the negotiations leading up to the Canadian-U.S. Free Trade agreement.[29]

Two-level game studies have often concentrated on the impact of domestic ratification constraints on international agreements. Yet ratification is only one aspect of the complex web of rules through which diverse preferences are aggregated into a common position. In the EU case, this complexity is amplified by the existence of three levels that interact in international bargaining: domestic, supranational (European), and international.[30] Moreover, the two-level game literature has generally not considered the existence of distinct negotiating contexts, based on the nature of the demands in the negotiation. Yet whether preferences are distributed on one side of the status quo or the other transforms the potential impact of institutional rules on the final outcome. I argue, therefore, that two central variables contribute to determining the EU's external bargaining power: the level of supranational competence (made up of internal EU voting rules and degree of delegation to the supranational level) and the nature of the negotiating context.

Supranational Competence and Negotiating Context

The members of the European Union negotiate international trade agreements as a single entity, in spite of their diverging preferences. Different formal and informal rules, both for making decisions and for delegat-

---

[25] Putnam (1988).
[26] Mayer (1992).
[27] Evans, Jacobson, and Putnam (1993).
[28] Milner and Rosendorff (1997).
[29] Clark and Duchesne (1995).
[30] On the EU case, see Patterson (1997); Hug and Konig (2002).

ing negotiating authority, can be put in place to fulfill this obligation of "speaking with one voice." Which rules provide the EU with the stronger bargaining capabilities on the international scene? The ways in which these institutional processes influence the divergence between the reservation prices of the negotiators and domestic veto players need to be analyzed in a systematic fashion.

Internal EU Decision-making Rules

By joining the European Union, individual member states have delegated their authority to make trade policy to the collective Council of Ministers. National preferences have to be aggregated into a supranational common position before they can be defended at the international level. The conduct of trade policy reveals a second level of delegation, this time from the Council of Ministers to its negotiating agent, the European Commission. EU Commission officials conduct international trade negotiations, within the limits set by the Council's mandate. At the conclusion of the negotiations, the Council approves or rejects the trade agreement. Although the trade policymaking process has been the longest and most successfully integrated in the EU, a central characteristic of it has been the uncertainty surrounding the voting rules in use for both the mandate and the ratification stages. This uncertainty has worsened throughout the 1990s under the pressure of the changing nature of trade. In spite of formal rules laying down the procedures for majority voting, the Council has often agreed to the mandate by unanimity because of the existence of a formal or informal veto right by individual member states.

In the following model of pooled representation, I use a simple spatial mapping of the EU internal voting process where the issue-specific policy preferences of the member states are ordered along a single dimension from the status quo to a higher degree of preferred policy change.[31] For instance, if the issue being voted on is the reduction of agricultural subsidies, some countries may prefer to keep the current level, while others may want their complete elimination, and the majority may be somewhere in between. If the issue is about genetically modified foods, some countries may want to keep the moratorium, others may want their complete ban, and others may want to approve them completely. In many cases of trade negotiations that are about removing impediments to trade, the alignment of preferences mirrors the protectionist versus liberal dichotomy: the

---

[31] For the same type of spatial models applied to other policy areas, see, for instance, Garrett (1995); Garrett and Tsebelis (1996); Frieden (2003).

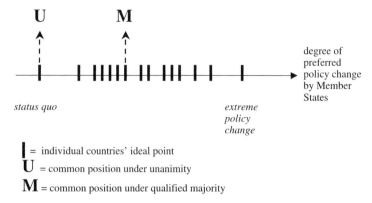

1. Impact of Internal Voting Rules on the EU Common Position

countries closest to the status quo are protectionist, while the countries farthest from the status quo are pushing for international liberalization.[32]

Whether member states follow the voting rule of unanimity or qualified majority to make their decision produces different common bargaining positions under a given set of policy preferences (see figure 1).

UNANIMITY

The voting rule of unanimity gives each country a veto. When each member state possesses the power of veto, whether at the outset of a negotiation or at the ratification stage, the common position eventually reached is the lowest common denominator.[33] Indeed, in case member states fail to agree on any other common position, the status quo is the default position, which enables the most conservative state to set the terms of the collective message. By contrast, this power to dictate the terms of the final decision to fellow Community members does not apply to the state with the other extreme preferences because, theoretically, it prefers any proposal that provides an improvement over the status quo. Therefore, unanimity has the effect of amplifying the most conservative voice by giving it the weight of all member states when it becomes the common EU position. It could be argued that, in practice, not all states share an equal veto right: a threat of veto from one of the big countries (e.g., France, Germany, the UK) carries more weight than a threat of veto from a smaller

---

[32] For the sake of simplification, I make the additional assumption that all countries are on the same side of the status quo.

[33] See Garrett and Tsebelis (1996: 281).

member state. In theory, however, any country could rally the collective position around its preferences in the case of unanimity rule.

MAJORITY

By contrast, majority rule has the effect of mitigating extreme positions. Under the qualified majority system in place until November 2004, states had to gather about one-third of the total EU votes to block a proposal. After the implementation of the Nice Treaty, the number of votes allocated to each member state was reweighted, and in order to pass, a qualified majority must now fulfill the following conditions: the decision receives a set number of votes; the decision is agreed to by a majority of the member states; and the majority represents at least 62 percent of the population of the European Union.

Several studies of the EU decision-making system have tried to highlight the ability of particular governments to influence the outcome of Council decisions by analyzing the possible winning coalitions to which each member state is pivotal.[34] Applied to the configuration of preferences displayed in figure 1, the studies' results suggest that the common position under qualified majority usually falls around the proposal originally made by the Commission—except when the Commission has extreme preferences, in which case it lies at the limit of what the qualified majority will accept.[35] Therefore, most member states benefit from this voting rule because qualified majority gives their preferred position the support of the whole Community. The losers from this voting rule are the states with extreme preferences, since they can be outvoted.

A cautionary note is in order here: the focus on the formal decision rules may overlook the importance of the informal decision rules. The de jure distinction and history of disagreements between cases settled by unanimity and cases settled by qualified majority was presented in chapter 1. De facto, however, the distinction is more blurred, as voting is rarely used and the modus operandi in most cases seems to be consensus.[36] Case evidence suggests that the norms of consensual decision making run deep in the EU, and national representatives preparing Council decisions try hard to avoid outvoting each other, seeking instead common solutions to

[34] See, for instance, Hosli (1996) for an application of the power indices method to the study of decision making in the Council of Ministers. Subsequent criticism of this literature, however, has shown that it has systematically overestimated the power of governments with extreme preferences and underestimated the power of more centrist governments because of its lack of emphasis of the policy preferences of the member states. For a thorough analysis of the complexities of EU voting rules, see Garrett and Tsebelis (1996, 1997).

[35] Jupille (1999).

[36] On the practice of consensus, see Lewis (1998); Neyer (2004).

the problems faced. How can the informal norm of consensus properly be accounted for in the formal model? Indeed, thanks to consensus, states with extreme preferences may not be outvoted under QMV but partially accommodated. In that sense, the effect of consensus on the single voice may be to shift the equilibrium position toward the preferences of the most conservative country, to the left of the position expected under qualified majority. While the widespread recourse to consensus does muddy the conceptual clarity of the present model, it nevertheless leaves the broad lines of analysis intact.

The one-dimensional spatial model presented in figure 1 illustrates the mechanical effects of different voting rules on policy decisions, under a given set of preferences. It shows that unanimity (ex ante or ex post) amplifies the most conservative voice, while majority mitigates the extremes. Of course this presentation is extremely simplified. For one, it does not take into account the reality that states with outlying preferences can often be appeased through side-payments, issue-linkages, and temporal trade-offs, which diminish the likelihood that they will recourse to veto.[37] Yet despite its simplified assumptions, this model provides a first step toward analyzing the impact of the EU's institutional structure on its external bargaining capabilities.

Negotiating Competence

A related institutional variable, which may impact the external bargaining power of the EU, is the competence delegated by member states to Commission negotiators. The practical conduct of international trade negotiations involves some delegation of competence by the Council (principal) to the Commission (agent).[38] Nicolaïdis has established a useful distinction between three attributes of the negotiating mandate that helps us operationalize the variable "delegation of competence": flexibility, autonomy, and authority.

- *Flexibility* refers to the nature of the mandate that the principals give to their agents at the outset of an international negotiation. A mandate can be vague and flexible, with the negotiators being instructed to do "the best they can," or it can be more restricted, with a specification of the concessions that are acceptable. It can

[37] See Mayer (1992) for an analysis of the strategic use of internal side-payments. For an analysis of cross-issue linkages, see Davis (2003).

[38] Studies stemming out of the rational choice institutionalist tradition have analyzed the act of delegation of authority for certain functions by a group of principals (i.e., the member

also serve for the entire duration of the negotiation or it can be subject to updating to fit changes in the political environment.

- *Autonomy* refers to the extent to which the principals are actually involved in the negotiations. The autonomy of the agent can be limited for instance by "obligations of reporting regularly to the principals" and by having the principals actually "sitting at the negotiating table alongside the agent."[39]
- *Authority* refers to the ability of the agent to make promises and deliver on these promises. The authority of the negotiator depends on the procedures used for ratification and on the uncertainty associated with these procedures. As Nicolaïdis rightly observes, "this is the only one of our three attributes which is used in the analysis of two-level games. It is indeed the most visible and quantifiable constraint."[40]

These three attributes of the delegation depend as much on the formal rules as on the current political climate. De jure, EU negotiators work within the limits set by the negotiating mandate agreed to by the Council but are left free to conduct the bargaining as they wish until the final agreement is submitted to the member states for approval. De facto, the authority of the Commission is a day-to-day struggle. Commission representatives attempt to exercise as much autonomy as possible without asserting it in such a manner that it could provoke a backlash from sovereignty-wary member states.

The nature of the delegation is an important variable to consider because the agent's own preferences may potentially affect the content of the final agreement. As Pollack has argued, the EU Commission does have preferences distinct from those of the member states.[41] Since the Commission is a complex organization composed of multiple individuals from multiple countries working in multiple areas, it is difficult to talk globally about its substantive preferences. In the specific case of international trade negotiations, however, the Commission can be generally characterized as more liberal than the majority of the member states. Thus, if the Commission is more of a free-trader than its principals, and if it enjoys some supranational competence, it can be expected to move the location of the agreement within the bargaining space further up on the protectionist-to-liberal scale. It is more difficult for member states to veto an agreement once it has been negotiated and presented to them as a fait accompli

---

states in the Council) to an agent (i.e., the Commission) in the European Community context. See, for instance, Pollack (1997) and Nicolaïdis (1998).

[39] Nicolaïdis (1998: 11).

[40] Ibid.

[41] Pollack (1996).

than to change specific provisions as the negotiations proceed. This is also the rationale behind the U.S. administration's push for the fast-track procedure.

The variables of voting rules and negotiating competence are quite distinct in theory. They each produce specific effects on the process and outcome of international bargaining. Nevertheless, in practice, they are most often positively correlated. Commission autonomy is fundamentally endogenous to the voting rules in place, which are largely determined by the will of the member states. When unanimity is used (formally or informally), less policy-making functions are delegated to the agent: the most conservative member state tends to keep a tight leash on the Commission to ensure that the negotiating mandate is respected.[42] Member states may be reluctant to delegate extensively when the issue at stake is particularly salient for them, even though the treaties require them to do so. In that case, the most conservative country will insist that EU negotiators report every step in the bargaining process and wait for orders before making any concessions. Under majority voting, by contrast, negotiators usually have more bargaining latitude. The mandate given is more vague, thereby giving the negotiators more flexibility. Therefore, the most conservative state does not need to keep the negotiators in check since it will not have the final say on the agreement anyway.

For these reasons, I have chosen to bundle together the two variables of voting rules and delegation under the single heading of "supranational competence" for the remainder of this book.

Nature of the Negotiating Context

The final variable central to this model is the nature of the negotiating context. The distribution of the policy preferences of the EU and of its negotiating opponent relative to the status quo determines distinct negotiating situations. In turn, these distinctive contexts influence the impact of EU institutional mechanisms on the external bargaining capabilities of the EU.

First, several assumptions need to be made. I assume that the distribution of policy preferences of the member states is observable by all agents. Information, or lack thereof, is therefore not a crucial element in the model.[43] Member states as well as third countries can roughly observe the preferences of a country on a given issue—for instance by following de-

---

[42] Argument made by Franchino (1998).

[43] See Clark, Duchesne, and Meunier (2000) for a model of EU-U.S. trade negotiations based partly on incomplete information.

bates in national parliaments, holding formal and informal conversations with members of government, reading the national press, and following opinion polls.

I also make the simplifying assumption that the EU and its opponent do not have the choice of accepting or rejecting a negotiation when it is initiated by the other party. There are two main empirical rationales for this assumption. First, negotiations on a given issue cannot be examined separately from negotiations on other issues: in today's multilateral trade regime, all negotiations are linked. In the "prenegotiation" phase, the actors identify the problems to be addressed and agree on the issues to include in the negotiations.[44] This first phase can take years to complete, during which the parties weigh their chances of obtaining favorable outcomes on a given issue and balance them against issues from which their opponent is expected to derive greater relative gains. For instance, the EU was drawn into negotiating agricultural liberalization in the Uruguay Round of the GATT only under the promise that financial and other services would be included in the multilateral negotiation. The second phase is the actual conduct of the negotiations on substantive issues, during which concessions are made and details are hammered out. This is why it is fair to assume, for the purpose of my model, that after the prenegotiation phase has occurred, neither party can refuse to negotiate.

A second practical rationale is that most trade negotiations are of an "integrative" nature—also referred to as "non-zero sum game."[45] Countries accept entrance into these negotiations in the first place because they each hope to derive some benefit. This is in stark contrast with many foreign policy negotiations, which are about dividing a "fixed pie"—for instance, with a given piece of land as the coveted prize that both parties try to appropriate. In an integrative negotiation, which is about increasing the size of the pie, each side is likely to try to maximize the benefits the opponent is willing to extend, while minimizing its own concessions. If the issue being negotiated is the liberalization of a particular sector and its opening up to foreign competition, for instance, each side agrees to the negotiation based on its belief that gaining new markets will be beneficial. Each party, however, may try to obtain the freest possible access to its opponent's market while keeping as many restrictions as possible on the entry to its own market. The transatlantic disputes on aircraft subsidies and public procurement are good examples of such negotiations. For the purpose of this model, it is therefore fair to assume that each party accepts the negotiation initiated by the other party.

---

[44] See Hampson (1995) for a discussion of the multiple phases of a multilateral negotiation. See Davis (2003) on issue linkage.

[45] The distinction comes from Walton and McKersie (1965).

A further assumption is that the preferences of the actors are not symmetrically distributed around the status quo. One can assume that governments prefer too little rather than too much policy change. If the issue being discussed is the reduction of agricultural subsidies, for instance, it is politically more costly (mostly for reasons of collective action problems) to reduce them too much rather than preserving them at the current level.

Finally, I make the assumption that the EU's negotiating opponent is a unitary actor. This is a strong simplification that assumes one side in the negotiation has a domestic ratification constraint, while the other side is treated as if having no necessary domestic ratification.[46] I therefore treat the opponent as a "black box," whose internal institutional procedures have no impact on the international negotiation.[47]

Let us distinguish between two negotiating contexts (see figure 2). For reasons of simplification, I refer to the EU's negotiating opponent as the United States—but the model can account for the bargaining of the EU with any other third country.

CASE 1 ("CONSERVATIVE")

The first configuration is called "conservative" because it is about conserving the status quo policy, while the negotiating opponent demands change. Negotiators often refer to this type of case as "defensive." In a conservative case, the preferences of the EU member states and of the negotiating opponent are distributed so that the opponent is the furthest away from the status quo. This definition rules out cases in which the preferences of the member states are distributed on both sides of the status quo. If unanimity is equated with the status quo position, while majority yields a common position further remote from the opponent than was the status quo, then I argue that the opponent will not challenge the EU into a negotiation. This would be a Quixotic fight since, in the best case, all the opponent would obtain from the EU would be the status quo and, in the worst case, it would have the potential to obtain a bargaining outcome worse than the current status quo. In other words, the negotiating opponent challenges the EU to change its policy, based on its assessment that the worst possible outcome is the status quo.

A large number of conflictual EU-U.S. trade negotiations since the 1960s have involved the preservation of the European policy status quo. Transatlantic negotiations on agriculture, for instance, have typically

[46] See Tarar (2001) for an analysis of the dynamics of international bargaining in a situation where both sides are similarly constrained.

[47] Since the opponent's institutions have an impact in the real world, I therefore always speak of the EU's "potential" (and not actual) bargaining capabilities. Interesting results would surely emerge from relaxing this assumption.

Conservative case

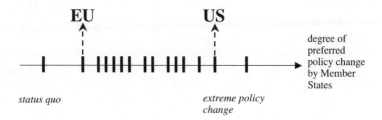

EU   US

degree of
preferred
policy change
by Member
States

status quo   *extreme policy*
                                change

Reformist case

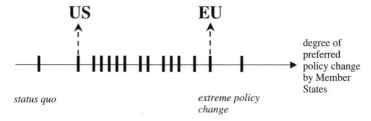

US   EU

degree of
preferred
policy change
by Member
States

status quo   *extreme policy*
                                change

2. Conservative vs. Reformist Negotiation

been characterized by U.S. demands for change in the EU's protectionist Common Agricultural Policy (CAP). Other, similar negotiating contexts have included the dispute over the national content of broadcast programs during the Uruguay Round, the EU banana import regime, and the beef hormones dispute.

CASE 2 ("REFORMIST")

The second configuration is called "reformist" because it is about the EU demanding changes in the policies of its negotiating opponent. Negotiators often refer to this type of case as "offensive." In a reformist case, the opponent's preferences are closer to the status quo than the preferences of the EU member states. In other words, the EU is the one making demands on the policy status quo of a recalcitrant negotiating opponent.[48]

[48] The assumption of uncertainty over the decision-making rules enables us to make abstraction of the strategic behavior of member states over whether to use their veto. There

The advent of the Single Market program, which made the EU more powerful and more attractive to investors, and the simultaneous return to unilateralism in U.S. trade policy produced a rapid increase of trade negotiations in which the EU became the "demandeur" since the late 1980s.[49] For instance the EU tried to pry open its competitors' markets with negotiations on reciprocity in the original Second Banking Directive in 1988 and in the Utilities Directive on public procurement in 1990.

EU Institutions and International Trade Negotiations

By what mechanisms do internal institutions affect external outcomes? Under what conditions are EU institutions an asset or a liability in international trade negotiations, and how can they maximize the potential bargaining power of the EU? The institutionalist model illustrated in figure 3 stresses processes of precommitment in the EU bargaining strategy, which allows negotiators to strike the optimal balance between maximizing distributional gains and minimizing the chance for involuntary defection. This simple model combines the central variables of supranational competence and negotiating context to try to answer these questions.

The pooling of external representation has a direct impact on the outcomes of international trade negotiations. Internal voting rules, coupled with parallel delegations of competence, affect the EU's potential international bargaining power differently whether preferences are distributed according to the first or the second configuration.

Conservative Negotiation

As long as the EU as a whole is closer to the status quo than its negotiating opponent, bargaining theory predicts that the outcome of the negotiation will be equated with the Community's position.[50] In this case, the opponent cannot obtain departures from the status quo greater than what the EU is willing to offer. By shifting the equilibrium outcome closer to the

---

have been many documented cases in the EU where member states have vetoed a deal that they did not care about, only to obtain internal concessions in other issue areas. For instance, in 1994 Spain threatened to veto the accession of Austria, Finland, and Sweden, unless its fishermen were allowed to fish in British and Irish waters. In 1992 Italy blocked a big budget-reform package in order to get a higher quota for milk production and an assurance it would not be prosecuted for earlier cheating on its milk quota. This give-and-take game between the member states is outside the focus of this book.

[49] See, for instance, Hocking and Smith (1997).

[50] The outcomes were determined using the Nash bargaining solution. I am grateful to William Clark and Ariel Rubinstein for helping me identify the most appropriate tools for analyzing the possible outcomes of these negotiations.

A. CONSERVATIVE CASE

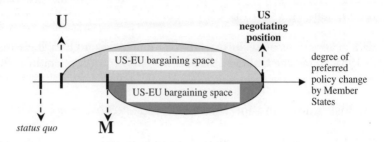

B. REFORMIST CASE

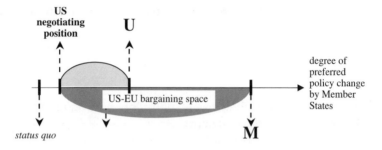

$\mathbf{U}$ = EU common position under unanimity

$\mathbf{M}$ = EU common position under qualified majority

3. Impact of EU Voting Rules on Bargaining Space with Third Countries

EU position, pooling makes the negotiating opponent worse off. Nevertheless, the third country can potentially win greater or fewer concessions depending on the extent of supranational competence demonstrated by the EU.

RESTRICTED COMPETENCE

Unanimity amplifies the power of the EU's most conservative state by ensuring that the negotiating position adopted is the lowest common denominator, while enabling this position to resonate internationally through the combined weight of the whole Community. Unanimity has the effect of restricting the likelihood that an agreement will be reached, since the negotiating opponent would be only marginally better off from the negotiation than from the status quo.[51] The institutional difficulties associated with altering the common position make the EU a very tough bargainer. When it is known to the negotiating opponent that the EU cannot deviate from its offer, the Community can use its institutional constraints as an excuse for not coming up with enough concessions. Therefore, the threat of having one outlying country eventually overturn the international agreement leads to minimal, or even no, gains for the opponent. In that sense, unanimity reinforces the potential bargaining power of the Community.

Negotiators with limited flexibility have very little room for maneuver and cannot hide their bottom line, since the EU reservation value becomes common knowledge. Negotiators with little autonomy are required to constantly report to the member states and await further negotiating instructions. Negotiators with limited authority cannot guarantee that the principals will uphold the agreement negotiated on their behalf. In a conservative case, tight constraints exerted by the member states on the negotiators can enhance the credibility that the offer made is of a "take it or leave it" nature. The negotiating opponent is aware that the hands of the EU negotiators are "tied": each bargaining move by the agent has to be cleared by the principals—that is, by the most conservative principal. As a result of the EU negotiators' "tied hands," the challenger may settle for only limited concession, for fear of being left with no agreement at all. Hence, limited negotiating delegation ensures that the final outcome does not deviate from the preferred position of the EU. It can thus be used strategically to enhance the bargaining power of the EU as a whole. This hypothesis is consistent with the Schelling conjecture, while at the same time restricting its application to specific conditions.

From the perspective of individual member states, the pooling of external representation through unanimity benefits overall the states whose preferences are closest to the status quo—that is, the most conservative. If all the EU member states have close preferences, "trading voices" makes all of them better off. The closer these preferences are to each other and the farther they are from those of the negotiating opponent, the greater the benefits of a common position.[52]

EXTENSIVE COMPETENCE

Qualified majority, by contrast, mitigates the extremes. The most conservative state cannot impose upon others its preference to preserve the status quo. Qualified majority increases the likelihood that an agreement

---

[51] See Putnam (1988). The "win-set" is defined as the set of potential agreements that would be ratified by domestic constituencies.

[52] See Frieden (2004).

will be reached, since there is no uncertainty that the final deal will be approved by the Council. The challenging opponent benefits from being faced with a Community governed by majority rule in this case. It can expect greater gains than it would have obtained, with the same distribution of European preferences, under unanimity. In that sense, qualified majority does not enhance the EU external bargaining power as much as unanimity does. Yet it still makes the negotiating opponent worse off than in the absence of pooled representation.

A more extensive delegation of negotiating competence has one immediate effect on the process of bargaining with third countries: it improves the chances of conclusion of an international agreement. When the negotiators have been delegated more extensive flexibility, autonomy, and authority by the principals, they have more institutional latitude to find creative bargaining solutions. They can successfully negotiate an international agreement, knowing that their principals will not be allowed to bicker on the details of the deal. This is the rationale behind the "fast track" process of executive delegation in U.S. trade policy. When the EU common position is closer to the status quo than that of its opponent, an extensive delegation of competence entails a more liberalizing outcome than would have been achieved under restricted delegation. On the other hand, an extensive delegation of competence in the EU brings greater rewards for the negotiating opponent. EU negotiators cannot exploit the "tied hands" strategy, and the opponent knows that EU negotiators will be able to "sell" the agreement as a whole to their principals.

The pooling of external representation in a conservative case benefits the majority of member states when supranational competence is extensive. The country with the most conservative preferences is worse off than in the unanimity case, although better off than it would be in the absence of pooling.

Reformist Negotiation

When the EU stands further away from the status quo than its negotiating opponent, bargaining theory predicts that the outcome of the negotiation will be equated with the opponent's position. Therefore, the internal EU voting rules have a less decisive impact on the final outcome of the international negotiation than in the first case, even though they still influence the likelihood and the process of the negotiation. Yet if, for an external reason, the negotiation has to proceed, once again unanimity and qualified majority inside the EU will produce different bargaining outcomes.

RESTRICTED COMPETENCE

Unanimity ensures that the common negotiating position stands as close as possible to the position of the third country. Since it takes only one member state to cancel EU demands for change, the unanimity requirement makes a Community-led offensive less likely. It is easy to imagine that the negotiating opponent can try to "divide and rule" the member states by introducing its own Trojan Horse in the EU (for instance, through promises of side-payments, such as a major public purchase, or a trade-off with another area, such as defense). This Trojan Horse can use the threat of veto in order to get EU demands for policy change dropped. If the negotiation were to proceed, the outcome would stand at the opponent's ideal point. Most offensives, however, never materialize into actual negotiations.

As in the conservative case, a restricted delegation of negotiating competence ensures the capture of the negotiating process by the most conservative state in the EU. In a reformist context, it means the state with the preferences closest to those of the negotiating opponent. Therefore, unlike in the conservative case, limited EU competence plays to the advantage of the opponent. The Schellingesque strategy of "tied hands" does not apply in this case. As for the likelihood of an agreement, it is low since the negotiators do not have much latitude over the details of the deal.

For individual member states, unanimity benefits the state with the most conservative preferences since it can capture the collective EU position. This is similar to what happens in the conservative case, where the most conservative state can dictate the terms of the final agreement. Contrary to the conservative case, however, this time unanimity decreases the overall bargaining power of the EU since the negotiating opponent can more easily obtain what it desires—that is, little or no change in the status quo.

EXTENSIVE COMPETENCE

Qualified majority has the effect of making the negotiation more likely in a case of extensive competence since only a majority of member states are needed to challenge the policies of third countries. The absence of veto power deprives the negotiating opponent of the option of driving a wedge among member states by convincing only one country to derail the EU's offensive. If the negotiation must proceed (for instance, if reciprocity is involved), the EU is a tougher bargainer than in the case of restricted competence. As long as the opponent holds the keys to the preservation of the status quo, however, the negotiation outcome will also stand at the opponent's ideal point.[53]

An extensive delegation of competence means that EU negotiators can make demands, offers, and concessions without waiting for the member states' approval. It increases the likelihood that a final agreement will be concluded. The Schelling conjecture does not apply in this case either. Extensive supranational competence enhances the EU's ability to implement effective offensive actions against trade rivals; the majority can maintain an offensive even if a few member states defect; and the negotiating opponent will find it difficult to induce sufficient defection. Table 2 summarizes the findings and the predictions about the institutional determinants of the EU's external bargaining capabilities.

The main finding that EU supranational competence, as well as negotiating context, have a profound effect on the outcomes of international trade negotiations explains why the fight over the sharing of competence in trade policy has been so fierce in recent years. To the question of what is the optimal institutional design for maximizing the EU external bargaining strength in trade negotiations, this model answered that it depends on the situation, and it depends on for whom.

From the opponent's point of view, qualified majority voting is preferable. In the conservative case, when the European common position is closer to the status quo, majority voting clearly improves the final outcome for the negotiating opponent. In the reformist case, however, the EU does not hold the keys to the final outcome anyway. For maximizing EU bargaining strength in international negotiations, therefore, the design should be reversed: unanimity produces a stubborn, "tied hands" international bargainer. From the point of view of individual member states, the optimal institutional design differs depending on their preferences. Limited supranational competence should be favored by a state at the conservative extreme of the preference distribution, since such competence amplifies its external voice by giving it the weight of the whole EU. By contrast, relatively higher supranational competence is desirable for states with median preferences because it attenuates the extremes and gives their own position the support of the whole EU.

A logical extension of this model would be to release the assumption that the negotiating opponent is not domestically constrained. Would the combination of voting rules/delegation/negotiating context be expected to produce different outcomes if the United States is treated not as a

[53] In cases where the EU can use retaliation and alter the context of the negotiation, as in the EU-U.S. negotiations over public procurement in 1990–1994, internal voting rules start again to have an impact on the outcome of the negotiation: majority voting can enhance the collective bargaining power of the Community, while unanimity is more desirable for the opponent. Note that these effects are reversed from case 1.

TABLE 2
The EU's Institutional Structure and International Trade Negotiations

Supranational Competence	Negotiating Context/Status Quo	
	Conservative (Case 1)	Reformist (Case 2)
Unanimity	*Likelihood of agreement*: Low.	*Likelihood of agreement*: Low.
	Bargaining outcome: Stands at the ideal point of the most conservative EU member state.	*Bargaining outcome*: Stands at the ideal point of the negotiating opponent.
	Winners and losers: The EU collective bargaining power is high. The most conservative state wins. Most other member states would have benefited from a different voting rule.	*Winners and losers*: The opponent is protected from change; thus the EU bargaining power is low. The opponent can play "divide and rule." The amplified preferences of the most conservative country have only a limited impact on the final outcome.
Restricted delegation	The tied hands strategy and the Schelling conjecture apply. They work to the advantage of the EU as a whole.	No tied hands strategy. The opponent benefits from the capture of the agent by the less reformist member state.
Qualified majority	*Likelihood of agreement*: High.	*Likelihood of agreement*: High.
	Bargaining outcome: Stands at the ideal point of the pivotal EU state.	*Bargaining outcome*: Stands at the ideal point of the opponent.
	Winners and losers: The EU collective bargaining power (measured from the opponent's viewpoint) is lower than under unanimity. The most conservative states lose from this voting rule.	*Winners and losers*: The opponent holds the keys to the agreement, but cannot use a "divide and rule" strategy. The reformist countries benefit from having the issue put on the negotiating table, even if no agreement is reached.
Extensive delegation	No tied hands strategy since the agents have some bargaining latitude. The negotiation is more likely to progress successfully when the negotiators can find creative compromises.	No tied hands strategy. The likelihood of agreement is increased by the bargaining latitude available to the negotiating agent.

"black box" but as a complex, multilevel polity also subject to domestic ratification constraints? Tarar has tried to reevaluate whether the Schelling conjecture still holds when both sides in the negotiation face internal constraints.[54] He found that if both sides' constraints are low, the constraints have no effect on bargaining. If only one side's constraint is high, that side obtains an advantage. If both sides' constraints are high, the executive from the side moving second in the negotiation has the advantage. The results of my model seem not to be in contradiction with Tarar's, especially when the conservative/reformist dichotomy is understood as a substitute for the second-mover/first-mover dichotomy. Nevertheless, further work on this subject seems warranted.

The combination of negotiating context and supranational competence points to the existence of a link between the EU's institutions and external bargaining power. It also highlights a link between the EU's institutions and the nature of the international political economy. Most trade negotiations today are about market access and "behind the border issues," not tariff reductions.[55] Member states' preferences can be ordered along a continuum going from protectionism to liberalism. For a given set of member states' preferences, the supranational competence exerted by the EU can have a different impact on the potential for world trade liberalization. Unanimity voting and restricted delegation are likely to exert a protectionist influence on the international political economy. In the first case, where the EU's opponent attempts to lift access restrictions to the European market, unanimity subjects the collective EU position to the whims of its most protectionist member. In the second case, where the EU attempts to get its opponent to lift restrictions against access to its own market, unanimity makes the EU more likely to stop pursuing negotiations, thereby failing to promote liberalization. Majority voting, by contrast, has a liberalizing influence on the world economy, since it prevents states with conservative preferences from holding the EU position hostage. The influence of the EU's institutional structure on international economic liberalization is worth considering since the EU is the world's largest trader and, along with the United States and Japan, sets almost all of the world's economic rules.

THIS chapter presented a model linking preferences, institutions, and outcomes. It argued that the bargaining leverage of the EU in international trade negotiations is not driven entirely by its aggregate power, nor by the intensity of its preferences. Instead, the capability of the EU to affect the distributional outcomes of international trade negotiations also stems

[54] Tarar (2001).
[55] See, for instance, Peterson and Cowles (1998).

from the institutions through which these preferences are aggregated. Indeed, the pooling of sovereignty reshapes power relations in the international arena, as the first part of this book argued. The following chapters will operationalize these institutional variables and examine the propositions about the impact of the institutional aspects of the pooling of external representation on its bargaining leverage in a series of case studies of past and ongoing trade negotiations between the European Union and the United States.

The United States is the EU's main trading and investment partner. If the EU institutions indeed impact its external bargaining capabilities, it should be particularly apparent in transatlantic trade negotiations, since the desire to put Europe on an equal basis with the United States in the conduct of world affairs was one of the less avowed rationales behind the initial creation of the European Community. Negotiations with the United States also provide a nice test of the institutional determinants of the EU bargaining leverage since the United States has enjoyed a fairly balanced trade relationship with the EU and is almost structurally equal to it— whether in terms of economic output, population, level of development, or standard of living. Moreover, the EU and the United States have successfully reached trade agreements on nonconflictual issues when their bargaining position easily converged or when trade-offs between sectors were possible, such as the successive reductions of industrial tariffs since the 1960s. Most other EU-U.S. trade negotiations have been conflictual, sometimes very publicly, such as on agriculture, audiovisual services, and aeronautics. In several cases since the late 1980s, the EU made "reformist" demands, trying to pry open the U.S. market—such as the reciprocity provisions of the 1988 Second Banking Directive, and the third-country provisions of the 1990 Utilities Directive on public procurement. Except for these few market-opening efforts, however, the majority of conflictual trade negotiations in which the EU participated have involved some challenge of the European policy status quo.

The cases of EU-U.S. trade negotiations examined in this book are the agricultural negotiations during the Kennedy Round (1964–1967), the agricultural negotiations during the Uruguay Round (1986–1993), the negotiations on reciprocity in public procurement (1990–1994), and the ongoing transatlantic negotiations on open skies agreements in international aviation (since 1992). All these cases resulted in agreements, but often after protracted negotiations and years of impasse. In some instances, the final international agreement reflected disproportionately one party's preferences. In others, the EU and the United States had to make similar concessions in order to reach an agreement. In some instances, the final international agreement was disproportionately weighed in favor of one member state. In others, the agreement satisfied a majority of member

TABLE 3
EU Institutions and Specific EU-US Trade Negotiations

	Negotiating Context/Status Quo	
Supranational Competence	Conservative (Case 1)	Reformist (Case 2)
No EU competence	Open skies agreements (phase 1)	
Restricted (Unanimity voting and restricted Commission autonomy)	Kennedy Round agricultural negotiations Uruguay Round agricultural negotiations (phase 2) Open skies agreements (phase 2)	[none]
Extensive (Qualified majority voting and some Commission autonomy)	Uruguay Round agricultural negotiations (phase 1)	Public procurement negotiations

states. The institutionalist argument developed in this chapter will help explain the variance in outcomes between these cases.

These particular cases were selected because they provide institutional variation, as illustrated by table 3. In two cases, the institutions remained constant throughout the negotiation; in two other cases, the rules of the game changed in the middle. The agricultural negotiations during the Kennedy Round are an example of conservative negotiation in which the supranational autonomy was nonexistent and the mode of decision making in the EC was unanimity. The United States capitulated to an inflexible Common Market, especially in the wake of de Gaulle's "empty chair" policy, and the final deal reflected the EC's lowest-common-denominator position. The agricultural negotiations during the Uruguay Round offer a rare example of agreement in a conservative negotiation resulting from a sizable degree of supranational competence, especially when contrasted to the recapture of national competence through the reinstatement of the veto power after 1992. The dispute over reciprocity in public procurement represents the first successful reformist attempt by a Community deciding under qualified majority rule and enjoying some supranational competence. The open skies negotiations in international aviation illustrate in a first stage what happens when member states are not obligated to negotiate with a single voice, and in a second stage how the transfer of negotiating competence to the supranational level affects the international agreement. As noticed in table 3, there is no case of offensive negotiations coupled with low supranational competence because by definition the Community can afford to attack others' markets only when it has successfully liberalized its own, which implies some surrendering of national sovereignty.

Additionally, the cases selected provide some variation in issue areas (agriculture, procurement, air transport), thereby avoiding outcomes biased by the "special" nature of one issue. Moreover, these cases offer some variation in the time factor. They make possible intertemporal comparisons, since one case took place in the 1960s, one in the 1980s, and two in the 1990s. Each of these cases also unfolded over periods of several years, which provide for institutional change within almost each case. Yet several of these cases overlap in time, thus enabling the elimination of outside factors, such as changes in the security environment, in the comparison.

These four cases allow us to address the question of the external consequences of institutional integration and to test the institutionalist hypotheses. They contribute to empirical knowledge about EU-U.S. trade negotiations, and more specifically about the role played by the EU's use or nonuse of a single voice. The case studies all point to the fact that, given exogenous member states' preferences and depending on the conservative/reformist negotiating context, the degree to which member states were willing to let go of their sovereignty affected the process and outcome of the final international trade agreement.

3

EC-U.S. Agricultural Negotiations in the Kennedy Round, 1964–1967

THE KENNEDY ROUND of the General Agreement of Tariffs and Trade was the first real test of the effect of the integration of the six members of the European Community on international trade negotiations. The rapid economic successes of the Common Market prompted the American administration to engage in global negotiations with the EC to ensure that it would not turn into a protectionist fortress. Industrial tariffs were the primary issue negotiated in the round. Nevertheless, the fear generated by the formation of the Common Agricultural Policy in Europe led the U.S. administration to make agriculture the benchmark by which to judge the success or failure of the round. A central agricultural disagreement between the United States and the EC rapidly deadlocked the negotiations, at times jeopardizing progress in other sectors. Eventually, the Europeans obtained an international agricultural agreement on their own terms. Why did the EC gain favorable outcomes in negotiations with the United States when the former was still institutionally weak and inexperienced? Why was the United States defeated in the Kennedy Round on "grounds of its own choosing" at a time of U.S. hegemony and fledgling integration in Western Europe?[1]

This chapter argues that the European institutional constraints partly determined the preponderant influence exerted by the EC on the final agreement in agriculture. In this exemplar "conservative" case, where the EC was trying to preserve externally the hard-won internal European status quo on agricultural policy in the face of American demands for change, the strict intergovernmentalist decision-making process served as formidable bargaining leverage. On several occasions the EC used its incomplete transition from national to collective policies as an excuse for not making progress in the negotiations. Given the inflexibility of the European position and the tied hands of the Commission negotiators, rendered even more credible by the 1965 crisis of the EC institutions, the U.S. administration was forced to give way to an incapacitated Common Market and to accept agreements it disliked, for fear of being left with no agreement at all.

[1] Warley (1976: 387).

American and European Objectives in the Kennedy Round

Even though the Kennedy Round was formally launched only in May 1964, its beginnings are often traced to the GATT Ministerial Conference of May 16–21, 1963, during which the principal protagonists agreed on the broad principles and objectives of the negotiation. In particular, it is during this conference that the EC and the United States decided to include agriculture in the Kennedy Round but, unable to agree on the specifics because of their divergent preferences, left resolving the controversial details to later.

American Objectives in the Kennedy Round

The Kennedy Round was the first real test of the external effects of the integration of trade policy and trade negotiating authority in the European Economic Community. The Dillon Round (1960–1962) aimed at resolving technical problems caused by the creation of the Common External Tariff in the EEC; only a small part of the negotiations was devoted to true tariff reductions. By contrast, the Kennedy Round was called in direct response to the challenge posed to the United States by the rapid success of the Common Market and the impending establishment of the Common Agricultural Policy.

A REACTION TO THE SUCCESSES OF THE COMMON MARKET

The most pressing international economic issue facing the United States in the early 1960s was the impact of the formation of the European Economic Community: it could affect both the growing unemployment rate in the United States and the deficit of the U.S. balance of payments, two central themes of the Kennedy electoral campaign in 1960. In July 1961 Britain had announced its decision to apply for membership in the EEC. The strong belief shared among Kennedy administration officials that the British government's application for membership into the Common Market was going to be successful increased the urgency of an American response to the potential external effects of the EEC and prompted the United States to demand a new round of multilateral trade negotiations. In his January 1962 special message to Congress, President Kennedy emphasized the obsolescence of U.S. trade policy as a result of "the growth of the European Common Market": "An economy which may soon nearly equal our own, protected by a single external tariff similar to our own, has progressed with such success and momentum that it has surpassed its original timetable, convinced those initially skeptical that there is now no turning back, and laid the groundwork for a radical alteration of the economics of the Atlantic Alliance."[2]

Even after France vetoed the entry of Great Britain in January 1963, the United States still pledged to succeed with a new round of negotiations designed to prevent the EEC from turning inward-looking. American policy was to prevent an EEC market of 190 million people, providing production potential equal to that of the United States, from fragmenting the Western world into competing trade blocs and provoking the demise of the multilateral trading system. Preserving access for U.S. goods into the Common Market was absolutely crucial to the U.S. economy, since in the years since the creation of the European Community U.S. exports to the EEC had grown roughly three times as fast as U.S. trade with any other major destination.[3] Moreover, American officials worried about the newfound bargaining strength of the Common Market countries and about the necessity "to deal with them as a group."[4]

In launching the preparatory steps for the Kennedy Round in 1962, the central objective of the United States was therefore to curtail any protectionist tendencies of the Common Market in both the industrial and the agricultural sectors. The bargaining principle proposed by the United States was to cut all tariffs (industrial and agricultural) in half over five years, with a minimum of exceptions. This would ensure that all product groups would be subject to substantial tariff reductions. The longer-term goal of the United States was to set a precedent for dealing with the "unified and coequal bargaining force with the United States"[5] and learning to share power in the determination of world trade rules.

THE INCLUSION OF AGRICULTURE

The initial impetus for including agriculture in the Kennedy round negotiations was American. The Treaty of Rome founding the European Economic Community had provided an obligation to establish common rules

[2] Kennedy (1962: 68).
[3] See "Components of a Strategy for the Kennedy Round," preliminary draft, December 10, 1963: "Our trade with Western Europe is important not only in absolute terms but because of the rapid rate of growth it has enjoyed. Reflecting the prosperity that has accompanied the Common Market, U.S. exports to the EEC in recent years have grown roughly three times as fast as our trade to any other major destination. . . . Since the growth rate of the Common Market countries is beginning to slow down, it is doubtful that the previous growth rate of American exports to that area will continue." George Ball Box 7, John F. Kennedy Presidential Library, Boston.
[4] Seymour E. Harris, Memorandum on trade policy, December 4, 1961, NSF Box 309–310, Trade, General, 1962, John F. Kennedy Presidential Library, Boston.
[5] Preeg (1970: 13).

for agriculture, but little guidance on how to proceed. So much uncertainty surrounded the nature of the emerging agricultural arrangements in the Common Market that the United States wanted to anchor agriculture firmly in multilateral trading rules. The Kennedy administration expected that these negotiations would curtail the potentially protectionist nascent CAP and result in fair access for U.S. agricultural exports in Europe. At the time of the Kennedy Round, agricultural products represented 40 percent of U.S. exports to the EEC. It was therefore vital to ensure that American producers would not suffer from discriminatory measures resulting from the integration of the agricultural sector in Europe. Hence, U.S. officials emphasized unambiguously that the Kennedy Round would be a success only if liberalization applied to agricultural products.[6] Indeed, the United States set the rules of the game and, at the outset, selected agriculture as the key issue by which to judge the success of the round, as opposed to industrial goods.[7]

The first encounter of the United States with the CAP, over the issue of poultry exports, occurred during the preliminary negotiations for the Kennedy Round.[8] By mid-1962 Germany was the biggest customer of American chicken, accounting for 56 percent of total U.S. poultry exports.[9] When the EEC initiated its variable levy system in July 1962 as a result of the implementation of the first CAP measures, the immediate impact on U.S. chicken exports to Germany was more than a doubling of the previous tariff—from less than 5 cents a pound in July 1962 to 13.5 cents in July 1963. In nine months under the new system, U.S. exports of poultry to Germany had dropped to 40 percent of the previous year's level. By 1965 there were virtually no more exports of U.S. chickens to the German market. After months of trying to negotiate a rollback of the higher tariffs from the EEC, the United States decided to retaliate against the Common Market by raising tariffs on forty-six million dollars of EEC

[6] Christian Herter, U.S. special trade representative, quoted in *The Journal of Commerce*, May 15, 1963: "The participants in the Kennedy Round have laid down as their object the liberalization of trade because it is seen to be to their advantage. But such liberalization cannot be achieved in any field unless it applies as much to agricultural products as to industrial products. With agricultural exports to the EEC running at the rate of $1.6 billion per annum, the USA would find it difficult to estimate what tariff reductions on industrial products that interest the Community it could reasonably offer if significant offers were not forthcoming from the EEC in the agricultural field."

[7] Why, then, as Shonfield asked, "had the Americans decided to make this essentially secondary, and exceptionally difficult, matter the key issue in the biggest multilateral tariff negotiation ever undertaken? The answer which suggested itself was that they had come to the conclusion that they now had a decisive competitive edge in agricultural trade and were determined to exploit it in full." Shonfield (1976: 33).

[8] Talbot (1978). On the Chicken War, see also Evans (1971); Conybeare (1987).

[9] Preeg (1970: 74–77).

exports. Eventually a GATT panel ruled that the United States could impose sanctions in the amount of twenty-six million dollars, which officially ended the "Chicken War." This had been the first concrete test of the new agricultural policy of the EEC members and had suggested that the Common Agricultural Policy would surely have a variety of other negative trade effects on third countries. Therefore, the 1963 "Chicken War" reinforced the determination of the United States to prevent a potential disruption of world trade in agriculture caused by newly or soon-to-be enacted rules in the Common Market.

The Kennedy administration had other motivations for limiting the anticipated negative effects of the CAP. First, U.S. officials initially believed that Great Britain would join the EEC. Since Britain was the world's largest agricultural importer, the United States became worried at the prospect that it might adopt the CAP. Second, farm exports were expected to reverse the deterioration of the U.S. balance of payments.[10] Moreover, President Kennedy needed to curb the protectionist tendencies of the CAP because of a deal struck with Congress, which agreed to support the 1962 Trade Expansion Act in return for the promise that U.S. agricultural exports would be facilitated.[11] Finally, the technological revolution that had ensured the productivity and competitiveness of American agriculture was starting to reach the Common Market. U.S. officials feared that European politicians would have great difficulty resisting domestic demands for an expanding share of the European agricultural market.[12] For all these reasons, the United States elected to make the preservation of its access to European agricultural markets its primary objective in the upcoming round of multilateral trade negotiations.

MAIN U.S. AGRICULTURAL OBJECTIVES IN THE
KENNEDY ROUND NEGOTIATIONS

The central U.S. strategy in the Kennedy Round was to ensure that GATT rules would apply equally to industrial and agricultural products, and in particular that agricultural production and trade would be determined by

[10] "There was a spreading awareness that agriculture was one of the few industries in which the United States had an unassailable economic advantage and in which it could meet foreign competition head to head and win. . . . Thus, progressively over the course of the 1960s, agriculture gradually moved in official thinking from being an expensive problem to the status of a glamour industry, capable, were it not for the policies of others, of meeting a trinity of priority policy objectives and delivering a huge prize to the American economy." Warley (1976: 320).

[11] According to Warley (ibid.: 378), congressional support could be obtained only "if the negotiations manifestly held out some promise to the farm lobbies that opportunities for their agricultural exports to the European market would be improved by rolling back the protectionist tendencies evidenced in the CAP."

[12] "Components of a Strategy for the Kennedy Round."

comparative advantage and market mechanisms. To confront the EEC on its proposed CAP, the United States was thus ready to abandon its traditionally protectionist agricultural policy.[13] The main American objectives in the Kennedy Round negotiations were to prevent the acceleration of the movement of Community countries toward agricultural self-sufficiency as a result of the existence of incentives for uneconomic production, "to liberalize to the maximum extent possible the Communities' common barriers to trade, and to establish a precedent for further efforts in the future to keep the Communities outward looking in both political and economic terms."[14]

U.S. preferences in the agricultural negotiations with the Common Market were initially threefold. First, the United States wanted tariff concessions on agricultural goods similar to the tariff concessions on industrial goods, that is, cuts of 50 percent.[15] Second, the United States wanted the removal of nontariff barriers not justified under the GATT, since nontariff barriers had restrained American agricultural exports to Western Europe more than tariff barriers. U.S. projections for agricultural exports in 1970 estimated that if foreign tariffs remained at their 1963 levels but nontariff barriers were removed, the United States could expect to export roughly $4.6 billion, as compared with roughly $4 billion if nontariff barriers remained in effect.[16] Finally, the United States hoped for, if not the abandonment, at least an accommodation of the system of "variable levies" adopted by the Europeans in 1961, which would obviously distort competition.[17]

[13] Until 1952, far from playing a trade liberalizing leadership in agricultural matters, the United States was seeking ways of protecting its agriculture through means such as import restrictions, disposal of surplus stocks, use of export subsidies, and a formal waiver from GATT obligations (which it obtained in 1955). Indeed, since the 1933 Agricultural Adjustment Act (AAA), the United States was pursuing protectionist domestic agricultural policy.

[14] Memorandum from Bernard Norwood to Christian Herter, Subject: Country committee evaluations of concessions to be sought by the United States in the Kennedy Round, October 27, 1964, Box 12, Bernard Norwood, 10/8/64–2/10/66, John F. Kennedy Presidential Library, Boston.

[15] "The vital importance of the inclusion of agriculture in the Sixth Round has been emphasized by the United States from the outset. The United States has repeatedly insisted that the objective of the agricultural negotiations should be trade liberalization equal to that achieved in the nonagricultural sector, meaning 50% tariff cuts where tariffs provide the effective protection, and, where other forms of protection are employed, such as variable levies, liberalization equivalent to a 50% cut in fixed tariffs" (Herter, Hearings, 1966: 25).

[16] USDA, Major agricultural objectives in trade negotiations, August 7, 1963, NSF Box 309–310, Trade General 8/63, John F. Kennedy Presidential Library, Boston.

[17] "One type of arrangement which we could accept would be a limit on EEC protection at a level which would permit United States (and Free World) access to the Community's markets. This was the first alternative proposed to the Community as a means of accommodating our poultry trade in the West German market. In effect this arrangement, which in the case of the EEC would require a negotiated limit on the variable levy, also places a limit on the prices which internal producers receive for the same product. "The same objective

In sum, realizing the potential dangers of the not-yet-established Common Agricultural Policy, the American administration vowed to use the Kennedy Round to bring European agricultural policy provisions in consonance with the rules of the GATT. As summarized in a memorandum setting the U.S. negotiating objectives on agriculture, "the U.S. should stress the need for the EEC to fit its Common Agricultural Policy to solutions to these problems and to the requirements of the GATT rather than to try to fit solutions and the requirements of the GATT to its Common Agricultural Policy."[18]

The EC's Objectives in the Kennedy Round

The Europeans received the invitation for a new round of GATT talks favorably, but with sizable reservations and without much enthusiasm. On one hand, Europeans viewed the premise of the Kennedy Round as a recognition of the newfound economic power and potential bargaining strength of the Community. They could use the opportunity of the round to legitimize internationally their internal arrangements. On the other hand, the six member states sought to avoid a round of difficult negotiations that might shatter their fragile unity and jeopardize the foundations laid for the Common Agricultural Policy, a cornerstone in the European bargain struck between France and Germany.

DIVERSITY OF MEMBER STATES' PREFERENCES ON AGRICULTURE

The European Economic Community officially agreed to the inclusion of agriculture in the Kennedy Round during the prenegotiations of May

---

could be secured by starting with EEC producer prices. For example, for grains, if the EEC were to agree to hold producer prices in France to the 1962–63 crop levels, there would not be an unduly large inducement to expand output in that country. Since the danger to world trade comes primarily from the threat of expanded French output, the freezing of French prices at current levels would largely remove the danger. If this were done, we could look with sympathy on the use of deficit payments to other EEC grain producers. But even in this case, we would have to have an understanding with the Community about the level of the levy since it could be manipulated to induce higher internal EEC prices and thus greater output.

"Another type of arrangement which we could accept in order to accommodate these items would be a low-duty (or levy) quota for a United States (or Free World) share of the markets of the Community. This type of arrangement was an alternative proposal to the EEC as a means of obtaining access for our poultry. Also, as a third alternative, we might accept arrangements under international commodity agreements which would enable us to obtain reasonable access to the markets of the Community." USDA, Major agricultural objectives in trade negotiations, August 7, 1963.

[18] Ibid.

1963, but on the sine qua non condition that its own agricultural policy be set and completed before any international accord on agricultural exports could be reached. The Community's common negotiating position on agriculture was not set at the beginning of the round, however, since the member states, especially France and Germany, had conflicting interests. The Common Agricultural Policy was a complex edifice based on the principles of uniform price levels throughout the Community, on the existence of target prices for certain products such as grains, and on variable levies amounting to the difference between target and import prices in order to prevent imports from underselling domestic production. Under this system, imports were only residual supplies, which could be tapped only if domestic production could not meet demand. As a result, an increase in domestic production would automatically substitute imports. Additionally, export subsidies could be provided for selling surpluses outside the Community.

The Franco-German disagreement was particularly acute on the issue of grains prices. France was the largest and most efficient farm producer in the Common Market. On one hand, French agriculture was vulnerable to competition from outside the Community because of the traditional protection it enjoyed, including higher domestic prices than those prevailing on world markets. On the other hand, the productivity of French agriculture was rapidly increasing as a result of technological developments. Since the French farm labor force was not declining at the same rate as productivity was increasing, France needed some outlets, within or outside the Common Market, for its potentially increasing surpluses. For that reason, French President de Gaulle insisted repeatedly that "France considers it a condition of its membership in the Community that the other Five import from France the products France produces and that they have heretofore imported from outside the Community, and that any French surpluses not absorbed within the Community be treated as Community surpluses whose sale on world markets is subsidized from Community resources."[19]

The French position on agriculture with respect to both the establishment of the CAP and the Kennedy Round agricultural negotiations was therefore clear. Inside the Community, France desired as free a market as possible in order to benefit from its competitive advantage. On the particular issue of grains prices, France demanded unified prices sufficiently low to dominate cereal production in the Community. In that sense, French interests were quite compatible with U.S. interests, even though the unified grains prices proposed by France were higher than those favored by

[19] "French Attitudes toward the Kennedy Round," March 11, 1964, Box 7 Ambassador Charles Bohlen, Background Paper for Christian Herter, John F. Kennedy Presidential Library, Boston.

the United States.[20] On the external front, however, France had a rather autarkic view of what Europe's agricultural policy should be. The French government wanted external protection to shield European producers from outside competition and demanded the collective financing of export subsidies.

Germany, by contrast, was the most expensively protected and least competitive agricultural producer in the Community. Were the French agricultural proposal adopted, Germany would have to make the largest downward price adjustment and at the same time would have to contribute heavily to the financing of the export subsidies benefiting French farmers. Therefore, the German government proposed instead to agree on a European unified grains price sufficiently high to maintain the competitiveness of German farmers. Chancellor Erhard hoped to use the pretext of the Kennedy Round to speed up the rationalization of German agriculture, but not to the extent of gravely alienating the German farm vote.[21]

The other four member states also exhibited diverse preferences on agriculture, but none carried as much weight on the final decision as France and Germany. The Italian economy was heavily dependent on foreign trade. Therefore, Italy attached a lot of importance to the successful conclusion of the Kennedy Round, which it expected would prevent French, or Franco-German, hegemony over the Community. The Netherlands also hoped that the agricultural solution chosen by the Europeans would enable the successful completion of the Kennedy Round, since it had already had to raise its traditionally low tariffs in order to align with the Common External Tariff. Belgium's attitude toward the agricultural negotiations was somewhat ambivalent, balancing between Prime Minister Spaak's desire for a successful multilateral negotiation and the necessity to take into account domestic protectionist pressures. As for Luxembourg, it hoped that the trade negotiations would succeed but had only a limited role to play.[22]

Despite their divergences, the six member states could easily agree on one central feature of agricultural policy: agriculture was not a sector like the others. As T. K. Warley reported,

> the EEC's posture in the Kennedy Round was liberal in all areas but agriculture. Its common external tariff was lower on average than most; it had offered to reduce it in the Dillon Round by more than the U.S. negotiators could match; and . . . the Community was perfectly willing to negotiate on the basis of a 50

---

[20] "Components of a Strategy for the Kennedy Round."
[21] Ibid.
[22] Ibid.

percent linear reduction of tariffs on manufactures. However, it took the view that agriculture was different by reason of the universal involvement of governments in agricultural policies and the consequent distortions in world markets which resulted from the interactions of national support policies.[23]

Therefore, the central objective of the Common Market countries in the Kennedy Round was to prevent negotiations with the United States from hindering the formation of the CAP, whose rules were going to be created as the multilateral negotiations progressed. The Community agreed to discuss the regulation of world agricultural trade, but with the hope that it could set up the CAP without foreign intervention. In that sense the agricultural component of the Kennedy Round can be characterized as a purely "conservative" case, to reprise the terminology established in chapter 2: the United States launched the Kennedy Round to change preemptively EC agricultural policy, on which the Europeans themselves had not yet found a status quo. Once they agreed on the status quo, their objective would become to defend it from foreign attacks.

THE SYNCHRONIZATION ISSUE: INTERNAL VS. EXTERNAL DEVELOPMENTS OF AGRICULTURAL POLICY

The preparatory negotiations for the Kennedy Round started as the Community had not yet put in place the Common Agricultural Policy or even agreed on its main principles. The variable levy system, so much criticized by the American administration, was adopted in 1961. Some other provisions, including the levy on poultry, were adopted in 1962. The rest of the CAP, including the controversial unified grains price, took time to put in place. Since the outset of the Kennedy Round prenegotiations, the EC had made clear that it would not settle on an international agricultural agreement until its own internal system of protection and common agricultural policies were completed. A major issue in the prenegotiations became the so-called synchronization of the establishment of the CAP with the international agreement in the Kennedy Round.

The United States worried that France might demand the full implementation of the CAP as a condition for the Kennedy Round. Indeed, the French position was that no agricultural offers would be possible in the multilateral negotiations until the Six had reached an agreement on the CAP and on EEC agricultural prices. The U.S. administration was concerned about the establishment of the CAP prior to the launching of the Kennedy Round negotiations because it felt that "since the EEC's

---

[23] Warley (1976).

internal difficulties in securing agreement on agricultural policy are so great, there are grave doubts as to whether it can or will be willing to negotiate changes in its agricultural regulations even after they are adopted by the EEC Council."[24] The "tied hands" argument is indeed a constant in real-life bargaining.

The German foreign minister, Schröder, proposed the "synchronization" principle according to which the internal and external negotiations on agriculture would proceed simultaneously. Under this plan, Germany would trade off acquiescence in common agricultural policies for beef, rice, and dairy products (but not common grain prices) in return for French cooperation in the Kennedy Round. The United States silently but greatly favored this proposal because it could increase its influence on the eventual design of the CAP and could therefore prevent the "lock-in" of an unfavorable European agricultural policy. Yet the synchronization principle could not be followed through, and the rest of the Kennedy Round negotiations confirmed the worst fears of the U.S. administration with respect to both the content of the CAP and the negative impact of the EC's institutional difficulties on American bargaining leverage.

Internal Institutional Paralysis and Deadlocked External Negotiations

The Kennedy Round officially opened on May 4, 1964, with no common position on agriculture from the six members of the Common Market. The absence of internal European agreement on a Common Agricultural Policy paralyzed the international negotiating process until December 1964. The United States was put in the singular position of having to wait for the Europeans to resolve their internal divisions before any progress could be made in the bilateral EC-U.S. negotiations. This eventually resulted in the "decouplage" of industrial and agricultural negotiations, a situation that the U.S. administration had forcefully rejected at the outset of the round. Subsequent institutional paralysis in the EC prevented the U.S. negotiators from making any gains in agriculture, instead of playing to their advantage. Despite U.S. attempts to further divide the six member states in order to change the EC's internal decision-making rules, France's de Gaulle went through with the "empty chair crisis," which the U.S. administration was forced to witness helplessly.

[24] The trade negotiations, December 10, 1963, Box 14, Special Representative for trade negotiations memoranda, 11/14/62–3/29/63, John F. Kennedy Presidential Library, Boston.

Internal EC Deadlocks

The U.S. negotiators found themselves in the awkward situation of having to wait for the European farm policy to be implemented before negotiations with the goal of altering this policy could begin. As a result of its unfinished CAP, the EC by and large determined the agenda and, consequently, the outcomes of the Kennedy Round negotiations on agriculture.

THE MANSHOLT PLAN

In February 1964 the EEC finally made a negotiating proposal for the agricultural negotiations through its agriculture commissioner. Under the so-called Mansholt Plan, the Common Market would first agree on the remainder of its common agricultural policy (including the grains price). Then, the various parties to the Kennedy Round negotiations would attempt to calculate and compare their total amounts of agricultural support, subsidization, and protection. This was called the principle of *montants de soutien* (margins of support): after this comprehensive calculation of government protection in agriculture, the United States and the EEC would negotiate the reduction of margins of support, which were the difference between the price of products on the international market and the price received by domestic producers. Importers would be allowed to assess an additional levy if export prices were lower than a negotiated reference price. This proposal focused the debate specifically on the trade distorting effects of government intervention and placed limits for the first time on domestic agricultural policies. The plan also promised an end to export subsidy wars.

For the EC, the *montants de soutien* proposal represented a real concession, which had been difficult to agree upon internally. But the United States rejected the proposal because it represented a special code for agricultural products, and the United States wanted the application of the 50 percent GATT rule to every sector, including agriculture. On the contrary, the European proposal was eliminating price as a mechanism for determining production and trade patterns. Instead, it introduced a rule tailored to the developing CAP, which would allow for a temporary freeze of EC common support prices and would enable the variable levy system to continue unchanged. In rejecting this proposal, however, the U.S. administration had apparently not measured the extent to which it was difficult for the EC to reach a common bargaining position—and its inflexibility once it was reached.

THE DECOUPLAGE, FIRST AMERICAN CONCESSION

The Kennedy Round started without a common negotiating position from the Community on agriculture. For the first few months, the central issue of the round progressively became the question of whether the negotiations on industry and agriculture would progress in parallel. The "decouplage" (uncoupling) of the two sectors could affect dramatically the progress of the round. First, U.S. officials believed that if the industrial negotiations went ahead on their own, agriculture would be left out of the final agreement, as it had been under all the other GATT rounds. This should not be allowed to happen since the United States had made agriculture the benchmark by which to judge the success of the Kennedy Round. Second, the simultaneous progress of industrial and agricultural negotiations would enable negotiators to use linkage between the two sectors to conclude deals.

As the deadline of November 16, 1964, for the tabling of exceptions and offers approached, the Six were stalemated. They had not reached an agreement on a unified grains price, and they had made such an agreement a prerequisite to their Kennedy Round agricultural offers. The United States refused to get into the internal EEC debate and continued to insist that both industrial and agricultural offers would be presented at the same time. American officials hoped that the parallel progress of the two would force the rapid conclusion of the European agricultural deadlock. France, however, seized this opportunity to suggest that perhaps the EEC should postpone as well the submission of its list of exceptions in the industrial sector until the conclusion of an internal EEC agreement on agriculture. The U.S. administration apparently believed de Gaulle's threats that there would be no negotiation with the United States as long as the CAP had not been established, and that if the member states failed to resolve their differences on the CAP, there would be no more Common Market at all.[25]

These internal divisions in the EEC had a direct impact on the GATT negotiations. Thanks to its inability to reach the required common position, and therefore its inability to negotiate with a single voice, the Common Market achieved one of its initial objectives in the negotiations, which was to delay the link between the submission of offers in the industrial and the agricultural sectors. Tired of waiting for a European decision on agriculture, the U.S. administration radically changed its negotiating strategy and in November 1964 dropped what U.S. officials qualified as a "bomb"—the decision to proceed in the Kennedy Round negotiations on industrial goods without waiting for agricultural

[25] Peyrefitte (1997: chap. 10).

rules to be tabled as well. This was a major concession on the part of the United States.

THE GRAINS AGREEMENT

The decouplage was supposed to facilitate the resolution of the long-drawn-out debate in the EEC over the setting of the unified grains price. The central issue to resolve was the level of this price: would it be closer to the lower French level or to the higher German level? The United States was particularly worried about a higher level than the current French price, since it might artificially stimulate extra production in France and reduce exports to the Community. According to the internal EC decision-making rules, laid out in article 113 of the Treaty of Rome, no common bargaining position could be presented in the GATT negotiations until all member states approved it. In December 1963 Germany rejected the Commission proposal on a unified price level for grains midway between the French and German prices, thereby creating a major stalemate in the EEC and in the GATT. Preeg explained German opposition by arguing that after France vetoed the entry of Great Britain into the Community in January 1963 and strains arose between France and Germany on nuclear issues, in spite of the Franco-German friendship treaty, Germany became less inclined to make commitments on agriculture that would primarily benefit France.[26]

After years of unsuccessful negotiations prior to the Kennedy Round and months of debate while the round was already under way, an internal EEC agreement on grains prices and financing of the subsidy system was finally achieved in December 1964. The price eventually adopted was higher than the French price (by about 15 percent), but lower than the German. Previsions at the time estimated that these unified grains prices would result in an increment of about three million tons in production, or roughly 30 percent of net imports, by 1970.[27]

The "Empty Chair" Crisis

The December 1964 internal EEC agreement on grains prices had eased the stalemate on agriculture, and by March 1965 the parties to the Kennedy Round agreed to set a timetable for specific agricultural offers: they would start negotiations on a world grains arrangement soon after April, they would negotiate on government protection between May and Sep-

[26] Preeg (1970: 72).
[27] Krause (1968: 102–107). Also quoted in Preeg (1970: 34).

tember, and they would make specific negotiating offers by September. This timetable could not be followed, however, as the internal and external dimensions of the Common Agricultural Policy clashed when France decided to temporarily boycott the EC institutions.[28]

THE ORIGINS OF THE CRISIS

The December 1964 meeting on grains prices had directed the Commission to make a proposal addressing the financing of the CAP for the period covering the next five years. In early 1965 the Commission proposed that agricultural export subsidies be paid by a fund contributed to by all member states. French farmers would be the main beneficiaries of this subsidy arrangement. After 1967 the Commission proposed that the revenues from the common external tariffs on industrial goods be gradually transferred to the Community budget, in turn used in its majority to finance agricultural policy. Aside from the financing issue, the Commission also introduced in the proposal a clause to implement greater supranational decision making in the EC. The Commission hoped that, in exchange for the collective financing of export subsidies, France would accept the participation of the European Parliament in determining the Community budget, as well as other measures designed to increase supranational powers in the EC.

This was a risky move by the Commission since the conflict between the supranational aspirations of the Commission and the intergovernmentalist views of de Gaulle's "Europe des patries" had not been resolved. Several analysts argued that the Commission felt strengthened by the success of the December 1964 meeting on grains prices, in which agriculture commissioner Mansholt had played a crucial role and which, as a result, had legitimized the Commission even in the eyes of the suspicious French leader.

France, expectedly, disagreed with all aspects of the proposal, especially the part about the transfer of powers to the Parliament. The other five member states generally supported the Commission's proposal, considering that since France was going to benefit the most from the agreement on financial regulations, it could make some trade-offs on institutional issues. Up until the moment of the meeting on June 28–30, 1965, where the Commission proposal was to be discussed by the Council, a compromise seemed plausible. At the actual meeting, however, last-minute attempts for conciliation failed. Yet instead of stopping the clock and resuming discussions in July, Couve de Murville, the French president of the

---

[28] On the "empty chair" crisis, see, for instance, Newhouse (1967); Preeg (1970: chap. 7); and Moravcsik (1998).

Council, ended the discussions and announced to the press that it had been impossible to find an agreement.

The pretext for the crisis had been the Commission's proposal bundling the financing of the CAP with a delegation of power to the European Parliament. Yet the threat of a crisis had been brewing for quite a while. Already in July 1964 de Gaulle suggested that were Germany to reject French proposals for the Common Agricultural Policy, then France would stop going to Brussels.[29] If the Franco-German disagreement on agriculture was the trigger for the crisis, the underlying cause was institutional.[30] The real objection of de Gaulle was to the rule of qualified majority voting in the Council, which, according to the Treaty of Rome, was scheduled to replace unanimity as of January 1, 1966. De Gaulle used the opportunity of the crisis triggered by the Commission's proposal to settle once and for all his disagreement with the institutional trend taken by the Common Market.[31] Rather than abdicating France's veto power and delegating more authority to the supranational institutions, the general preferred to have France boycott the Community institutions altogether—leaving an "empty chair" in all Council meetings. Since full membership was required on voting matters, the French boycott led to a suspension of all EEC operations starting on July 1, 1965.

THE "EMPTY CHAIR" AND THE KENNEDY ROUND

With no meeting of the Council, the Community had no authority to decide on offers for the Kennedy Round. Yet the internal EC crisis started as the Europeans were expected to present their agricultural offers to their GATT negotiating partners. Some technical work could continue under the existing mandate, but for any significant breakthrough in the negotia-

---

[29] Reported in Peyrefitte (1997: 263).

[30] Peyrefitte (ibid.: 286) reports that on June 12, 1965, the General already warned him of his intentions by telling him: "Hallstein believes he is the President of the supranational Government. He does not even hide his plan, which is to transpose to the European level the institutional structure of federal Germany. The Commission would become the federal Government. The European Parliament would become what is today the Bundestag. The Council of Ministers would become the Bundesrat—that is, the Senate! This is crazy. But do not be mistaken: this is an institutional stray that would end up succeeding if we do not stop it now. And we are the only ones who can do this" (my translation).

[31] "We should use this crisis to end once and for all these ulterior political motives. It is unthinkable that, on January 1, 1966, our economy will be subjected to the rule of majority, which will be able to impose upon us the will of our partners who, as we have seen, can coalesce against us. We should use this opportunity to revise the wrong rationales which have been exposing us to endure the diktat of others. Let's revise this silliness! As for the Commission, it has exhibited a partiality which suits neither its mission, nor even good manners. It must be replaced by another one in its entirety." General de Gaulle, reported in ibid. (292, my translation).

tions, the Council needed to give the Commission a new mandate—and France needed to participate.[32] As a result, the internal EC crisis in effect shut down the agricultural talks in GATT, since one of the main participants was unable to come up with a negotiating position.

The U.S. administration adopted a very strict policy of not attempting to intervene in the European institutional conflict. Instead, the Americans stayed out of the debate, maintained an explicit "no comment" attitude, and, in the Special Trade Representative Christian Herter's words, greeted de Gaulle's "efforts to dominate or destroy the Common Market with sad silence."[33]

The internal EC crisis put the Kennedy Round, in which all offers on remaining agricultural products had to be presented by September 16, in jeopardy. The participants to the Kennedy Round were facing a dilemma as a result of the Community's institutional inability to make its negotiating offers on schedule: should they proceed or not with the negotiations? One option was to postpone the negotiations until the EEC was in a position to reciprocate. This option entailed several dangers, including the possibility, taken seriously for the first time, that time could run out on the U.S. negotiating authority, which was due to expire on June 30, 1967. As a result, agriculture might drop out of the negotiation altogether, were the other GATT participants to insist on the conclusion of the industrial negotiations before the expiration of U.S. negotiating authority. The alternative option was to proceed without the EEC. This would restore momentum to the talks and push them toward a successful conclusion. At the same time, going ahead without the EEC could reduce pressure for the Community to make significant offers at a later time, since there would no longer be the leverage of parallel schedule for all countries.

After carefully weighing the pros and cons of each option, the U.S. administration decided to move ahead on schedule and put forth its offers on September 16. Nevertheless, U.S. negotiators withheld their offers on products of particular export interests to the EEC, to minimize any future negotiating advantage that the delay might give the Community.[34] Herter also explicitly warned that U.S. offers "are made in the expectation that the other major participants will make . . . offers of like degree. If this proves not to be the case, the U.S. will withdraw or modify its offers on both agricultural and industrial products to the extent it deems necessary to achieve reciprocity in the negotiations."[35]

[32] See Preeg (1970: 113).

[33] Letter to McGeorge Bundy by Christian Herter, July 20, 1965, Box 7 McGeorge Bundy, John F. Kennedy Presidential Library, Boston.

[34] Evans (1971: 216).

[35] Quoted in Preeg (1970: 115).

The Kennedy Round proceeded in the following months in a quite discouraging manner for the negotiators, who could work only on marginal issues, without the presence of one of the two central participants. The year 1965 was therefore a year of stagnation and fear that if no progress was made, many countries would return to restrictive and protectionist policies. The United States also tried to elaborate alternative courses of action if the EEC were to cease participation in the talks altogether. Among the options discussed were the formation of a broader economic bloc without the EEC, the Atlantic Common Market, as well as the conclusion of a GATT agreement withdrawing the most favored nation clause for the EEC, as long as it could not make concessions. Nevertheless, both options might exacerbate the European split and make reconciliation even more difficult. In short, there was no good alternative to EEC participation in the Kennedy Round, and all the United States could do was to wait for the Europeans to overcome their institutional crisis.

THE LUXEMBOURG COMPROMISE

The tide started turning in early 1966, soon after the French presidential election of December 1965 in which de Gaulle had to face a runoff election against his competitor, partly as a result of the opposition of farm groups, who strongly supported the Common Market. The "empty chair" crisis was eased at the Council meeting in Luxembourg on January 30, 1966, where the Six agreed to disagree. The question of qualified majority voting was left open. Noting that there was a divergence of views on the issue, the member states unanimously agreed to get back to work on the backlog of Community business—that is, internal farm policy and the Kennedy Round.

The "empty chair" crisis officially ended in May 1966 with the so-called Luxembourg Compromise, which authorized member states to keep a veto power on matters of vital importance to them. This compromise voided, in effect, the passage from unanimity to qualified majority voting envisioned by the Treaty of Rome. For the rest of the Kennedy Round negotiations, it meant that the EC position would always be the lowest common denominator position of the six member states.

The Council also reached in May an agreement on the financial regulations that had caused the crisis a year earlier. The compromise included a complicated burden-sharing procedure until 1970 (with France paying a larger share than Germany), a declaration of intent about the use of receipts from the common external tariff for the Community budget after 1970, and a declaration of intent by the Five to reinforce the authority of the European Parliament. The Germans made the accord on farm financing conditional upon reaching the necessary decisions for the Kennedy Round. In July the EEC finally agreed to its Kennedy Round agricultural offers.

Institutional Constraints, "Tied Hands," and the Conclusion of the Kennedy Round

The long blockage of the EC institutions had a direct impact on the Kennedy Round negotiations. Faced with the severe institutional crisis in the EC and with undesirable European agricultural offers when the negotiations resumed in September 1966 after the end of the "empty chair" crisis, the United States finally came to the conclusion that any solution representing small progress in the farm sector was better than no solution at all.[36] Given the institutional weaknesses of its opponent, the United States had few options available but to make concessions and, ultimately, accept the lowest common denominator EC position by fear of obtaining nothing otherwise.

Negotiators with Tied Hands

The story of the "empty chair" crisis and, more generally, of the Kennedy Round agricultural negotiations suggests that the EC used its institutional constraints as bargaining assets, willingly or not. The internal voting rules in the EC and the lack of latitude granted to European negotiators contributed heavily to the American team's inability to reach a better deal for the United States.

THE FAIT ACCOMPLI

Even before the Kennedy Round had started, American negotiators knew that they were facing a difficult task as a result of the Community's internal procedures—and lack of familiarity with the use of such procedures. U.S. officials believed at the outset of the round that whatever decisions would be made in Brussels would be difficult, if not impossible, to alter in the multilateral context. Yet they believed that they could avoid being presented with a fait accompli: "With respect to the assumption that the United States must conduct negotiations within the limits of the Common Agricultural Policy as it has thus far evolved, there does not seem to be any

[36] From archival research in various U.S. documents on the Kennedy Round negotiations, John F. Kennedy Library, Boston. See also Zeiler (1992: 183).

real reason why we should place ourselves in such a negotiating straight jacket."[37]

The strategy they devised was mostly "to influence the establishment of the common price *before* it was set, rather than to attempt to negotiate a reduction in this price after its establishment."[38] The American strategy to prevent decisions made in Brussels from being unalterable in the Kennedy Round is best stated by George Ball in the following excerpt of the December 1963 "Components of a Strategy for the Kennedy Round":

> Recognizing that the EEC positions and policies once negotiated internally are difficult to negotiate externally, we should
> a) seek skillfully to influence EEC decisions before they are taken;
> b) develop further our bilateral relations with the member states and the Commission.
> c) seek more formal prior bilateral consultative arrangements with the Commission, with Germany, and also with one or more other EEC states, perhaps including France;
> d) urge the Commission to explain to GATT members its agricultural proposals and to take into consideration third country comments prior to EEC decisions.
> e) seek to encourage the EEC to grant a flexible negotiating mandate to the Commission.[39]

Getting themselves out of the EC institutional straight jacket, however, proved impossible to do for U.S. negotiators. Ex post, when asked why they failed to reach a more favorable agricultural agreement in the Kennedy Round, American policymakers often contended that the transitional stage of European integration prevented effective negotiations. George Ball, for instance, declared that "the reason for the disappointments in bargaining . . . result primarily from the difficulties the Six have had in trying to put their individual agricultural policies together."[40] Similarly, Christian Herter, the U.S. special trade representative, asserted that "the lack of progress in the Kennedy Round goes right back to the fact that the largest trading partner in the world, the Common Market, has taken so long to develop a comprehensive negotiating position. . . . Until the Common Market could adjust itself and get a trading position, there was no way of negotiating."[41]

---

[37] USDA, Major agricultural objectives in trade negotiations.

[38] Memorandum for the files, August 16, 1963, subject: August 15 meeting with under secretary Murphy (Agricultural Policy, 8/13/63–12/31/63), John F. Kennedy Presidential Library, Boston. Emphasis is in original text.

[39] "Components of a Strategy for the Kennedy Round," preliminary draft, December 10, 1963, Box 7 George Ball, John F. Kennedy Presidential Library, Boston.

[40] Hearings (1966: 6).

[41] Ibid., p. 44.

ABSENCE OF NEGOTIATING FLEXIBILITY AND AUTONOMY

The U.S. administration realized early on that the flexibility of the Community's agricultural mandate was crucial to the American bargaining position. In 1964 U.S. officials, looking ahead to the upcoming negotiations, argued that "the effectiveness of the year-end decisions would depend to a considerable extent upon the flexibility and imagination of the Commission in its negotiations on the Kennedy Round. If the Commission exploited to the maximum its mandate and reflected the expressed desire of the Germans, Dutch and others for negotiations with some real flexibility, then perhaps the importance of the sticky points could be minimized and maybe some significant progress could be made."[42] At the same time the U.S. administration realized that the Commission could be one of its best allies.[43] Therefore American officials were careful not to antagonize the Commission by having informal bilateral talks with the individual member states and instead insisted on having the Commission as their exclusive interlocutor.[44] Yet the U.S. preference for EC negotiating flexibility and autonomy did not materialize during the negotiations.

One major innovation of the Treaty of Rome had been the creation of a Community with external personality. In particular, the EC took over negotiating functions from the member states in international trade negotiations. Under article 111, decisions on bargaining positions were to be taken by the Council of Ministers under the unanimity rule until January 1966, the end of the transitional period. Had France not obtained the Luxembourg Compromise ending the "empty chair" crisis, qualified majority voting would have been automatically instituted after this date. While the mandate to negotiate was agreed to unanimously by the repre-

[42] Letter from Tuthill to Robert Schaetzel, deputy assistant secretary for Atlantic affairs, Department of State, January 9, 1964, Box 16 Ambassador John W. Tuthill, 7/30/63–7/20/64, John F. Kennedy Presidential Library, Boston.

[43] "The Commission is clearly much more receptive to negotiations along the lines we envisage than several of the national states and would be inclined to be considerably more liberal in its approach to the solution of the problems involved" (Objectives for Governor Herter's trip to Brussels, January 25, 1963, Box 16, Trips-Europe, 1/24/63–2/4/63, John F. Kennedy Presidential Library, Boston).

[44] "We must be very careful in these bilaterals not to create the suspicion of wishing in any way to divide the six and I intend to go to the particular pains to avoid any such impression. At the same time, since the idea of having an exchange of views was first raised with us by the Germans and the French, we should be equally clear that we consider it our right, and quite proper, to have informal exchanges with each of the EEC member states without in any way abrogating the Commission's role as chief EEC spokesman. I certainly agree with Ambassador Tuthill's view that throughout the negotiations we must establish the principle of negotiating with the Commission (hoping they have a mandate) while maintaining bilateral contacts with the member states as a means of gaining a better understanding of individual viewpoints." W. Michael Blumenthal to Christian Herter, October 16, 1963, Box 7 Ambassador Blumenthal 6/19/63–8/28/64, John F. Kennedy Presidential Library, Boston.

sentatives of the member states, the actual negotiations were carried out by members of the Commission on behalf of the EC.[45] This procedure led to awkward situations where the EC negotiators were powerless to make any compromise or counterproposal until they received a new negotiating mandate, agreed to once again by unanimity, from the Council.[46]

As a result of the desire of member states (especially France) to keep a complete check on the progress of the GATT talks, EC negotiators had their hands tied during the Kennedy Round, and the EC bargaining position was therefore quite rigid. In that sense, Community negotiators were mere messengers with no ability to make constructive proposals in the heat of the negotiations. As stated by Warley, "the Kennedy Round agricultural negotiations were in fact bedeviled by the limited authority of the negotiators. . . . The Commission had constantly to return to Brussels for instructions and was, for most of the time, a carrier of messages from the Council of Ministers."[47] Throughout the round, American negotiators kept complaining about the hurdles created by the EC internal arrangements.[48] Indeed, this inflexibility of the EC position had important consequences for the bargaining process with the United States, which had to make sensible proposals and counteroffers with a high chance of being accepted by the EC member states.

The inflexible negotiating position of the Community also came from the absence of secrecy surrounding the EC decision-making process.

> Council decisions—debated at length and attended by large numbers of people—quickly became public knowledge. It was virtually impossible to maintain security at Brussels (a consideration aggravated by the widely held belief that the Americans, in particular, had ready access to Community information). As a consequence of rigid, publicly known mandates, the Community spokesmen at Geneva could not effectively negotiate, and their main role became primarily to convey messages to and from Brussels.[49]

[45] The Belgian Jean Rey, later president of the EC Commission, was the chief EC negotiator in the Kennedy Round.

[46] Representatives of the member states were present during the negotiations in Geneva, but they were not allowed to negotiate directly.

[47] Warley (1976: 389).

[48] Archival material on the Kennedy Round at the Kennedy Library shows that U.S. negotiators were extremely preoccupied with internal EC decision-making procedures and tried to influence some EC member states to soften and majoritize the procedures. See, for instance, Memorandum from Governor Herter to Mr. Rehm, February 4, 1963: "Please let me have the answer to the following question: If the EEC Commission makes recommendations to the Council favorable to us in modifying sections of the Common Agricultural Policy, and those recommendations are vetoed in the Council by one nation, can the United States take retaliatory action against that one nation, or must it consider the EEC as a single entity?" (Box 14 John Rehm, 2/4/63–6/3/64, John F. Kennedy Presidential Library, Boston).

[49] Preeg (1970: 38).

Because internal Community debates were well known, the United States knew what the EC's reservation value was in the negotiation, but it also knew that the EC could not accept anything beyond this reservation value.

Finally, the inflexibility of the EC negotiating position came from the fear of endangering the fragile Community structure. Each internal decision (grains prices, exports subsidies, etc.) had been so painful and difficult to reach that the member states felt that what had been agreed to became a binding commitment. They worried that any type of pressure for renegotiating these commitments, and particularly outside pressure, would disturb the fragile balance arduously achieved in the Community and jeopardize the chances of future internal compromises. Therefore, "once an accord had been reached in the Council it was too fragile to permit significant changes in the Geneva negotiations."[50] In consequence, the Community derived some leverage out of its inflexibility.

The Kennedy Round Agricultural Agreement

The Kennedy Round negotiations were concluded under the pending threat of expiration of the U.S. executive authority to negotiate. In 1962 President Kennedy had obtained the passage of the Trade Expansion Act (TEA), which was the centerpiece of his legislative agenda.[51] The TEA authorized the president, for a period of five years, to reduce tariffs by as much as 50 percent, and even eliminate them completely on products for which the United States and the Common Market accounted for 80 percent of the world market. At the end of the period, Congress would simply accept or reject the agreement negotiated by the President, without being allowed to bicker on the details. The succession of crises and deadlocks in the Kennedy Round pushed the multilateral negotiations close to the date of expiration of the presidential authority. By June 30, 1967, any negotiated reduction on a particular item would have had to be approved by Congress. To avoid this occurrence, the Kennedy Round ended in a marathon session between the United States and the EC in May 1967.

The United States and the EEC disagreed over the level of agricultural offers until the last day of the negotiations. In the end, however, the United States was very disappointed by the EEC's agricultural offers but had no option but to acknowledge defeat. To conclude the whole Kennedy Round, which was being held up by the agricultural negotiations, the United States had been forced to make many concessions throughout the

[50] Warley (1976: 388).
[51] See Zeiler (1992) for a history of the Trade Expansion Act.

negotiating process: it had retreated on the issue of food access guarantees, decided not to wait for an accord on cereals within the Common Market to proceed with agricultural negotiations, and allowed the *decouplage* of industrial and agricultural negotiations. These concessions resulted in the signing of a final agreement that did not include the changes in agricultural trade originally intended by the Kennedy administration.[52]

It would not be fair to say that the United States "lost" the Kennedy Round, for it gained important trading benefits in several sectors, and its overall exports grew as a result of the final agreement. But the United States clearly was the loser in the agricultural negotiations, having achieved none of its initial objectives. Therefore, "in the economic folklore of the United States in the late 1960s and early 1970s, the Kennedy Round was firmly established as a failure."[53] By contrast, the final outcomes satisfied the European Community and established its reputation as a strong bargainer.

---

[52] It was already clear in 1966 that the United States was going to be the big loser of the agricultural negotiations. See Box 5 agriculture + EEC, Memorandum to the President from the Secretary of Agriculture, August 1, 1966, Subject: Kennedy Round negotiations—Tabling offers, Agriculture department exceptions:
"1. The United States agricultural offer to the EEC is a very generous one, encompassing a 50 percent cut in tariff on some $315 million of US agricultural imports in 1965. The items covered include some that are very sensitive politically, such as tobacco. At the same time we are being called on to make offers on dairy and meat products, specifically beef. If it should become known that such offers are being considered, particularly in the absence of anything even remotely commensurate by the EEC, there would be a swift and serious political repercussion in the United States, and there is every reason to expect that they will become known through the EEC.
"2. The EEC will make no meaningful offer. From advance information we have, it seems likely that their offer, rather than representing progress, would result in a more protectionist rather than more liberal trade position. It is argued that we have made progress in the negotiation because the EEC has on some few items abandoned its completely unrealistic montant de soutien position, which would have only frozen high EEC support levels and which would not have liberalized trade. Initially the EEC insisted this system cover all products. The fact that the EEC will now offer shallow duty cuts on a few items does not represent any real progress in my judgment. Their offers, overall, still do not constitute a basis for negotiating anything but increased protection in the EEC market. It appears that all the EEC is trying to do is legalize internationally its notorious variable levy and gate price system, which relegates third countries to a residual supplier position. The EEC has just finished setting its internal agricultural support prices. The EEC internal price levels on many products are now at least half again as high as the United States price levels, and considerably higher than was previously the case. Such an uneconomic high level of internal pricing can have only one effect. It will certainly increase domestic production within the EEC. With the application of the notorious variable fee system which protects the most inefficient internal producer from any outside competition, it will limit trade possibilities. Moreover, the process of setting these prices is difficult, time-consuming and both economically and politically hazardous. This being the case, it is impossible to conceive the EEC ministers will now turn around and reverse these decisions."
[53] Shonfield (1976: 26).

In the nongrains agricultural sector, the Europeans ultimately made few concessions.[54] The United States and the EC mutually obtained tariff reductions of 20 percent on average on only a few items (other than cereals, meat, and dairy products). Faced with a relative defeat in the nongrains negotiations, the American administration pinned its hopes on the International Grain Agreement instead, only to be resisted once again by the EC. The United States finally accepted a less than favorable agreement. The negotiations to provide access to markets protected by a self-sufficiency ratio commitment (mainly the EC) were unsuccessful. The deadlock in the sector of cereals was finally broken when the United States agreed to drop its demands for access guarantees in exchange for the EC's abandonment of its margin of support plan. As a consequence, a comprehensive approach to an international grains arrangement was ultimately dropped. The only accord to be reached was on a joint food aid commitment and minimum wheat prices. In sum, the final outcomes were quite fruitless relative to the original expectations of the United States. While a small agreement was reached in the grains negotiations, the broader issue of market access and accommodation of the practices of the Common Agricultural Policy remained unresolved.

Overall, the final outcome of the negotiations in the grains sector was rather negative compared to the original expectations of the United States on three fronts: the price levels agreed upon were too high to advantage U.S. farmers; U.S. farm exports were not guaranteed access to EC markets; and the commitment in food aid to developing countries was far below the initial target. When not complaining about the "modest success"[55] of the negotiation on agriculture, U.S. officials confessed that the American expectations had not been met.[56] Nevertheless, despite their disappointment, the American administration endorsed the Kennedy Round agreement, partly because the overall tariff reductions on industrial goods were impressive and advantageous for U.S. exporters, and partly to prevent the likely resurgence of protectionism at home if the negotiations were to fail. The final Kennedy Round agreement spurred many criticisms in the United States, mainly in the agricultural sector where, at best, the results were judged moderate. Others were less forgiving about the deal finally struck in Geneva, such as Congressman Odin Langen (R-MN) who, on behalf of the House Republican Task Force on Agriculture, called

[54] See Preeg (1970) and Evans (1971) for an analysis of the results.

[55] John Schnittker, undersecretary of agriculture (in Zeiler 1992: 239).

[56] Worthington: "I am afraid you have to come to the conclusion that certainly we cannot hope to get out of this negotiation in agriculture what we hoped we would get when we went into it. We did have high hopes that the massive bargaining authorities which the Congress gave us would enable us to deal successfully with the developing variable levy systems of the European Economic Community" (Hearings 1966: 66).

the Kennedy Round a "failure" and complained that U.S. farmers had been "sold out" by negotiators.[57]

In contrast, the Common Market concluded the agricultural negotiations triumphantly. Against most expectations, the EC had proven its ability to resist effectively U.S. demands for market access and even to dictate the terms of the final agreement. The initial goal of the EC in the Kennedy Round—to ensure that the Americans accepted in principle letting "agricultural trade accommodate itself to the CAP and not the converse"—was reached.[58] This led a historian to conclude that, in short, "the Europeans enjoyed more decisive leverage at international trade negotiations than ever before."[59]

Conclusion

As a consequence of the failure of the EC and the United States to reach a substantial agreement on agriculture, the Common Market was left free to maintain its support prices at a very high level, which eventually gave rise to enormous surpluses exported with the help of subsidies. As predicted by the model central to this book, in this purely "conservative" case the final agricultural agreement of the Kennedy Round was extremely favorable to the EC, thanks to the institutional paralysis in Europe epitomized by the "empty chair" crisis and the complete lack of autonomy for the Commission's negotiators. It was only after France blocked the policymaking process in the EC that the Kennedy Round was concluded on European terms. Thus, contrary to expectations derived from the conventional wisdom about unity and strength, the study of the bargaining processes in the Kennedy Round agricultural negotiations reveals that internal strife and institutional constraints can indeed be turned into bargaining assets—or bargaining handicaps from the viewpoint of third parties.

Because the EC polity was weak—that is, no institutional rule besides veto existed to mediate the divergent interests of the member states—the terms of the final agreement were dictated by the most reluctant country. In this "conservative" case where the EC was trying to preserve the status quo on its newly enacted Common Agricultural Policy, the unanimity rule meant that the common position adopted was the lowest common denominator. Moreover, unanimity resulted in inflexibility of the agreed upon negotiating position. The U.S. administration was presented with a fait

[57] Zeiler (1992: 240).
[58] Krause (1968: 214).
[59] Zeiler (1992: 2).

accompli: the internal EC difficulties in agreeing on the CAP had been so obvious that the policy adopted by the Europeans had become an established fact. It was unthinkable for U.S. negotiators to ask for changes in the CAP after the "empty chair" crisis. Finally, unanimity enhanced the credibility that the offer made was of the "take it or leave it" form, since the negotiators had no room to maneuver. The lack of Commission autonomy made a renegotiation of the agricultural package impracticable before the deadline provided by the expiration of the U.S. negotiating authority.

This chapter also suggests that the EC obtained favorable outcomes in the Kennedy Round because integration was still in its early stages. The first phase of European integration, which began in 1958 and covered the whole Kennedy Round period, was a time of elaboration and consolidation of the European Community. Most policy decisions had not been transferred yet to the supranational level; the EC supranational institutions were not strong and autonomous; the Community had not yet become a *fait acquis* in the eyes of its partners. In this first period, the European nations forming the Community moved from totally uncoordinated to partially coordinated positions in trade negotiations, while linked together by a relatively weak supranational polity. The unanimity rule prevailed as the only policymaking procedure, and the EC had no experience yet in resolving internal conflicts. In a situation where the weakness of the EC's institutional mechanisms prevented an automatic resolution of disputes, the complete inability of the Community to offer concessions beyond the lowest common denominator appeared extremely credible. Hence, despite its important political and economic superiority, the United States was unable to unlock the position of the EC and therefore had to accept this "tied hands" position as the final outcome of the negotiations. It thus seems that the partially integrated EC derived unexpected negotiating strength from its institutional weaknesses.

Moreover, the actual and perceived fragility of the European Community in its early phase also served as a bargaining asset in favor of the Europeans. The member states were still in the process of building the foundations of the Community when the United States demanded the first trade concessions. Such concessions could have destroyed the fragile balance of interests holding together the various EC countries. In particular, the CAP was a keystone of the European edifice, which could disintegrate if its fundamental principles were jeopardized. Therefore, even if some EC member states (especially Germany) disagreed with the French proposed policy on agriculture, they finally agreed to hang together to preserve the fragile Community, as if having the CAP was more important than having a successful Kennedy Round. American policymakers were also particularly sensitive to this argument for security reasons. The United States had supported Western European efforts to integrate their economies in the hope that the EC would create a strong border against the East, perhaps complete with a defense component in the long term. American negotiators had to weigh seriously the threat of a disintegration of the Six that could be partly caused by American demands for changes in agricultural policy.

The reverse side of this argument suggests that a stronger and more integrated Europe might be less able to resist American demands. The second phase in the development of European integration can be loosely defined as a state in which an important number of policy decisions have been transferred to the supranational level, the central institutions have grown stronger, collective-integrated policymaking has become routine, and the scope of EC decision making has extended. A consequence of its increasing unitary character and centralized decision-making procedures might be to render the EC negotiating positions less prone to capture by a radical country. The next chapter will examine, by contrast, the well-oiled EC institutional machinery in the Uruguay Round of the GATT (1986–1993), during which the Community was no longer a fragile construction but had become a *fait acquis*.

4

EC-U.S. Agricultural Negotiations in the Uruguay Round, 1986–1993

THE NEGOTIATIONS on agriculture between the European Community and the United States during the Uruguay Round of GATT provide a particularly good illustration of the external consequences of the EU's single negotiating voice in a "conservative" situation, in spite of the liberal preferences of many member states. At the same time, these negotiations offer some unusual institutional contrast between the apex of Commission autonomy and the subsequent reining in of Commission negotiators, and between the institutional confusion following the Single European Act and the subsequent de facto reinstatement of veto power.

When agricultural liberalization was tackled once again in multilateral negotiations, after the blatant failures of the Kennedy and Tokyo Rounds, it was put on top of the negotiating agenda by the United States but resisted by the EC. The wide gap between the positions of the member states at the start of the Uruguay Round prevented the Community from making any concessions departing from the status quo. The European Community and the United States therefore negotiated for six years without any result. The decision finally to undertake a reform of the Common Agricultural Policy in 1992 paved the way for an agricultural agreement with the United States. The so-called Blair House agreement on agriculture was really made possible by the combination of a weakened unanimity rule and greater autonomy seized by Commission negotiators. Yet Blair House represented a turning point for the delegation of negotiating authority to the supranational representatives. The institutional rules that had enabled the conclusion of the agreement were subsequently altered to limit the Commission's negotiating autonomy and informally reaffirm unanimity as the mode of decision making in the Community. This institutional change eventually resulted in the renegotiation of the EC-U.S. agricultural agreement, which was less satisfactory for the United States and the majority of member states than the original one.

Deadlocked Negotiations

Negotiations between the EC and the United States on agriculture made no notable progress for six years, threatening to thwart the whole Uruguay Round in the wake of their failure. The wide divergences about agricultural liberalization between the member states paralyzed the EC's bargaining potential and enabled the EC to offer to the world only a perpetuation of the status quo as its bargaining position. In a "conservative" situation, the institutional practice of consensual decision making leads to the adoption of the lowest common denominator as the single position and therefore diminishes the likelihood of a final international agreement. The first six years of the agricultural negotiations in the Uruguay Round are a perfect illustration of this hypothesis.

Initial Negotiating Demands

The initial impetus for the Uruguay Round was American. The United States wanted to bring trade in services within the multilateral system, strengthen GATT rules and disciplines, and once and for all tackle agricultural liberalization.[1] Agricultural trade disputes between the United States and the EC had intensified in the early 1980s, while each side retaliated with the imposition of costly protectionist measures. Between 1981 and 1986 U.S. agricultural exports declined in both volume and value, while the EC performed well, largely because of the Common Agricultural Policy's export subsidy program. In retaliation, the United States Department of Agriculture (USDA) established in May 1985 the Export Enhancement Program, which distributed government subsidies to U.S. exporters, while Congress provided for lower loan rates to U.S. agricultural exporters through the Food Security Act.[2] In response, the EC further increased its compensation to European producers. In 1986 U.S. and EC domestic agricultural support programs were estimated at about $25 billion each. Also in 1986, for the first time the EC temporarily surpassed the United States as the world's largest agricultural exporter (even though at the same time it remained the world's largest importer of agricultural products). One of the central U.S. objectives in the Uruguay Round was therefore to get rid of the CAP because the EC-U.S. "subsidy war" was becoming too expensive.

The EC first rejected the concept of a new round of multilateral trade negotiations with special emphasis on agriculture when the United States introduced the idea at the GATT ministerial meeting of November 1982. Given its own economic recession, the weakness of its central institutions, and the ambient "Europessimism," the EC found new multilateral trade talks premature. Moreover, the Europeans perceived the negotiations as

---

[1] See Hampson (1995: esp. 180–185) for a clear analysis of the players in the Uruguay Round and their objectives. See also Schott (1994) and Bayard and Elliott (1994) about the U.S. impetus for the round.

[2] Libby (1992).

a means for the United States to respond to its own problems (mainly the overvaluation of the dollar) at the expense of EC producers. The context was not very favorable to a positive reception of a new U.S.-led trade initiative anyway: the United States and the EC were engaged in a series of trade disputes over steel, various agricultural issues, and the Soviet gas pipeline.

Most importantly, the reopening of agricultural talks just four years after the conclusion of the Tokyo Round had the potential for being highly divisive within the Community. The ten, and then twelve, EC countries had extremely divergent interests with respect to agriculture. Great Britain and the Netherlands, both net financial contributors to the CAP, hoped that the multilateral negotiations would provide an external push enabling the EC to slow the increasing costs of the CAP. Other member states, above all France but also to some extent Belgium, Ireland, Italy, and Germany, wanted to keep a high degree of agricultural protection in Europe. As Europe's first and the world's second agricultural exporter, France was particularly adamant about maintaining the current system of export subsidies and protected market access for agricultural products, especially given the importance of the rural vote in French domestic politics.[3]

The EC was therefore put in a defensive position on agriculture even before the start of the Uruguay Round, as it had been in all previous rounds of multilateral trade negotiations in which the issue was raised. Given the "centrifugal forces"[4] within the Community coupled with the practice of consensual decision making on such an important issue, the only common position on which the EC could initially agree was the preservation of the status quo.

Although considered a "failure" at the time, the 1982 GATT meeting set in motion important preparatory technical work for a new round of multilateral negotiations, which intensified in 1985, as the EC boosted efforts to consolidate its internal market. On March 19, 1985, the EC Council declared itself in favor of launching a new round of multilateral negotiations in order to halt protectionism and correct the imbalances whose origins lie in the financial and monetary areas.[5] The EC Commission took six months of in-depth consultations with the member states to prepare the negotiating directives forming the "Overall Approach" toward the new round of multilateral negotiations, but neither France, Italy, nor Greece wished to commit themselves, and no qualified majority could be found in support of the Commission's text at the June 17, 1986, meeting of the Council in Luxembourg.[6]

[3] See Keeler (1996).
[4] Paemen and Bensch (1995: 46).
[5] Ibid., p. 36.
[6] Ibid., p. 47.

France, in particular, had three requests for the upcoming round. First, the section on agriculture would have to be rewritten entirely to ensure "the defense of the Common Agricultural Policy." Second, France wanted to raise the question of exchange rate fluctuations. Third, it wanted to obtain the "rebalancing of rights and obligations" (in other words, attack the waiver on agriculture gained by the United States in the 1950s). As a result, External Relations Commissioner Willy de Clercq went to the inaugural Uruguay Round meeting at Punta del Este with a tough mandate.[7] The EC mandate was to "limit the damage" in agriculture and at the same time open up the Japanese market and restrict American exceptions. As Paemen and Bensch relate, "unable to agree, but constrained to act by the pressure of events, the Ministers of the Twelve Member States decided to pass the buck to the European Commission."[8] After prenegotiation posturing by each party at the inaugural meeting, a breakthrough occurred that enabled the EC to finally accept the launching of a new round of multilateral trade negotiations. France, a major services provider, agreed to discuss agriculture in exchange for the inclusion in GATT talks of its most important concerns, such as liberalization of investment and services, the issue of exchange rate fluctuations, and the "rebalancing" of former privileges.[9] The EC had agreed that world trade in agriculture was problematic and that support was costly, but it hoped to replicate the scenario of the Kennedy Round: to get agricultural reform on its own terms and to receive confirmation that the CAP would be allowed to continue.

The launching of the Uruguay Round in September 1986 was followed by a long series of negotiating stalemates in the agricultural sector as a result of the wide divergences separating the European from the American positions. The United States was first to officially put up its negotiating proposal before the GATT group dealing with agriculture in July 1987. It called for a complete elimination of all subsidies in agriculture by the year 2000—a negotiating position called the "zero option" by analogy to ongoing arms control negotiations.[10] It also demanded a phase-out over ten years of the quantities exported with the aid of export subsidies, and a phase-out of all import barriers over ten years.

The EC was taken aback by the extreme nature of the American negotiating proposal, which could not be dismissed purely as a bluff.[11] The Euro-

---

[7] Ibid., p. 48. See also Hampson (1996: 202–215).

[8] Paemen and Bensch (1995: 56).

[9] Ibid., pp. 36, 46–48.

[10] Paarlberg (1993).

[11] In his own account of the negotiations, Paemen wrote: "The European Community immediately claimed that the Americans were bluffing. Proposals like these would cause problems even for US agriculture, because the Americans too used subsidies, even to support their exports. But no matter how loudly the European Community yelled, there was no changing the facts. If they were really serious about liberalizing, the Americans had the resources to get by without aid. The same could not be said of the Community. There were

peans did not submit their own proposal until late October, reiterating their initial plea for short-term measures, nonnegotiability of the CAP, and reduction of all forms of support. A divided Community was ready to make some concessions on the issue of domestic support but was unable to offer anything on either market access or export subsidies. As one of the key negotiators for the EC himself acknowledged, "seeing no scope for a compromise on the basis of such a bold position as that of the US, the EC decided to opt for splendid isolation."[12]

Negotiating Stalemates

The wide gap separating the U.S. and EC positions and the inability of the EC to offer concessions going beyond its lowest common denominator led to a series of negotiating stalemates, which almost terminated the Uruguay Round altogether. The December 1988 Montreal ministerial meeting, initially conceived as a midterm review for the Uruguay Round, ended in failure because there was no room for compromise between two widely opposite positions. Some progress was made in early 1989 after a new U.S. negotiating team, headed by Secretary of Agriculture Clayton Yeutter, gave a lot of ground in order to quickly reach an agreement on agriculture, but a series of crises throughout 1990 slowed down progress in the negotiations. It seemed that EC negotiators "evidently assumed that, as in past GATT rounds, agriculture would be taken off the table before the end of the negotiations."[13]

The Commission, however, was resolved to cut back agricultural support, which was costing up to 60 percent of the total EC budget. The Agriculture Council rejected the Commission's agriculture proposal in September 1990 for going too far. Most ministers vigorously defended their farmers' interests in Brussels, especially Germany, which was in the midst of reunification. The Council adopted a much watered-down text in November, which proposed a 30 percent cut in domestic support over five years, to be calculated from 1986, as well as a correcting mechanism to take into account currency fluctuations and improved conditions for export competition.

The EC representatives' lack of negotiating autonomy prevented a successful conclusion of the Brussels ministerial meeting of December 1990, originally intended to close the Uruguay Round. After an initial crisis triggered by an American ultimatum, Renato Ruggiero, the Italian trade

---

good reasons for thinking the Americans' proposal might be a bluff. Then again, no one could be certain." Paemen and Bensch (1995: 106).

[12] Ibid., p. 107.

[13] Schott (1994).

minister and president of the Council, asked the Commission to continue the negotiation while exercising "a degree of flexibility in keeping with the spirit of its mandate." "In the bustling microcosm of the Heysel, the news traveled fast. The Commission had been granted flexibility!"[14] The United States and other countries agreed to a compromise proposed by Swedish Agriculture Minister Mats Hellstrøm, which included a reduction of 30 percent in export subsidies, import restrictions, and domestic supports from 1990 levels to be implemented over five years. Ray Mac-Sharry, the agriculture commissioner, tried to use up this flexibility, but in the end the Hellstrøm proposal proved to be beyond the Commission's negotiating mandate. The Brussels meeting consequently collapsed, and participants criticized the crucial lack of flexibility of EC negotiators. This collapse conforms to one of the central hypotheses of this book: the lack of supranational competence in a conservative situation decreases the likelihood of reaching an international agreement.

Negotiations resumed but made no progress until December 1991 when Arthur Dunkel, the director general of the GATT, drafted a proposal providing specific terms for reductions in export subsidies, domestic support, and import restrictions. Most countries accepted the Dunkel Draft as a basis for the final agreement on agriculture, but the EC Council rejected the text for several reasons.[15] Dunkel also introduced the principle whereby no amendment to his draft would be taken into consideration unless the proposing country had held informal negotiations beforehand with the other parties and obtained their support. For the European Community, this meant that a bilateral preagreement on agriculture had to be concluded with the United States.

Capping the CAP: The 1992 Reform

The EC-U.S. agricultural negotiations were put on hold while the EC, facing increasing isolation internationally and rising budgetary pressures, undertook an internal reform of its Common Agricultural Policy.[16] By redefining the negotiating mandate, quieting internal divisions, and granting more flexibility to Commission negotiators, this reform enabled the bilateral negotiations to move forward and eventually result in an agreement.

[14] For a detailed account of the 1990 Heysel negotiations, see Paemen and Bensch (1995: 185–186).

[15] Including the absence of a "rebalancing" agreement and the nonexemption of the EC's compensation payments from GATT discipline. Schott (1994: 46).

[16] See Keeler (1996) on the relationship between the CAP reform and the GATT negotiations.

THE 1992 CAP REFORM

On May 21, 1992, after a year of intense debate, the EC Council of Ministers adopted the reform of the CAP presented by Agriculture Commissioner Ray MacSharry. The reform was revolutionary because it capped
production, entailed a substantial reduction in support prices (to be compensated by aids), and proposed to set aside land out of production. The
main internal disagreements, opposing northern versus southern states,
and large-farm states versus small-farm states, focused on the proposed
levels of price and quota cuts, the distribution and duration of compensa-
tory payments, and the effects of the reform on farm income and production. Reforming the CAP in order to control spending and limit surplus
production had been a subject of debate in the EC since the end of the
Kennedy Round. Previous CAP reforms, however, managed only to modify existing policy mechanisms. The 1992 reform was more drastic. Unlike
the negotiations in the GATT, however, the reform did not address the
crucial issues of market access and export subsidies.

Agriculture Commissioner MacSharry played a very active role in setting the agenda for a CAP reform, designing the actual reform, and getting
it approved by the Council. The Commission wanted a reform in order
to avoid a budgetary crisis and diffuse internal criticism of the EC's waste-
ful and protectionist policies. The Commission also hoped to derive a
more flexible negotiating mandate from the reform in order to successfully reach a deal with the United States. Countries reluctant to change in
the functioning of the CAP, such as France, eventually agreed to the reform because the combination of budget constraints, Commission
agenda-setting, and outside pressures made such a reform inevitable.[17]
France could also use the strategic advantage of locking in the CAP reform
now to avoid making further concessions to the United States later.

INTERNATIONAL BARGAINING CONSEQUENCES OF THE CAP REFORM

European and American officials disagreed over the meaning of the CAP
reform. European policymakers argued that this reform represented the
upper limit of changes that the EC could make to its agricultural policy.
By contrast, the United States argued that the reform was an internal EC
matter, addressing only the issue of internal support. It was interpreted
as the basis for a future U.S.-EC agreement that would also include provisions on market access and export subsidies. Above all, the United States
wanted to avoid rigidity in the European position and therefore rejected
EC attempts to lock in a negotiating position by reaching internal

[17] Ibid.

agreements first—that is, in Schelling's words, having its "hands tied" by a prior internal agreement. When EC negotiators first demanded reciprocal concessions as a result of the CAP reform, Carla Hills, the United States trade representative (USTR), suggested instead several ways in which the reform could be expanded to deal directly with the issues in the trade talks.[18]

EC-U.S. agricultural negotiations were stalled for many years because divisions between the member states had prevented the EC from departing from its conservative bargaining position. The absence of a real institutional mechanism to settle internal differences and the lack of autonomy granted to EC negotiators resulted in paralysis of the negotiating process. The CAP reform broke the long deadlock in the negotiations because it forced the member states to reach an internal agreement and therefore define a common position. The reform delimited the Commission representatives' new negotiating mandate. The CAP reform also enabled the bilateral negotiations to move forward and eventually result in an agreement because in effect the vagueness of the new mandate granted more autonomy to Commission negotiators.

Internal Divisions, Commission Autonomy, and Conclusion of the Blair House Agreement

Negotiations between the United States and the EC accelerated after the adoption of the CAP reform, leading to the so-called Blair House agreement of November 20, 1992, which almost brought the Uruguay Round negotiations on agriculture to a successful end. The combination of a weakened unanimity rule and greater autonomy seized by Commission negotiators made the conclusion of the agreement really possible. This illustrates the hypothesis that supranational competence in a conservative case makes the conclusion of an international agreement more likely.

Internal EC Crisis

A series of intense bilateral negotiations on agriculture at a high political level started in Brussels in October 1992. It failed to produce results, as France pressured the Community to make new demands and brandished its veto threat, suggesting that the Commission negotiators were going

---

[18] Stuart Auerbach, "No Concessions Offered to Europeans in Washington Trade Talks, US Says," *Washington Post*, May 28, 1992.

beyond their mandate as defined by the CAP reform.[19] The United States responded to the failure of the negotiations by linking the oilseeds dispute to the ongoing discussions and menacing the EC with the threat of a full-blown trade war.[20] Carla Hills announced a retaliatory 200 percent punitive tariff on $300 million of European food imports effective December 5 if the EC did not reduce its oilseeds production from 13 to 8 million tons. By targeting French, but also German and Italian, products for retaliation, the United States tried to "divide and rule" the EC by increasing the member states' pressure on France, in order to avoid the final capture of the collective EC position by the preferences of the most extreme member state. The U.S. administration also tried to exploit the obvious lack of cohesiveness in the EC by forcing the member states favorable to its views to simply disregard the outliers and reach a bilateral agreement.

Negotiations resumed in Chicago on November 2 in this tense bilateral context, although the American administration was particularly eager for a deal that would come before the presidential election. The talks did not produce any progress in the bilateral negotiations but resulted in a major internal crisis in the Community. Before concluding a deal, American negotiators wanted to ensure that the agreement negotiated by the Commission representatives would be supported by the Council. In a surprise move, Agriculture Commissioner MacSharry offered proof of the Council's likely support in the person of Mr. John Gummer, the British president of the Agriculture Council, who was secretly in Chicago to monitor the talks and assured U.S. Agriculture Secretary Edward Madigan that the EC would back the deal.[21] This created a scandal in EC circles: "The Commission and the presidency were going behind the backs of their Community partners in order to stitch up the deal!"[22] That same evening, Commission President Jacques Delors told MacSharry that the agreement being negotiated would be voted down in Brussels because it was too costly for the Community and exceeded the Commission's negotiating mandate. Denouncing Delors' interference and infringement on the nego-

[19] Pascal Riché, "GATT: Bruxelles négocie, Paris agite son veto," *Libération*, October 12, 1992.

[20] In the 1961–1962 Dillon Round negotiations, the EC granted zero-duty access to oilseeds and cereal substitutes, which at the time were not used much. Since then, the EC started to provide internal support to European production of oilseeds in order to limit oilseeds imports. The dispute erupted when the United States challenged the EC oilseeds subsidy program in the GATT. Successive GATT panels found against the EC, which refused to comply.

[21] Sean Flynn, "Sutherland, MacSharry Played Key Roles in Complex Agreement," *Irish Times*, December 15, 1993.

[22] Paemen and Bensch (1995: 214).

tiators' autonomy, MacSharry presented his resignation from the Commission on his way back to Brussels.[23]

This internal EC crisis influenced the course of subsequent EC-U.S. negotiations, even though Delors and MacSharry settled their differences a couple of days later (with MacSharry returning to his post as agriculture commissioner). Beyond a conflict of personalities, the crisis revealed that the EC institutional system was not functioning properly. According to a Commission official, "the Commission does not meet anymore, leaving the Commissioner in charge of the negotiation to act as he wishes. In other words, it is a mess. We have been in free wheel for two years."[24] The crisis further revealed the extent of internal divisions in the EC, not only between the member states but also between and within the various EC institutions. As a French analyst wrote at the time,

> [In Chicago] the Americans understood that their adversaries were at loggerheads. As long as the American offers were too remote from their own proposals, divergences between the Europeans were of no consequence. . . . But on November 2 and 3, the Americans witnessed the explosion of European divisions. . . . The Commission and its Commissioners are divided on the opportunity of counter-retaliatory measures. The Americans now have everything to gain from an immediate resumption of the negotiations.[25]

Internal EC divisions appeared even more clearly in the following Council meetings. On November 9 EC foreign ministers denied French demands for European retaliation against U.S. trade sanctions. At the Agriculture Council of November 16, expected to adopt a common position for the GATT negotiations to resume that week, an isolated France tried to convince the other member states that the proposed agreement

---

[23] "During that evening Mr. Delors called Mr. MacSharry from Brussels. He told him that his offer would require more cuts in output than those planned under the latest reform of the common agricultural policy, and that the gesture therefore went beyond the Commission's negotiating mandate. Mr. Delors also said, apparently, that he would oppose such a deal; that the Commission would vote it down; and that if it went to the Council two countries would invoke the "Luxembourg Compromise." . . . Mr. Delors maintains that, as one of four commissioners charged with the GATT talks, he has every right to call a commissioner if he believes he is exceeding his mandate. Furthermore, Mr. Delors believes that the Commission president has a duty to try to prevent any country becoming isolated in the defense of its essential interests. In the past he has protected Germany on coal subsidies. This time the country happened to be France. Many view Mr. Delors' efforts to block a deal less charitably, putting them down to his ambitions for the French presidency." "Blood Is Thicker than Rape Oil," *The Economist*, November 14, 1992.

[24] Jean Quatremer and Pascal Riché, "GATT: Le vin blanc européen trinque pour le colza," *Libération*, November 6, 1992. Author's translation.

[25] François Wenz-Dumas, "GATT: une manche aux Etats-Unis," *Libération*, November 12, 1992. Author's translation.

with the United States was going far beyond the CAP reform. MacSharry did not answer France's question about the compatibility with the reform and proceeded with a new round of bilateral talks.

The Blair House Agreement

On November 18 and 19, 1992, MacSharry and External Affairs Commissioner Frans Andriessen met with Madigan and Hills in the Blair House residence in Washington, DC. After a series of proposals and counterproposals, MacSharry enabled a breakthrough in the negotiations by offering a reduction of 21 percent in the volume of subsidized exports (not 24, as in the Dunkel Draft), as well as 36 percent reduction in budget over six years, using 1986–1990 as the base period. The Blair House compromise also provided for a 20 percent reduction in internal price support over six years, with the period 1986–1988 as reference. Finally, European and American negotiators agreed to a "peace clause" that would exempt from trade actions those internal support measures and export subsidies that do not violate the terms of the agreement. A separate deal on oilseeds was also concluded, ending several years of EC-U.S. disputes and GATT litigation and canceling the promised U.S. trade sanctions against the EC.

The increased autonomy seized by the EC negotiators made the Blair House compromise possible. Their fairly broad mandate and adequate flexibility to negotiate were apparent from the beginning of the talks, including to American negotiators.[26] When MacSharry agreed to return to the talks as agriculture commissioner, newspapers reported that he was given a "free hand."[27] As Andriessen was entering the actual negotiations, he told reporters that he was flexible in his position, shouting: "The message from Brussels? Go ahead and make a deal!"[28] Conscious that the EC representatives had a fairly broad mandate and adequate flexibility, U.S. negotiator Madigan, "speaking with reporters as he entered the Blair House, where the talks were being held, said that the EC negotiators reportedly were coming to the talks with 'enhanced flexibility.' "[29]

[26] Interview with senior USDA official, January 1995. See also Keith Bradsher, "The Anatomy of a Trade Agreement: US Gamble Pays Off in Deal with EC," *New York Times News Service*, November 23, 1992; "US, EC Trade Talks Adjourn, to Resume Later," *Reuters*, November 19, 1992; David Usborne, "Struggle Continues for GATT Formula," *The Independent*, November 20, 1992; "US, EC Begin Talks on Farm Subsidies as Officials Claim Agreement Is Near," *The Bureau of National Affairs*, November 19, 1992.

[27] Bradsher, "The Anatomy of a Trade Agreement.

[28] "US, EC Trade Talks Adjourn, to Resume Later." Also Usborne, "Struggle Continues for GATT Formula."

[29] "US, EC Begin Talks on Farm Subsidies."

This enhanced autonomy gave rise to accusations that the Commission had negotiated the agreement in secret.[30] And, if we are to believe this Commission official, when pressed by representatives of the member states to give some explanation, "instead we would read the newspaper, we would leave to go to the bathroom. . . . The Commission tried to encourage secret diplomacy."[31] The member states even ignored the exact content of the "ghost" compromise for several days after its negotiation.[32] The Commission argued that there was no formal text because the agreement was made in part by telephone and in part through exchange of notes. While the Commission held a meeting on November 20 to present the broad characteristics of the agreement, the only specific text that the member states had in hand for a week was a two-page, USTR press release. Only a week later did the Commission finally send a ten-page document to the member states, including five pages confirming the compatibility of the agreement with the CAP reform.

The Blair House agreement was interpreted at the time as a relative negotiating success for the EC. The agreement was able to occur in spite of strong opposition from France, the most recalcitrant country, because the Commission representatives exercised a particularly high degree of autonomy during the negotiations. The combination of weakened unanimity and a greater Commission autonomy actually freed the hands of EC negotiators, thereby breaking the negotiation paralysis. The agreement reflected the U.S. bargaining strength but served the interests of the majority of member states. The negotiating outcome would have been different had France been able to control the EC decision-making process by a stricter unanimity rule and a tighter check on the Commission negotiators.

Veto, Tied Hands, and Renegotiation of the Blair House Agreement

Despite the conclusion of the Blair House deal, the EC-U.S. agricultural negotiations were reopened before the end of the Uruguay Round. Since the vast majority of member states supported the Blair House agreement, why did the United States eventually agree to its renegotiation? Informal institutional change in the EC, characterized by the informal reinstating

[30] "Obfuscation by the Commission on EC-US GATT Deal," *Agra Europe*, December 4, 1992.

[31] Jean Quatremer and Pascal Riché, "Comment Paris s'est pris au piège agricole," *Libération*, May 14, 1993. Author's translation.

[32] Pascal Riché, "Accord de Washington, le texte fantôme," *Libération*, November 26, 1992. In a personal conversation, Pascal Riché told me that when the text of the agreement

of the veto power and tighter control over the Commission by member states, affected the process and outcome of the international negotiations. As a result of this rollback of EC supranational authority in international trade negotiations, the final bilateral agreement was heavily influenced by France, the most recalcitrant country in the EC.

French Opposition to Blair House

The French government opposed the Blair House agreement as soon as it was signed, on the grounds that it was not compatible with the CAP reform. Italy and Spain were also skeptical at first of Blair House, but only Belgium seemed ready to support France in its demand for a renegotiation of the accord.[33] Fueled by violent domestic protests from angry farmers and by crucial national elections in March 1993, the French government embarked on a crusade to denounce the content of the agreement and contest the conditions under which it had been reached. Above all, French policymakers blamed the EC negotiators who, they claimed, had exceeded their mandate. In private, French officials criticized the personalities of Andriessen and MacSharry, but they also denounced the EC institutions, which seemed to drift away from intergovernmentalism and allowed the overruling of fundamental objections by a member state.[34] The French goal thus became to reopen the agricultural negotiations and at the same time curb the erosion of "negotiating by consensus" and the growing autonomy of the EC negotiators.

A period of stagnation during which all the major actors changed followed the flurry of negotiating activity that preceded Blair House. Andriessen was replaced in January by Sir Leon Brittan, and MacSharry by René Steichen. Mickey Kantor succeeded Hills and Mike Espy replaced Madigan when the new U.S. administration came into office. In Germany, Ignaz Kiechle, the long-time Christian Social Union (CSU) agriculture minister known as a tireless defender of farming interests, was replaced by Jochen Borchert, a CDU member sympathetic to the Blair House agreement.[35] In France, after a long electoral campaign in which the protection of French farmers, the CAP reform, and opposition to the Blair House compromise were central issues, the Socialist government was

---

appeared in his newspaper *Libération*, it was the first time that many member states' officials had a look at it.

[33] Pascal Riché, "GATT: la France retrouve ses amis latins," *Libération*, November 28–29, 1992.

[34] Interviews with French officials, 1994.

[35] "Borchert Signals Change of Direction in German Policy," *Agra Europe*, February 12, 1993.

overwhelmingly replaced on March 28 by a center-right government known for its loyalty to farmers. During the campaign, Jacques Chirac, the leader of the Gaullist party, went so far as to denounce the "foreign" EC commissioners who negotiated the deal.[36]

The successive French governments attempted to reclaim some of the institutional competence delegated to the supranational Commission in order to alter the already negotiated "preagreement." They concentrated first on the reinstatement of the veto right in the EC. Starting in February, the socialist government officially threatened to invoke the Luxembourg Compromise against the Blair House agreement, which could provoke a major institutional crisis within the EC, not without resemblance to the "empty chair" crisis during the Kennedy Round. Observers noted that France could have difficulty in vetoing the deal because other member states might not agree that France's vital interests were at stake.[37] But the French threat to sabotage Blair House was plausible and the possibility of a veto was constantly in the minds of American negotiators, who were closely following the legal arguments in the EC about the constitutionality of a veto and the fact that the Luxembourg Compromise might no longer be applicable as a result of the 1986 Single European Act.[38] American officials took the threat of veto particularly seriously because the recent difficulties surrounding the Maastricht Treaty on European Union had created new uncertainties as to the future of European integration.

In April 1993 Agriculture Commissioner René Steichen tried to seek an accord on the separate oilseeds deal, which required EC endorsement independently from the rest of the Uruguay Round, but the vote was postponed until the newly elected French government had clarified its position on Blair House. The French stance was finally unveiled on May 12 in a memorandum accepting the oilseeds deal but vowing to fight the other parts of the agreement.[39] The memorandum disagreed primarily with the length of the "peace clause" and the concept of reducing the volume of agricultural exports; instead, France preferred to limit subsidies. The memorandum was well received in Ireland, which had hard-

[36] Julie Wolf, "Putting CAP on and Making Sure It Fits," *The Guardian*, March 27, 1993.

[37] "The first two attempts to invoke the Compromise—by Denmark in 1981 over fisheries and by Britain the following year over farm prices—were overruled. The other countries simply went ahead and voted the measures through. Since then the use of the veto has been formally accepted four times on farm disputes. France used it over farm exchange rates in 1982, Germany over cereals prices in 1985, Ireland over beef in 1986 and Greece over farm exchange rates in 1988." Peter Blackburn, "Luxembourg Compromise Reappears to Haunt EC GATT Talks," *Reuters*, September 15, 1993.

[38] Interviews with senior USDA official and USTR official, January 1995.

[39] "France Spells Out GATT Position," *Reuters*, May 13, 1993.

ened considerably its anti–Blair House stance throughout the spring of 1993 because it feared the consequences of the deal for the Irish beef industry.[40] The May 28 Agriculture Council meeting bought off French objections to the oilseeds agreement by a generous increase in the set-aside payments for land that farmers take out of production and other concessions. On June 8 the EC foreign ministers endorsed the oilseeds deal with the United States, which reduced subsidized exports by restricting the amount of land that EC farmers can sow with oilseeds.[41] Nevertheless, the strong opposition of the French government to the Blair House agreement dampened the celebratory mood of the oilseeds deal ratification.

Institutional Demands: New Trade Policy Instruments

France blamed the conclusion of the Blair House agreement on institutional flaws in the EC. French European Affairs Minister Alain Lamassoure said that EC decision making was not working properly and the Commission's methods were unsatisfactory, ending up "with a certain confusion of responsibilities." Citing the Blair House accord, he complained about the unclear definition of competences in the Community and asked governments to ensure that the Commission stick to its negotiating mandate and that national parliaments be associated with the aims of that mandate.[42] The Balladur government was seeking to regain more control over the Commission's conduct of the GATT talks. "It is necessary to recover a certain right to examine the way all this is going on so we don't find ourselves facing a fait accompli."[43]

The French memorandum also complained about the inadequacy of the EC's retaliatory trade policy instruments and argued that the EC decision-making process, which allows a minority of states to block use of such instruments, had to be reformed. The memorandum suggested a new commercial defense instrument that would speed up antidumping rules and pleaded for an improvement of the efficacy of the Community's existing

---

[40] Sean Flynn, "Sutherland's Appointment Presents the Government with a Dilemma," *Irish Times*, June 10, 1993. See also Sean Flynn, "Renegotiated GATT Deal Is Not on, Steichen Says," *Irish Times*, June 15, 1993.

[41] "EC Officials See Farm Price Aiding Oilseed, Corn Gluten Agreements," *The Bureau of National Affairs*, June 2, 1993. See also "France Wins Some Support for GATT Stance," *Reuters*, June 8, 1993; "EC Ministers Approve Oilseeds Accord after France Lifts Its Opposition," *The Bureau of National Affairs*, June 9, 1993.

[42] "EC Decision-making Is Not Working—French Minister," *Reuters*, April 22, 1993.

[43] "France to Regain Control over GATT Talks," *Reuters*, May 14, 1993.

trade instruments in order to match the "impressive arsenal of American unilateralism." The French goal was to change the institutional rules of the game in the EC by, on one hand, making it easier for one outlying member state to rally its reluctant Community partners to its conservative position and, on the other hand, making it more difficult for one outlying member state to resist launching a trade offensive or retaliatory action against a third country.

In June Belgium backed French demands for new trade instruments to fight unfair trade practices by third countries and for strengthening EC trade defense mechanisms. Ireland, Portugal, and Spain also supported the French view, but Germany disagreed. External Affairs Commissioner Leon Brittan argued that the Community had all the instruments it needed, notably the "New Commercial Policy Instrument" introduced in 1984 and modeled after the U.S. section 301 procedure. What was required was the political will to use them.[44] From then on, limiting Commission autonomy, reinstating the veto right, and providing the EC with offensive trade instruments became intertwined with the French demands for renegotiating the Blair House agreement.

From Divided to United: France's Rally for Renegotiation

The U.S. administration made clear that it had no intention of reopening the Blair House agreement and treated the renegotiation issue as an internal EC matter. The Commission and all member states, with the exception of France and Ireland, also opposed the renegotiation of a deal that had been legitimately agreed to by the EC representatives. "Opening up Pandora's Box," in Commissioner Steichen's words, could also prove risky, because many American agricultural groups felt that the United States had granted too many concessions to the EC. Finally, renegotiating Blair House could provoke a crisis in the EC about the legitimacy of the Commission's representation, especially in the current atmosphere of mistrust of the EC created by the Maastricht debate.

France spent the next five months trying to find some allies to reopen the Blair House deal. In June Belgium offered France some welcome support by making the compatibility of the Blair House agreement with the 1992 CAP reform a priority of its upcoming presidency.[45] In July the

[44] "France Wins Some Support for GATT Stance." See also "French Government Releases Official Position on GATT Talks," *International Trade Reporter*, May 19, 1993.
[45] "Belgium to Seek Changes to Blair House Deal," *Reuters*, June 23, 1993.

French government formally requested a special "jumbo" meeting of EC foreign affairs, trade, and agriculture ministers to discuss the reopening of the agreement. Despite the opposition of several member states, the Belgian government ultimately decided to organize the "jumbo Council" in order to reestablish Community coherence, fearing that France would have no remorse using its veto power if it felt isolated.[46] Belgium also hoped to improve confidence and communication between the Commission and the member states, in order to avoid a repeat of the crisis following the secrecy of the Blair House agreement negotiations.[47]

Germany, which initially expressed firm opposition to reopening the deal, played a crucial role in mediating the renegotiation crisis. In late August Chancellor Kohl surprised everyone by announcing that Germany shared some French concerns about the Blair House compromise: "Europe should affirm its personality and identity in the trade negotiations and have the means to defend its essential interests. . . . That means the Blair House agreement in its present form is unacceptable for us [and] that Europe should have trade policy instruments that make it equal to the others."[48] Kohl's concessions to France were interpreted as either a trade-off for the financial crisis of the summer or an extraordinary gesture of Franco-German solidarity.[49]

In a second memorandum sent to the Commission and the member states on September 1, the French government stated that the summer's monetary instability had rendered the Blair House agreement further incompatible with the CAP reform, and it demanded the addition of firm protection against currency fluctuations.[50] France also presented a separate paper on trade policy, proposing that the Community adopt more aggressive trade tactics against unfair competition and be more efficient in the defense of European trade interests.[51] More controversially, the French memorandum also called for changes in EC internal procedures to ensure

---

[46] "The prime objective of the [Belgian] Presidency was therefore to get France out of its corner" (Devuyst 1995: 452–453).

[47] Belgium could achieve such an objective because "as a federalist oriented Member State, Belgium was in a position to request greater Member States scrutiny over the Commission without being suspected of trying to restrict the Commission's treaty powers" (ibid.).

[48] "Kohl Leans toward France in GATT Farm Dispute," *Reuters*, August 26, 1993; "Bonn Says Not Seeking to Renegotiate Blair House," *Reuters*, August 27, 1993; "Germany Wavers on Farm Concessions to France," *Reuters*, August 27, 1993; "Kohl Says Germany Shares Some French GATT Concerns," *Reuters*, August 26, 1993.

[49] "Franco-German Alliance Sought over GATT/ERM Issues," *Agra Europe*, August 27, 1993.

[50] "Senior Farm Officials Prepare for Jumbo GATT Council," *Reuters*, September 14, 1993.

[51] "France Calls for Tougher EC Trade Stance," *Reuters*, September 1, 1993.

national governments' closer control over the Commission during multi-lateral negotiations and to avoid the scarcely transparent conditions under which previous agreements, such as Blair House, were negotiated.[52]

The French government simultaneously revived its veto threat for the first time in months. At the same time France and Ireland engaged in heavy lobbying of their Community partners before the jumbo Council. On September 13 the Spanish government, concerned about its own fruit, rice, sugar, and wine production, backed France in a memorandum arguing that several provisions of the Blair House accord had to be revised and calling for transparency in future negotiations. The Spanish paper said that the importance of the issues at hand made it crucial that the Council be kept informed at all times of the progress of negotiations, so as to avoid the Community being presented with a "fait accompli."[53] Greece also sent a memorandum objecting to certain provisions of Blair House on September 15. The subject of the delegation of trade negotiating authority to the Commission came back to the forefront of institutional discussions in the EC, given the influence that the autonomy seized by Commission negotiators during the Blair House negotiations had on the final agreement with the United States.

At the same time France attempted to pursue an alternative strategy. The French government tried to bypass the Community and negotiate directly with the United States in the hope of increasing its direct impact on the final outcome of the Uruguay Round. "We would not call this negotiations, but we believe we should speak directly with the United States either bilaterally or with the EC Commission," said a senior Balladur aide in September.[54] This strategy proved fruitless, however, as the United States had no interest in negotiating with France directly when the EC compromise position was less extreme than the French. Indeed, American officials made clear to France that the EC Commission is the sole European negotiator; they were determined not to be sucked into a bilateral negotiation with France on revising Blair House.[55] When an outlying member state is in a conservative position, the negotiating opponent is better off if decisions in the Community are taken according to majority

[52] "France Calls for Sweeping Changes to Blair House," *Agra Europe*, September 3, 1993.

[53] "Spain Backs French Demand for Revised Farm Trade Accord," *Reuters*, September 13, 1993; Nancy Dunne and David Gardner, "Spain Backs France on Farm Trade," *Financial Times*, September 14, 1993; "France Aiming for GATT Buy-off," *Agra Europe*, September 17, 1993.

[54] "France Urges Reopening Dialogue on Blair House Accord," *Bureau of National Affairs*, September 9, 1993.

[55] Interview with senior USDA official, January 1995. See also "Brittan Says US Moves on GATT Cultural Position," *Reuters*, September 29, 1993.

and if the supranational representatives have bargaining authority than if the outlier retains control of the decision-making and negotiating processes.

The Jumbo Council and the Reclaiming of Unanimity and Commission Control

The exceptional "jumbo Council" of September 20 eventually enabled the EC to present a common front in the multilateral negotiations, at the expense of Commission autonomy and majority decision making. After an intense session, thirty-five ministers of trade, agriculture, and foreign affairs agreed on the need for "clarification," "interpretation," and "amplification" of the Blair House agreement and reaffirmed the fundamental principles of the CAP. This was a compromise solution, which achieved the objective of preventing France's isolation while not jeopardizing the results of the Uruguay Round.

The Commission's negotiating autonomy proved to be the dominant and most controversial issue during the Council meeting. Complaining that a Franco-German proposal risked tying his hands in the negotiations, Brittan urged the ministers not to demand any new negotiating mandate.[56] French Foreign Minister Alain Juppé angrily retorted that Brittan, a "petty official who had exceeded his brief," had no right to oppose member states' negotiating instructions. This internal drama further strengthened suspicions of the Commission's excessive power.[57] Although in the end no new mandate was given to Brittan, only "certain general orientations" for maintaining the EC's export capabilities and ensuring that international commitments are compatible with the CAP reform, the Council decided to "monitor constantly the negotiations" on the basis of Commission reports during each session of the General Affairs Council.[58] This decision was the first step toward a return to strict intergovernmentalism in trade negotiating matters and a reining in of the Commission's negotiating powers.

Another result of the jumbo Council was the clear reinstatement of unanimity as the basic decision-making principle in trade negotiations. The Council decided to approve the Uruguay Round results by consensus.

[56] Tom Buerkle, "Rift Hits EC as Germany Backs France on Farm Pact," *International Herald Tribune*, September 21, 1993; Stephen Nisbet, "Vague EC Plan Defuses French Trade Row," *Reuters*, September 21, 1993; "EC Ministers Instruct Negotiators to Clarify Blair House Accord with US," *International Trade Reporter*, September 22, 1993.

[57] "Leap of Solidarity," *European Insight*, September 24, 1993.

[58] Devuyst (1995). See also Lionel Barber, "French Coaxed Back into Farm Trade Fold," *Financial Times*, September 22, 1993.

This important decision was confirmed informally during the November General Affairs Council, which also discussed the issue of Commission autonomy and decision making in external trade negotiations. In October, at France's demand, the member states agreed to ask the Commission for a written report on the trade talks every two weeks until the December deadline.[59]

Renegotiation of Blair House

The threat of a major crisis if the EC demands for "clarification" of Blair House were not met contributed to a reversal of the U.S. position on the renegotiation of the agreement. In November Kantor recognized that the French objections to Blair House had provoked an internal EC debate that somewhat hampered its ability to make a bigger offer.[60] The U.S. administration ultimately agreed to renegotiate specific elements of the agreement rather than confront a possible breakdown of the talks before the crucial ultimatum provided by the expiration of the U.S. Fast Track Authority on December 15, 1993.

The Commission's negotiating autonomy was severely limited during the final days of the negotiations. Brittan shuttled "virtually directly from the negotiating room to the EU Council meeting to report—and presumably seek approval—from EU foreign and trade ministers."[61] Negotiations had to be concluded ahead of the deadline so EC foreign ministers could review the final text of a GATT agreement before authorizing Brittan to sign it on their behalf. "One French official boasted that ministers were keeping Sir Leon on such a tight leash that officials were 'practically following him into his bedroom.'"[62]

The EC-U.S. agricultural agreement, finally concluded on December 6, changed several important elements of the original Blair House accord. The "peace clause" was extended from six to nine years, as well as the timetable for cutting subsidized farm exports (the bulk of the cuts were moved to the later years of the implementation period). Market access for imports was fixed according to the type of product (animal feed, meat,

---

[59] Emmanuel Jarry, "Balladur Says Trade Jockeying to Go Down to Wire," *Reuters*, October 15, 1993; "European Council: Franco-German Stratagem Sets Hare Running in Brussels," *European Report*, October 30, 1993.

[60] "Airbus, Agriculture Trade-off on GATT Not Impossible," *Agence France Presse*, November 2, 1993.

[61] David Dodwell, "Hopes Run High for Tariff Cutting Deal," *Financial Times*, December 1, 1993.

[62] Tom Buerkle, "France's Trump: US Wanted Pact," *International Herald Tribune*, December 16, 1993.

dairy products, etc.), instead of the more restrictive product-by-product curbs. Direct assistance to farmers provided under the 1992 CAP reform was not challenged. Finally, and most importantly, 1991–1992 was taken as the reference period instead of 1986–1988. This would allow the EC to export an additional eight million tons of grain compared to the original Blair House agreement.

In exchange for accepting the agricultural agreement, France demanded a toughening of the way the EC handles unfair trading procedures and changes in the voting system within the EC on antidumping.[63] To avoid a French veto, still plausible until the last day, Germany dropped on December 15 its longstanding opposition to a measure giving the Council greater power to impose antidumping duties on unfairly priced imports through a simple majority vote. The French government had succeeded in making it easier for a conservative member state to capture the negotiating position of the EC, while at the same time enhancing the EC's offensive capabilities by making it harder for reluctant member states to reject an offensive trade action.

The EC gained more than mere "clarification" in the final agreement on agriculture, while the United States was forced to retreat during the last weeks of the negotiations. As a result of the constraints created by the EC obligation to negotiate as a whole while retaining the principle of unanimity and tight Commission control, the most recalcitrant country exerted a preponderant influence on the final outcome. When the Uruguay Round was concluded on December 15, 1993, the veto right had been de facto reinstated, the Commission's autonomy was curtailed, and Juppé was able to "voice admiration for the way Brittan had obtained a better deal on subsidized farm exports than the 1992 Blair House accord."[64]

Conclusion

The obligation for member states to combine their external negotiating efforts into one single Community position influences the final outcome of international trade agreements in which the EC participates. This crucial instance of agricultural negotiations between the United States and the European Community under the auspices of the GATT provides an illustrative case in defense of Schelling's conjecture. Both sides in the international negotiation blamed internal tied hands for not being able to go further. On the one hand, the United States trade representative was prone

[63] Jeremy Gaunt, "EC-US Close to Framework Trade Pact, Problems Remain," *Reuters*, December 6, 1993.
[64] Paul Taylor, "France Could Back Brittan for EC President," *Reuters*, December 14, 1993.

to mention the willingness of Congress to initiate retaliation against what it considered unfair trade practices on the part of the Europeans. In the eyes of the American negotiators, their message to the European negotiators was simple: greatly reduce subsidies to your agricultural sector or face stifling American countervailing duties. On the other hand, European negotiators argued that they could be open to the American position, but the situation was complicated by the recalcitrant stance of the leaders of some of the member states. Consequently, American as well as European negotiators held their own trump cards. They all preferred an agreement to an outright trade war, but both sides were attempting to gain as much as possible from an eventual agreement without making too many concessions.[65] However, because the two sides put a high value on the agreement itself, they found ways to avoid the prospect of involuntary defection, in a situation where their "win-sets" did not overlap.[66] While the trade structure between the two international entities did not change significantly between the time the negotiations started in 1986 and their conclusion in 1993, institutional features such as domestic ratification processes evolved. The Europeans' move from a strong unanimity decision rule to an informal consensus rule helped untie the Gordian knot of failed negotiations.

As was hypothesized in chapter 2, supranational competence in a conservative context enhances the likelihood of a final international agreement, and this agreement reflects the preferences of the median states. The Blair House breakthrough was able to occur after six years of deadlock in the EC-U.S. negotiations thanks to an internal agreement on agriculture finally entrusting the Commission with some supranational competence in the form of a bargaining mandate. The Blair House agreement, negotiated in good faith between representatives of the EC and the United States, was renegotiated because the European negotiating authority was contested and the institutional rules of the game were altered. By reinstating the veto right and tightening member states' control over Commission negotiators, France forced a divided EC to accept its point of view and cornered the United States into partly renegotiating the Blair House deal. This case study conforms with the hypothesis that the use of unanimity in a conservative context makes the EC a tough bargainer and leads to the adoption of a final agreement closer to the status quo. The eventual capture of the EC voting rules and Commission latitude by the most recalcitrant member state resulted indeed in the "lowest common denominator" final agreement.

---

[65] This slippery situation is illustrative of the depiction of trade wars between two "large" states by Conybeare (1987) and Gates and Humes (1997).

[66] Putnam (1988).

From the perspective of the negotiating opponent, a Community where individual member states retain tight control over the negotiating process through unanimity voting and strict oversight of the Commission's negotiating activities is a much tougher adversary than a Community governed by majority rule and centralized Commission power. Had the EC member states not integrated their trade negotiating authority, the United States could have successfully negotiated bilateral agreements with the majority of these states, while remaining in disagreement with the outlier. It happened, for instance, in the case of the "open skies" agreements, discussed in chapter 6, which the United States was able to secure with several member states because air traffic regulation does not fall under Community competence. But by joining the European Union, the member states have committed to a unitary external trade policy in the areas covered by the single market, including agriculture. In this case, the majority of member states were eventually constrained by the institutional structure of the EC into accepting an agreement that they did not favor but that was forcefully negotiated by an inflexible EC ruled by its most recalcitrant member.

5

EC-U.S. Negotiations on Public Procurement, 1990–1994

THE DECISION to complete the Single Market by 1992 gave the EC a new impetus in international trade negotiations by providing it with the means to be "reformist." A large internal market was both more attractive and more threatening to third countries, as the EC now had the credible option of retreating domestically if international concessions were not satisfactory. In the late 1980s the Commission developed the concept of reciprocity in order to retain its international negotiating leverage by ensuring that its internal liberalization measures were not unilateral in those areas not yet covered by existing GATT rules, such as services. A corollary of this new offensiveness was the accompanying switch to majority voting, since the Community could afford to be offensive in those areas in which the Single Market liberalization was being shaped successfully. As a result, most cases of negotiations in which the EC went on the offensive, asking its negotiating opponent for change in the policy status quo, are also cases in which supranational competence was extensive.

The public procurement negotiations represent the first rather successful reformist attempt by the Community to open up American markets. The EC included a reciprocity clause in its 1990 utilities directive liberalizing public procurement in the transport, telecommunications, energy, and water sectors in order to pry open the American public procurement markets. Despite its intense attempts at dividing the member states through retaliatory measures and a clear "Trojan Horse" strategy that turned Germany against its European partners, the United States failed to dilute the EC offensive. The majority requirement coupled with the reformist nature of the EC common position in the bilateral negotiations made it difficult for the Community's defending opponent to successfully play divisive tactics for its own benefit. This eventually resulted in the 1994 EC-U.S. agreement on public procurement, which was generally held as a success for the European negotiators.

The Creation of the Internal Market in Public Procurement

As part of the Single Market program, the member states deregulated their public procurement markets, traditionally national bastions, through a series of directives. In September 1990 the Council adopted the so-called utilities directive, which opened up to competition public contracts in the previously excluded sectors of water, energy, transport, and telecommunications. After a long-fought internal battle, the Council agreed to include in the utilities directive the controversial article 29 (also known as the "reciprocity clause") in order to deal preemptively with the external consequences of the EC's internal liberalization measures. This reciprocity clause had also been introduced into the directive as bargaining leverage for the upcoming multilateral negotiations on public procurement.

Completing the Internal Market in Public Procurement

Public procurement has long been one of the most important sectors of European economies. Studies from 1989 estimated public procurement in EC countries to represent 9 percent of national GDP if only contracts placed by central and local governments were considered, and as much as 15 percent of GDP if nationalized industries were included.[1] Four-fifths of all public procurement takes place in the sectors of energy, telecommunications, transport, and water.

The public procurement sector had been traditionally dominated by "buy national" policies. Despite earlier attempts by the Commission to open up public procurement, cross-border competition remained minimal.[2] In 1989 it was estimated that the portion of public works granted by EC member states to nonnational contractors (including from other EC countries) was less than 2 percent.[3] Indeed, the Commission-sponsored Cecchini report calculated that the opening up of the public procurement market could increase the gross national product of the EC by as much as 1 percent.[4] In theory, savings would be achieved by using foreign suppliers who offer lower prices; competition from foreign suppliers and contractors would press nationals to reduce their offers, and all suppliers would have to restructure their production to face the competition.

The Commission argued for years that the procurement practices in the EC damaged both purchasers and suppliers. "Purchasers suffer because they get limited choice and poor value for money, while producers are increasingly victims of their closed home markets, which have fragmented

[1] United States International Trade Commission (1989: 4–8).

[2] In the 1970s the EC adopted two public procurement directives intended to increase transparency and reduce opportunities for discrimination in procurement of public works and supplies. See ibid., p. 6–4.

[3] Ibid., p. 4–9. See also "EC: Government Procurement and the Single Market," *Euromoney International Financial Law*, October 17, 1989.

[4] Cecchini (1988).

European industries narrowly along national lines. As a consequence, in businesses such as telecommunications and boiler making, Europe has long suffered from excess capacity and a surfeit of small manufacturers lacking the scale economies available to their U.S. and Japanese competitors."[5] Despite these economic realities, however, the Commission had failed to convince the member states to abandon their practice of overtly favoring their nationals in the award of public contracts.

The Single European Act and the 1992 program designed to complete the internal EC market provided the political momentum needed to integrate public procurement practices in the EC. Member states agreed to include procurement among the list of sectors to be liberalized by December 1992. Under the Commission's impulse, a legislative program was set up to address the trade distortions created by national procurement practices. The first part of the Commission's program was to strengthen the existing, but ineffectual, legislative provisions on public procurement. Second, the Commission planned to toughen up provisions for sanctions and enforcement, whose earlier weaknesses had hampered previous efforts at creating a single procurement market. To this effect, the member states adopted the so-called remedies directive, which sets up the procedures for appeals against discrimination in the award of public contracts.[6]

Finally, in October 1988, the Commission drafted its original proposal for tackling once and for all the "heartland of monopoly purchasing." Despite being responsible for over half of all EC public procurement, the "excluded sectors" of water, energy, and transport had previously been exempted from EC rules.[7] After intense internal discussion among the member states, the Commission revised its proposal in August 1989 to include the field of telecommunications, while withdrawing the energy sector from the proposal's range of application.[8] On September 17, 1990, the Council finally adopted the utilities directive.[9] This directive was to come into effect in January 1993 in all member states except Spain (January 1996) and Greece and Portugal (July 1997).[10]

---

[5] Guy de Jonquieres, "Hurdles too High," *Financial Times*, November 13, 1989, p. 24.

[6] Directive 89/665 on the coordination of the laws, regulations, and administrative provisions relating to the application of review procedures to the award of public supply and public works contracts, OJ 1989 L395/33.

[7] de Jonquieres, "Hurdles too High," p. 24.

[8] See "Commission Drops Energy from Public Procurement Proposals," *EC Energy Monthly* (September 1989).

[9] Directive 90/531 on the procurement procedures of entities operating in the water, energy, transport, and telecommunications sectors, OJ 1990 L297/1.

[10] Because the member states wanted to keep a portion of the market for their own firms, contracts valued at less than five million ecus for public works, 600,000 ecus for public supplies in the telecommunications sector, and 400,000 ecus for supplies contracts in other sectors were excluded from the directive's scope of application.

*External Consequences of the Internal Market
in Public Procurement*

The internal market program had an exclusively European focus. The member states and the Commission failed to address the external implications of their internal endeavor for several years after the initial drafting of the 1992 program, giving rise to suspicions of a Fortress Europe by the Community's trading partners. The measures taken by the Community after 1988 to deal with the external implications of the Single European Market only confirmed these suspicions by turning the EC into a champion of the "offensive reciprocity" strategy.

In the 1988 explanatory memorandum to the proposed directive, the Commission argued that "the Community is running a serious risk of unilaterally making its domestic market more accessible to third-country firms if the directives on the excluded sectors fail to take proper account of the external dimension." This risk was particularly salient since the sectors addressed by the Utilities directive were not yet covered by multilateral rules, although multilateral negotiations on public procurement were scheduled to begin in 1990. The absence of GATT coverage, however, provided the EC with the right to insist upon reciprocal access to others' markets on its own terms. This meant that the EC could use the lure of the expected benefits from the removal of trade and investment barriers under the EC 1992 program to extract reciprocal access rights to the markets of other countries.[11] In particular, the Commission hoped to get rid of the discriminatory preferences in the U.S. legislation.[12]

The Commission did not want to give away to the United States the benefits of EC internal liberalization when the public procurement practices of the United States were governed by the blatantly discriminatory "Buy American" provisions. The United States had enacted the Buy American Act in 1933 as a measure designed to help the American economy out of the Great Depression. Despite the disappearance of the economic conditions justifying its initial enactment and a gradual erosion of the scope of the act through bilateral treaties that waived some of its restrictions, it was never abolished.

At the time of consolidation of the EC internal market, the Buy American Act gave a preference to domestic over foreign products in the purchase of manufactured products and construction materials used in public works and public buildings throughout the United States. It did not apply

[11] United States International Trade Commission (1993: 159).
[12] "Public Procurement: Agreement on Principle on Utilities Directive," *European Report*, February 24, 1990, p. 11.

to services. The Buy American provisions imposed a mandatory 6 percent price preference in favor of U.S.-origin products on all purchases by U.S. federal agencies or those financed by federal funds. This preference increased to 12 percent for purchases from small or minority-owned businesses.[13] It can also be increased by Congress permanently for a particular sector, or on an ad hoc basis in the annual budgetary procedure.[14]

According to the EC, there were at least forty Buy American provisions at the federal level, a minimum of thirty-seven at the state level, and many more at the local government level in 1989.[15] The EC found that Buy American programs granted price preferences from 6 percent to 50 percent for products with a minimum 50 percent domestic content. Moreover, local preferences were scheduled to rise to 60 percent by October 1, 1991. Buy American restrictions were applied to procurement in many sectors, including the transportation sector, where the price preference in the mass transit and highway construction sector is 25 percent rather than the standard 6 percent.[16] The EC considered Buy American programs at the state and local level to be increasingly important because of the diminished opportunities for federal procurement due to budgetary constraints. According to the EC, state and local procurement represented 70 percent of total U.S. public procurement.[17]

To avoid the free-riding of outside countries on the liberalization of the EC internal public procurement practices, the Commission suggested that the utilities directive include a reciprocity provision—also known as the "Buy European" clause. The Commission's initial proposal in 1988 provided that the contracting entities could exclude offers in which less than half of the value of the goods or services to be provided is of EC origin, and that EC producers would receive a mandatory 3 percent price preference. This way, the Commission argued, the EC would defend its commercial interests and its negotiating position in the upcoming multilateral public procurement negotiations by making no unilateral concession but creating a positive incentive for third countries to give guarantees of equal access to similar markets.[18]

The member states were initially extremely divided on the issue of the reciprocity clause. The more liberal states—the UK, Germany, and the

[13] In extreme cases, U.S. small businesses can have as many as five thousand employees.

[14] Commission of the European Communities, "Commission Responds to U.S. Trade Measures in Telecoms and Procurement," *Rapid*, February 1, 1993.

[15] United States International Trade Commission (1989: III-5–6).

[16] Buy American restrictions apply to other sectors as well, including paper for currency, securities, and passports; hand and measuring tools; and procurement by the National Science Foundation, the Voice of America Program, and the Small Business Administration.

[17] United States International Trade Commission (1989: III-5–6).

[18] 1988 explanatory memorandum by the Commission, 377, quoted in ibid., pp. 4–17–18.

Netherlands—disagreed that barriers should be erected around the Community. They suggested, however, that they could accept some milder form of EC preference as a lever to negotiate reciprocal agreements with third countries.[19] Other member states, such as France and Italy, argued that the Community should protect its markets in public procurement, especially when other trading blocs had their own protectionist measures, and should agree on a strong system of Community preference for tactical reasons before the next round of international negotiations. Indeed, France claimed that the Commission's proposal was not aggressive enough and needed further strengthening.[20]

The member states failed to agree on the issue of reciprocity in 1989.[21] Another divisive issue was the energy sector. The UK had argued from the start that most of it (mainly hydrocarbon exploration and production of solid fuels) should be excluded from the directive's scope of application. France, by contrast, wanted to include energy under the new EC public procurement rules. Finally, a deal was hammered out by the French presidency of the Community in the second half of 1989: oil, gas, and coal exploration in the North Sea were excluded from the utilities directive on the grounds that the sector was already competitive. In exchange, the UK would go along with the Buy European clause.[22]

On February 22, 1990, therefore, the EC Council of Ministers agreed on the utilities directive, which included article 29, the reciprocity clause. The vote was 11 to 1. Despite the inclusion of the Buy European clause in the directive, Edith Cresson, French European affairs minister, voted against the text because its impact was considerably softened through partial exclusion of the water and energy sectors.[23] Only a qualified majority vote was needed for the directive to be adopted, however. The reciprocity clause had become part of EC law.

Hence, after a long internal fight, the EC decided to introduce a reciprocity provision as part of its new public procurement legislation to be used as an offensive device in the upcoming multilateral negotiations. Internal Market Commissioner Martin Bangemann assured the member states that the reciprocity clause would be revoked as soon as an agreement on public procurement opening American markets to a satisfactory degree was reached.[24]

[19] de Jonquieres, "Hurdles too High," p. 24.

[20] See Lucy Kellaway, "Public Procurement Pact Eludes EC," *Financial Times*, December 23, 1989, p. 3; Lucy Kellaway, "Progress Expected on Tough EC Single Market Issues," *Financial Times*, December 21, 1989, p. 2.

[21] "EEC–United States: Warning on GATT Public Procurement Code," *European Report*, February 26, 1992, p. 6.

[22] "Public procurement," p. 11.

[23] Ibid.

[24] "EEC–United States: Warning on GATT Public Procurement Code," *European Report*, February 26, 1992, p. 6.

Offensive Reciprocity in EC-U.S. Negotiations on Public Procurement

Multilateral negotiations on public procurement started in 1990. The Commission was responsible for negotiating the Government Procurement Agreement on behalf of the member states, who had agreed on the negotiating mandate according to qualified majority and had given EC negotiators some latitude in order to obtain concessions from the United States. As hypothesized in chapter 2, the "reformist" nature of the Community position in these negotiations coupled with the supranational competence conferred by the majority rule put the United States in a difficult negotiating situation.

The Government Procurement Negotiations

The discriminatory trade effects of public procurement practices were first addressed at the multilateral level during the 1973–1979 Tokyo Round of the GATT.[25] The Government Procurement Code was signed in 1979 by the EC, the United States, Canada, five European Free Trade Association countries (excluding Iceland), Japan, Hong Kong, Singapore, and Israel. The agreement established rules for transparency and nondiscrimination in the award of public contracts by a list of major government agencies. The code was incomplete, however: it covered contracts for goods but not for services. Also, it excluded government procurement in the energy, telecommunications, and transportation sectors partly because EC negotiators during the Tokyo Round did not have jurisdiction over the utility procurement procedures of the member states.[26]

The signatories to the code had agreed that they would commence negotiations to expand its coverage to purchases that were not initially covered within three years of its entry into force. The first phase of the renegotiations started in 1984 and was implemented on February 14, 1988.[27] The second phase of the renegotiations began in 1987. Its goal was to expand the code's coverage to the so-called excluded sectors, to services contracts, and to remaining government bodies—including central government agencies not yet covered, subcentral government agencies, and certain public utilities.[28] In effect, the negotiations to enlarge the Govern-

---

[25] For a history of the public procurement negotiations, see Winham (1986).

[26] United States International Trade Commission (1989: III-4–5).

[27] Ibid., pp. 14–15–16.

[28] Ibid., pp. 15–10, III-4–5. See also Commission of the European Communities, "GATT Government Procurement Agreement—Report of a Panel on the United States Procurement of a Sonar Mapping Systems," *Rapid*, May 15, 1992.

ment Procurement Code took place in parallel with the Uruguay Round, in the hope of taking advantage of its liberalizing momentum.[29]

The European Community and the United States entered these negotiations in an unusual situation: for once, the EC was the *demandeur* and the United States wanted to preserve the status quo, therefore making the public procurement negotiation an exemplar reformist case. Moreover, the EC approached the negotiating table with the leverage created by its strategy of "offensive reciprocity."

THE EC POSITION

Thanks to its own internal market program, the Community took the lead in the negotiations to liberalize public procurement practices.[30] The EC put forward the first, and most liberal, offer in August 1990. It proposed that all public procurement markets be opened up to competition under conditions similar to those prevailing within the EC under the new public procurement directives. In effect, this would mean transparency of procedures, publication of calls for bids, prohibition of discriminatory clauses, and recourse for companies excluded from competing for a contract.[31] The central objective of the EC in the negotiations was to expand the coverage of the code to subcentral procurement states, municipalities, and other lower levels of government. Its main targets were the U.S. states and the Buy American provisions.[32] The EC also hoped for increased access to U.S. utilities markets, such as urban transport, airports, and water supply. The carrot that the EC provided its negotiating partners was the access to the European internal procurement market. The stick was the utilities directive's reciprocity clause, which others had no right to contest as long as the sectors of water, energy, transport, and telecommunications were not covered by the multilateral rules.[33]

THE U.S. POSITION

The United States responded to the European reformist demands with a much more limited proposal. American negotiators agreed to discuss the

[29] Indeed, signatories of the 1979 procurement code met on the sidelines of the Uruguay Round from December 3 to 7, 1989, in Brussels to try to use the momentum of the multilateral talks to make some progress on opening up public procurement to greater competition worldwide. See "GATT/Public Procurement: American Inflexibility," *European Report*, December 11, 1990, p. 9.

[30] Commission of the European Communities, "GATT Government Procurement Agreement."

[31] "Possible Areas of Agreement," *European Report*, November 30, 1990, p. 16.

[32] United States International Trade Commission (1989: 4–18).

[33] Ibid.

coverage of central procurement currently excluded from the code.[34] They claimed, however, that subcentral procurement could be liberalized by states only on a voluntary basis. The main objectives of the United States in the procurement negotiations were, first, to include European utilities under the new Government Procurement Code and abolish the reciprocity clause in order to have full access to the EC procurement market, and second, to preserve the existing preferences to U.S. suppliers.

Reciprocity and Retaliation

The United States tried to counter the EC offensive. At first, the American government used the tactic of targeted retaliation to divide up the member states and hopefully change the EC consensus on the reciprocity clause.[35] This strategy led to threats of counterretaliation by the EC and further U.S. attempts at retaliation, despite the signing of an incomplete provisional agreement in April 1993.

U.S. RETALIATORY MEASURES

The multilateral negotiations on public procurement quickly turned into bilateral negotiations between the EC and the United States after the negotiators had reached an impasse at the end of 1990.[36] When no significant progress was made in the bilateral negotiations, the United States adopted the strategy of retaliation. In February 1992 Carla Hills, the United States trade representative, threatened to impose sanctions upon the entry into force of the utilities directive on public procurement in January 1993, unless the EC removed the reciprocity clause. These threatened sanctions were based on the identification of the EC by the U.S. administration as "a country that maintains, in government procurement, a significant and persistent pattern or practice of discrimination against U.S. products or services" in telecommunications and electrical utilities.[37]

The European member states were united in their outrage against these threatened U.S. sanctions directed against the Buy European provisions, which were introduced in the utilities directive precisely as a mirror-image to the discriminatory provisions in U.S. public procurement.

---

[34] "Possible Areas of Agreement," p. 16.

[35] The title of this section is borrowed from Bayard and Elliott (1994).

[36] Commission of the European Communities, "Commission Responds to U.S. Trade Measures in Telecoms and Procurement," *Rapid*, February 1, 1993.

[37] Commission of the European Communities, "U.S. Threat of Trade Measures against EC under Title VII of the US Trade Act," *Rapid*, May 12, 1992.

The United States' position shows little regard for the fact of the case, the multilateral consequences of its own behavior. The provision in question is intended to prevent the liberalization of public procurement within the Community, achieved under the EC Internal Market program, from giving unilateral rights to bidders in third countries which keep their own markets closed. . . . It is hard to understand why the country which operates the Buy American Act, whose sole aim is to discriminate systematically in government purchases, should consider that it has any grounds whatever for complaining of discrimination by others in the field of public procurement.[38]

Indeed, the EC had formally offered to ban all discrimination in public procurement in the negotiations, provided that the United States would be prepared to guarantee comparable access for EC suppliers to U.S. markets.[39]

The member states divided, however, as to the response to adopt to these threatened sanctions. France insisted that it would be risky to implement the directive on time if no agreement had been reached with the United States in the GATT negotiations. Spain and Belgium also supported this position and requested a delay in implementation of the directive. The Commission and the other member states took a different position, however, rejecting the idea of reworking or postponing the directive.[40] Given the institutional context of majority voting and supranational latitude governing public procurement, the solution adopted by the EC was to wait and hope for a quick resolution of the bilateral negotiations. Hence, the utilities directive entered into force on January 1, 1993.[41]

The U.S. administration extended the deadline for the application of the sanctions against the EC, but in February Mickey Kantor, the new USTR, announced the U.S. intention to prohibit awards of federal contracts for products and services from the EC, to take effect from March 22, 1993.

EC COUNTERRETALIATION

In reaction to the U.S. sanctions, the General Affairs Council discussed the possibility of counterretaliation. Its Danish president argued that "it

[38] Ibid.
[39] "Washington Says It Will Retaliate against EC Directive on Public Procurement," *Agence Europe*, February 25, 1992.
[40] "Public Procurement: France Asks to Postpone EC Directive on "Excluded" Sectors," *Transport Europe*, December 23, 1992.
[41] "EC/US: Entry into Force of Procurement Directive Causes Problems," *Europe Energy*, January 22, 1993.

is important that the Community speak with a single voice" during the bilateral contacts due to take place in the following days.[42] Trade observers estimated that the U.S. sanctions could cost the EC some forty to fifty million dollars.[43] Not every member state was touched the same way by the U.S. retaliation, however. France and Germany, with their companies Alcatel and Siemens, were expected to suffer the most from the U.S. sanctions.[44] Nevertheless, at the February 2 Council meeting, the member states gave External Trade Commissioner Leon Brittan their unequivocal support and mandate to continue defending the EC directive in the face of U.S. sanctions.[45]

After a meeting with Commission President Jacques Delors, speaking on behalf of a united Community, Kantor postponed the U.S. sanctions on March 19, 1993. The threatened sanctions were due to start on March 22.[46] The Commission tried to convince the Americans to have an independent body proceed with an objective analysis of the current state of the respective public procurement markets and thereby be able to seek fair reciprocity. The United States postponed the sanctions a second time in late March, with the hope that the Commission would begin the process of deciding not to implement article 29 of the directive on public procurement if a bilateral agreement was reached in April.[47]

To the satisfaction of France, the Commission confirmed that the EC would not unilaterally renounce its reciprocity clause. Brittan reiterated that article 29 would continue to be a "means of negotiations" for improving access to the American public procurement market. By contrast, Germany supported the withdrawal of the Community's discriminatory provisions. The German government had never favored the reciprocity provisions, and in the face of the potential damage inflicted on German companies by the U.S. sanctions, it preferred to abandon the clause on the condition of reaching a "balanced compromise," with the United States giving the EC guarantees.[48]

[42] "Council Unanimously Denounces Latest U.S. Trade Decisions," *Agence Europe*, February 3, 1993. See also "EC Council Reserves Right to Retaliate against U.S.," *European Report*, February 3, 1993.

[43] "EC/US: Last-Chance Discussions Continue," *European Report*, April 21, 1993.

[44] "EC: Reaction from Sir Leon Brittan to U.S. Restrictions on EC Countries in Public Procurement Sector," *Agence Europe*, February 3, 1993.

[45] "EC/US/GATT: Americans Play Down Brittan/Kantor Meeting," *European Report*, February 10, 1993.

[46] "EC/US: Last Minute Move by Kantor to Delay Sanctions," *European Report*, March 24, 1993.

[47] "EC: In the Public Procurement Dispute, Washington Will Not Retaliate until the Meeting of 19–20 April," *Agence Europe*, March 30, 1993.

[48] "EC: General Affairs Council Comments on Progress in Trade Negotiations with U.S.," *Agence Europe*, April 6, 1993.

THE APRIL 1993 PARTIAL EC-U.S. AGREEMENT

The EC and the United States concluded a partial deal in April 1993. According to the agreement, the EC would disapply the reciprocity clause in some cases (mostly in the electrical equipment sector). In exchange, the United States would remove all discrimination against EC bids for procurement by the five publicly owned federal electrical utilities, plus the Tennessee Valley Authority. The United States also agreed to set in motion a process designed eventually to eliminate Buy American provisions carried out at subfederal level. The U.S. administration committed to approach the governors of all fifty states as well as leaders of the largest U.S. cities and municipalities (with a population of over half a million) about the withdrawal of the American preferences in public procurement. Finally, both sides agreed to launch a joint, independent study of access to the EC and U.S. procurement markets.[49]

The member states were unanimous in their approval of the partial EC-U.S. deal. The Article 113 Committee met on April 22 to hear the initial reactions of member states.[50] Brittan recommended the deal to the EC, arguing that thanks to the agreement European firms would, for the first time in sixty years, start to have access to contracts at the subfederal level. Moreover, by representing a de-escalation of EC-U.S. tensions, the agreement would help the atmosphere in the GATT.[51] The May 10 Foreign Affairs Council agreed to drop article 29 of the EC's utilities directive in exchange for the United States removing the Buy American preferences on the Tennessee Valley Authority and the five federal power administrations of the U.S. Department of Energy.

This agreement was only partial, however. It covered mostly heavy electrical equipment but did not involve telecommunications at all. For the most part, the EC had kept the reciprocity clause. As a result, the United States decided to proceed with some limited sanctions anyway, while continuing negotiating on the remaining procurement issues such as telecom-

[49] The approach to local leaders "was crucial for the Community, as most of America's tenders for contracts are in ports, airports, urban transport and water supplies are offered out by the state and municipal authorities rather than the federal government (examples include the modernization and extension of airports, the dredging and extension of ports, the building of highways, the building of metro systems and rapid transit railways, the construction of dams and the purchase of school buses. All these contracts are currently effectively closed to EC companies, which often have to be as much as 25% cheaper than their US competitors to win the deal)." "Details of EC/US Partial Agreement on Public Procurement," *Reuters*, April 22, 1993.

[50] "EC/US: Partial Breakthrough but Sanctions Linger," *European Report*, April 24, 1993.

[51] "EC/US: Unanimous Approval of Public Procurement Text," *European Report*, May 12, 1993.

munications.[52] The American administration announced sanctions of about twenty million dollars a year against EC suppliers, supposed to represent the share of the utilities market in telecommunications.[53] In June the EC agreed to retaliate to these limited U.S. sanctions by applying its own countersanctions worth fifteen million dollars.

Hence, the U.S. strategy of fending off the EC public procurement offensive with threatened and actual retaliation failed to produce its expected results. The EC's institutional rules of qualified majority voting and supranational competence enabled the Community to carry through an offensive against American public procurement practices. In the face of U.S. retaliation, these institutional rules once again acted to strengthen the bargaining leverage of the EC as a whole by not letting internal disagreements among the member states, mostly France and Germany, derail the resolve of the majority of the EC's constituent states to go ahead with their strategy of offensive reciprocity.

Successes and Failures of the Trojan Horse Strategy

Given the limited success of its earlier retaliatory strategy, the U.S. administration changed tactics and attempted to introduce a "Trojan Horse" in the Community by heating up the opposition of one of the member states. Despite the successful conclusion of a U.S.-Germany deal on telecommunications and the ensuing political turmoil in the EC, the United States failed to break up the EC reformist offensive, which was led under majority rule. As a result, the final multilateral agreement on public procurement was generally held as a success for the European negotiators.

Germany as Target of the Trojan Horse Strategy

Shortly after the conclusion of the partial EC-U.S. procurement agreement and the resumption of the bilateral negotiations on the remaining issues, the EC Council passed a regulation seeking to restrict access by U.S. companies to EC public contracts in the telecommunications sector as a reprisal for the sanctions applied by the Americans in the same sector. Three days later, it was discovered that Germany had breached European solidarity by concluding a surprise telecommunications deal with the United States.

On June 11, 1993, three days after the adoption by the EC of countermeasures against American companies, U.S. officials revealed that Ger-

---

[52] United States International Trade Commission (1993: 88).
[53] "COREPER Sets Limited Counter-sanctions against US," *Reuters*, June 2, 1993.

many had concluded a secret deal with the United States on telecommunications procurement. On the basis of an obsolete German-U.S. friendship treaty, Germany agreed to ignore the public procurement directive mandating preferential treatment for EC suppliers in telecommunications. The bilateral move effectively freed German and U.S. suppliers from EC-U.S. sanctions and countersanctions imposed in a dispute over mutual charges of discrimination against outside suppliers.[54] The Commission argued that this surprise bilateral deal was illegal and immediately threatened legal action against Germany.

The German government first tried to deny that it had signed an agreement with the United States. German Economy Minister Guenter Rexrodt confirmed, however, that Germany had no intention of applying article 29's preferential clause to U.S. companies, and accordingly the U.S. sanctions no longer had any reason to apply. Bonn had a different interpretation of article 29, he argued, pointing out that in the German translation, the preference clause on prices is not mandatory.[55]

After its failure to deny the existence of the agreement, Germany attempted to justify its decision to make such an agreement by citing the existence of a 1954 friendship treaty between Germany and the United States prohibiting trade discrimination between the two countries. Moreover, Germany's ambassador to the EC said that Germany's opposition to the reciprocity clause had been known since the EC drew up the directive.[56]

This unexpected breach of European solidarity by one of the EC's foremost pro-integrationist members was initially expected to have external consequences. This is precisely why the U.S. administration pursued secret negotiations with Germany, concluded a secret deal, and then revealed very publicly the existence of this deal. "If the Americans' plan was to try to erode Europe's admirable yet shaky unified stance on trade policy, they succeeded," wrote an analyst at the time. "What Mr. Rexrodt thought would be an under-the-table agreement, Mr. Kantor made public with great fanfare, taking advantage of this opportunity to sow the seeds of discord among the member states and to put the Commission in a difficult position, right in the middle of GATT negotiations."[57]

After the initial bewilderment at the possible existence of the German-American deal, the Commission immediately attacked its legality and even talked about imposing sanctions against Germany, while waiting for

[54] "France Condemns US-German Telecoms Pact," *Reuters*, June 14, 1993.
[55] "EC/US: German Public Procurement Opt-Out Heading to the Top," *European Report*, June 16, 1993.
[56] "Bonn Defends Telecoms Stand, but Agrees to Talk," *Reuters*, June 16, 1993.
[57] "EC U.S.: German Public Procurement Opt-Out Heading to the Top."

the European Court of Justice to start summary proceedings. The position of the Commission, supported by several member states, was that the EC gave periodic authority to renew bilateral cooperation agreements between EC member states and non-EC countries only on the understanding that they did not run counter to EC trade policy. Otherwise they risked weakening the Community's position in multilateral negotiations.[58] France, in particular, had called on the Commission to investigate what it called "an infringement of Community solidarity."

In a June 11 statement, the Commission claimed that Germany was obliged to grant the preference clause and pointed out that EC trade policy is an exclusive competence of the Community. Therefore the member states have no right to encroach upon this competence by signing bilateral trade agreements with non-EC countries. Article 234 of the EC Treaty makes it quite clear that if agreements concluded prior to the application of the treaty are incompatible with the treaty, the member states are obliged to remove any incompatible features. Moreover, the Commission stressed that, like all the other member states, Germany signed on June 8 the countermeasures retaliating against the American sanctions in telecommunications procurement.[59] Therefore, Germany was compelled to apply the countermeasures.

Eventually, the Council adopted in December 1993 a decision according to which the member states' bilateral friendship, trade, and navigation treaties and trade agreements could be renewed only "as regards those areas not covered by agreements between the Community and the third countries concerned insofar as their provisions are not contrary to existing common policies."[60]

Institutional constraints in the EC were clearly one of the reasons why Germany had negotiated a secret deal with the United States. Had the internal market in public procurement been governed by a unanimity rule, Germany would simply have opposed the reciprocity provisions from the start. Later, pressed by its telecommunications firm Siemens, which is well established in the American market, Germany would have opposed the retaliatory countermeasures against American telecoms companies. The supranational competence over procurement issues forced Germany to break EC law by acting on its own. These institutional rules, however, also prevented the German defection from having a long-lasting impact on the Community's position in the procurement negotiations, despite the initial political shock that it caused.

[58] "Bonn Defends Telecoms Stand, but Agrees to Talk."
[59] "EC/U.S.: German Public Procurement Opt-Out Heading to the Top."
[60] Council decision 93/679/EC of December 6, 1993. OJEC, December 18, 1993, L317.

*Unity Is Strength: The 1994 EC-U.S. Bilateral Agreement
on Public Procurement*

Bilateral negotiations resumed after the German incident and accelerated frantically in the last days of the Uruguay Round. The EC and the United States, along with the other signatories to the 1979 Government Procurement Code, finally concluded on December 15 an Agreement on Government Procurement, amending the code negotiated during the Tokyo Round. The basic principle governing the new agreement, which included all large national procurement purchases beyond a high threshold, was that of "national treatment" or nondiscrimination against foreign bidders. The EC and the United States failed to complete their negotiations on other aspects of public procurement before the December 1993 deadline for the end of the Uruguay Round, but they agreed to try to reach an agreement before the signing of the Uruguay Round on April 15, 1994, in Marrakesh.

The remaining issues were, of course, the most contentious. On the one hand, the EC still wanted greater coverage of subcentral procurement under the new code and removal of the Buy American restrictions. European negotiators complained that the December 1993 agreement was likely to apply to less than half of the U.S. states and also that the United States intended to open only one of the "excluded" sectors—electricity—to competition from European bidders. The Commission therefore insisted that the EC would continue to adhere strictly to the principle of reciprocity.[61] On the other hand, the United States complained about the discriminatory restrictions on the participation by U.S. firms in the EU's telecommunications and electrical utilities sectors. The two sides agreed to commission the Anglo-American consulting firm Deloitte and Touche to produce a study estimating the nature, volume, and international competitive value of public procurement on both sides of the Atlantic and later agreed to accept this study as the basis for further discussions.[62]

---

[61] "GATT: Shackles Still on in US Public Procurement Contracts," *European Report*, January 22, 1994.

[62] "Irrespective of whether the specific figures in the Deloitte Touche report are accepted, the value of the markets under negotiation—and thus the potential gains to firms on both sides of the Atlantic—is enormous. Under the code's category B—purchases at sub-central level—the EU says that its offer would open up markets worth over $100 billion. According to EU estimates, the sectors that stand the most to gain are telecommunications equipment (public sector only; the rest falls under category C), computer and office equipment, instruments (especially medical and measuring instruments), chemicals (including pharmaceuticals), machinery and machine tools, metal fabrication, electrical equipment, gas equipment, plumbing equipment, foodstuffs, furniture, banking, and financial services. The value of the

The bilateral talks accelerated again before the signing of the Uruguay Round. In March 1994, thirty-six U.S. states—up from twenty-four—agreed to open their public contracts to European suppliers.[63] Finally, the United States and the EC finally struck a public procurement deal on April 14, 1994. It was expected to open up two hundred billion dollars of business in government contracts—that is, almost double what was expected to result from the December 1993 agreement. In the end, thirty-nine of the fifty American states (including California, New York, Illinois, Texas, and Florida) agreed to open up public procurement to the EC. European companies also gained free access to contracts passed by seven American cities: Boston, Dallas, Indianapolis, Chicago, Detroit, Nashville, and San Antonio. For their part, the Europeans agreed to give American companies access to public supply contracts, be they passed by cities, regions, or member states. One of the principal markets targeted by the Americans was the electronics sector, which alone accounted for twenty-eight billion dollars in Europe.

The two sides failed to find acceptable compromises on all issues in negotiation, however, so the Marrakesh accord excluded both the EC's huge telecommunications sector, controlled by monopolies in most of the member states, and some of the Buy American provisions (notably on public transport) on the U.S. side. A senior U.S. official blamed internal EU squabbling for the deadlock in telecommunications and vowed that the United States would try every possible route to gain access to the European telecommunications sector, which was estimated to be worth twenty billion dollars.[64] The official would not say, however, if the Americans were already holding other quiet negotiations with some member states, but Mickey Kantor, the USTR, admitted that such negotiations would be difficult as several member states were determined to hang on to control of public procurement contracts in this sector.[65] European negotiators, for their part, claimed that the EC refused to open up its telecom-

---

potential market under category C—utilities and state-owned enterprises—will depend on the success of U.S. negotiators in opening the EU's market. However, U.S. estimates place the value of the EU market for telecommunications equipment at about $30 billion. With regard to non-telecommunications sectors, the EU values its offer at between $40 billion and $50 billion, consisting of $24 billion for the electrical utilities and the remainder for airports, ports, urban transportation, and water authorities" Calingaert (1994). See also "GATT/Public Procurement: Brussels and Washington Near Agreement," *European Report*, April 9, 1994.

[63] "GATT/Public Procurement: Brussels and Washington Near Agreement," *European Report*, April 9, 1994.

[64] Lyndsay Griffiths, "US, EU Strike Government Contracts Deal," *Reuters*, April 14, 1994.

[65] "GATT/Public Procurement: EU and US Sign a Partial Accord on GATT Ministerial Sidelines," *European Report*, April 16, 1994.

munications sector because the Americans did not agree to completely
abandon their Buy American Act.

Hence, when the bilateral agreement on public procurement was concluded in April 1994, the United States had acquiesced to many of the
initial EC demands (at least on paper), while the EC withdrew concessions
on telecommunications, which had been the central U.S. objective in the
negotiations. This result, which reflected the position of the median rather
than extreme member states, was achieved partly thanks to the transfer
of negotiating competence to the supranational level.

Conclusion: From Single to Multiple Voices Again

The EC quite successfully negotiated changes in U.S. procurement practices thanks to its own institutional features. The Commission was responsible for negotiating the Government Procurement Agreement on behalf of the member states, who had agreed on the negotiating mandate
according to qualified majority and had given EC negotiators some latitude in order to obtain concessions from the U.S. side. This case study
highlighted one of the hypotheses made in chapter 2: the EC's extensive
supranational competence enabled the Community to carry through a
reformist offensive against American public procurement practices.
Moreover, the offensive nature of the Community position in these negotiations, coupled with the supranational competence conferred by the majority rule, put the United States in a difficult bargaining situation.

In the face of U.S. retaliation, these institutional rules once again acted
to strengthen the bargaining leverage of the EC as a whole by not letting
internal disagreements among the member states, mostly France and Germany, cut short the EC offensive. Despite U.S. efforts at undermining
European unity in the procurement dispute through the negotiation of a
secret agreement with Germany, the Trojan Horse strategy did not succeed. The EC immediately declared the deal illegal and therefore void.
Moreover, the EC did not have to be unanimous to pursue its offensive
on the U.S. public procurement policy.

A counterfactual analysis might shed additional light on this case: Germany had declared its opposition to the reciprocity clause from the start.
Had unanimity been the decision-making rule in place in the EC at the
time, two alternative scenarios could have occurred. Either the internal
market in public procurement would not have been completed because
countries such as France would not have agreed to internal liberalization
not accompanied by measures dealing with its external implications, or,
once the internal procurement market was in place, the international negotiations on public procurement would not have proceeded under the

shadow of Article 29 because countries such as Germany would have disapproved of the strategy of offensive reciprocity. It is precisely because the member states were constrained by the institutional requirement of majority that Germany felt the need to negotiate a "secret" agreement with the United States.

In the end, the absence of a unanimity requirement coupled with the strong Community reaction to the U.S.-German deal on telecommunications reinforced the bargaining power of the EC and influenced the final outcome of the Government Procurement Agreement. Unable to break through the "single voice" of the EC to single out the weakest supporter of the reciprocity strategy, the United States found itself obligated to negotiate on the basis of sheer numbers—or else the EC would withdraw concessions, as it ended up doing on telecommunications. In the two previous case studies of "conservative" negotiations, EC voting rules and Commission latitude were eventually captured by the most recalcitrant member state, which resulted in the lowest common denominator final agreement and diminished the bargaining strength of the EC's negotiating opponent. This chapter, by contrast, illustrated how the bargaining strength of the EC's negotiating opponent can be reduced by the use of majority voting and the granting of supranational negotiating competence in an offensive case, where the EC's opponent is the one hanging on to the status quo.

6

Transatlantic Open Skies Agreements, 1992–2003

It happened that there were in the two armies [the Alban and the Roman] at that time three brothers born at one birth, neither in age nor strength ill-matched. That they were called Horatii and Curiatii is certain enough. . . . The kings arranged with the three brothers that they should fight with swords, each in defense of their respective country. . . . The state whose champions should come off victorious in the combat should rule the other state without further dispute. . . . Having engaged hand to hand, . . . two of the Romans fell lifeless, the three Albans being wounded. . . . The Roman legions were breathless with apprehension at the dangerous position of this one man, whom the three Curiatii had surrounded. He happened to be unhurt, so that, though alone he was by no means a match for them all together, yet he was full of confidence against each singly. In order therefore to separate their attack, he took to flight, presuming that they would each pursue him with such swiftness as the wounded state of his body would permit. He had now fled a considerable distance from the place where the fight had taken place, when, looking back, he perceived that they were pursuing him at a great distance from each other, and that one of them was not far from him. On him he turned round with great fury, and Horatius by this time victorious, having slain his antagonist, was now proceeding to a second attack. . . . Wherefore before the other, who was not far off, could come up to him, he slew the second Curatius also. And now, the combat being brought to equal terms, one on each side remained, but unequally matched in hope and strength. The one was inspired with courage for a third contest by the fact that his body was uninjured by a weapon and by his double victory; the other dragging along his body exhausted from his wound, exhausted from running, and dispirited by the slaughter of his brothers before his eyes, thus met his victorious antagonist. And indeed there was no fight. The Roman thrust his sword down from above into his throat, while he with difficulty supported the weight of his arms, and stripped him as he lay prostrate.

— Titus Livius, 672–640 B.C.

WHEN NO supranational competence has been delegated to the EU level, third countries interested in changing the European status quo have the opportunity to conclude bilateral agreements with the member states open to compromise without being held up by the recalcitrant member states. The EU-U.S. row over the "open skies" agreement offers an interesting illustration of how third countries can strike better deals when the member states are free agents in the external sphere than they would have under EU competence. This case provides elements for a counterfactual analysis of the previous three cases in which the "single voice" obligation had consequences for the process and outcomes of negotiations between the EU and the United States. At the same time, as in the Blair House chapter, the open skies negotiations are characterized by a change in the institutional variable midway through the case, which offers control and contrast invaluable for the analysis.

Air transportation follows distinct legal rules, since it is not subject to multilateral trade agreements. Unlike most areas of international trade, transatlantic air services are governed by bilateral agreements—not WTO global trading rules, and not EU competence. In the case of negotiating the deregulation of international aviation, the United States exploited the absence of an EU single voice by concluding a series of bilateral agreements with several small member states. These agreements would not have been reached had the Commission been the sole negotiator for the EU, and whatever the voting mode in place, because the three big member states initially opposed this U.S.-led liberalization. The open skies agreements with the small member states eventually had a domino effect in the EU, leading one state after another to alter its preferences and choose to conclude an open skies agreement with the United States. Eventually, after Germany reached an open skies deal of its own, representatives of the member states agreed to transfer some authority over the aviation negotiations to the Commission. This chapter argues that the transatlantic negotiations over open skies have been fundamentally altered, first, by the bilateral agreements negotiated prior to the transfer of competence to the supranational level and second, by the eventual adoption of a "single voice" requirement.

The Dispute over Negotiating Authority in Aviation

The original founders of the European Community excluded air transport from the sectors for which the Commission could take over external negotiating responsibilities. The issue of liberalization of transatlantic air transport emerged in the late 1970s under the impulse of the U.S. liberalization of its domestic aviation market, but with no success. When the United States addressed the issue again in the early 1990s, the institutional question of competence was formally raised in the Community. The Commission suggested that, as in other sectors being negotiated at the international level, the Community would benefit from negotiating the proposed transatlantic aviation agreements with a single voice. If there was any doubt about Community authority on the issue, why not reform the treaty by finally transferring the negotiating competence over air transport to the supranational level? Without reforming the treaty, why not at least give the Commission temporary competence until the completion of the open skies negotiations with the United States, as the member states had done for the negotiations on services taking place simultaneously in the Uruguay Round?

Absence of Supranational Competence in the Aviation Sector

The Treaty of Rome explicitly treated air and sea transport differently from other sectors of the economy. Article 84 stated that "the Council may, acting unanimously, decide whether, to what extent and by what procedure appropriate provisions may be laid down for sea and air transport." In the absence of clear legal support for the extension of supranational competence to the aviation sector and given the salience of the sovereignty feelings on aviation justified by concerns about the "national interest," no one challenged the member states' authority on the matter. Therefore, these categories of transport were simply considered to fall outside the scope of the treaty.[1]

A couple of legal and political developments occurred in the 1970s and 1980s. First, the European Court of Justice declared in a 1974 judgment that in principle the provisions of the Community's competition laws, articles 85 and 86, did apply to aviation. The opening paragraphs of both those articles prohibited collusion that would distort the market and the abuse of dominant positions. "However, it was one thing to declare that airlines should be subject to competition laws, it was another matter to implement this. In fact means of implementation were inadequate and attempts by the Commission to develop airline policy were largely unsuccessful and a decade slipped by without significant progress being made."[2]

Slow progress was made toward a single aviation market in the mid-1980s. Until then, European air transport was strictly regulated on a national basis. Capacity was restricted; rates were regulated at a high level; competition was almost nonexistent (except for charter flights); and all major airlines were state-owned and heavily subsidized.[3] In a 1984 memorandum on airline policy, the Commission proposed a gradual deregulation of air transport in Europe. Under the impulse of Great Britain and the Netherlands, who began unilateral deregulation, and as a reaction to

[1] Dobson (1995: 187).
[2] Ibid., p. 191.
[3] Ibid., p. 188.

the deregulation of the U.S. domestic aviation market, the EC had felt pressure to design a common policy in air transport. The member states temporarily rejected the recommendations of the Commission.

Nevertheless, continuing political and institutional pressure eventually triggered a change in the course of the Community's common air transport policy. The 1986 Single European Act changed the institutional requirement of unanimity to qualified majority regarding the "appropriate provisions" that could be laid down for air and sea transport.[4] Moreover, the 1986 "Nouvelles Frontières" ruling by the European Court of Justice opened up a means to implement competition rules in aviation. Finally, with the support of the British presidency, the Commission presented a modest liberalization package, which the Council adopted in December 1987. It was supplemented in November 1990 by a second package, which expanded the possibility of fare discounting, eased market access, and liberalized seat capacity. Yet despite these internal reforms, the member states had not addressed the issue of external powers and of who would be responsible for translating these reforms at the international level.

The Early 1990s' Feud over Competences

International aviation has operated since 1944 under the framework of the Chicago Convention and the ensuing thousands of bilateral Air Service Agreements (ASAs), which determine the routes, frequency, seat capacity, and fare regulations[5] applicable to airline carriers. Since the deregulation of its domestic airline industry in 1978, the United States has led the international effort to liberalize international air transport through open skies agreements. The Community was not institutionally ready, however, to tackle aviation liberalization as a single entity.

The United States undertook a revolutionary reform of its domestic aviation policy in 1978, opening up for the first time air transport across state boundaries to competition. The realization of economies of scale made possible by deregulation gradually led to the emergence of megacarriers, such as American Airlines and United Airlines. The U.S. deregulation had direct consequences for the European airline industry. As Dobson observed, it "affected Europe in three ways: it created an example of what a market-led airline industry could achieve; it resulted in U.S. diplomatic pressures for a more liberal international airline system; and

[4] Article 84(2), Single European Act: "The Council may, acting by a qualified majority, decide whether, to what extent and by what procedure appropriate provisions may be laid down for sea and air transport."

[5] Organized through IATA conferences.

it released market dynamics to which European airlines would eventually have to respond."[6]

The expansion of U.S. carriers into transatlantic routes was to some extent a matter of need—and survival. They were overequipped, they had heavily invested in hubs, and in many cases they badly needed the profits that transatlantic routes would bring them.[7] Therefore, the large U.S. carriers pressed the American administration to allow them to compete without restriction on the international market to achieve even greater economies of scale. As a result, the United States stepped up its demands to renegotiate the old ASAs that were concluded with the different European countries in the 1940s and 1950s. In 1989 the International Air Transport Association organized a conference designed to renegotiate the ASAs to adapt them to the new realities of air transport. "By the time of the IATA Marrakesh Conference in 1989, Americans were 'paranoid' about the prospect of 'Fortress Europe' reducing commercial opportunities for their airlines."[8]

For the first time, the member states were forced to consider the implications of the open skies negotiations on the EC and address the issue of competence. British Airways, in particular, complained about the handicaps it felt in the transatlantic market as a result of the absence of a single EC market in aviation.[9] Frustrated about the lack of access to the U.S. market, it favored a single European response to U.S. deregulation in the hope of using the bargaining leverage of Europe as a whole to obtain higher concessions from its American counterparts. The member states had, however, divided preferences regarding the open skies agreements and the desirable institutional framework for such agreements.

Great Britain and the Netherlands were most open to the idea of air transport deregulation.[10] Yet Great Britain, along with France and Germany, went on the defensive, resisting U.S. attempts to open up the transatlantic skies because of the large international stakes held by their national carriers. The big member states disagreed, however, on the best institutional design to fend off the American offensive. Through the voice of their foreign affairs ministries, France and Germany were not reluctant to having the EC negotiate as a whole in international aviation, even

[6] Dobson (1995: 179).

[7] I am thankful to Martin Staniland for raising this issue.

[8] Dobson (1995: 194).

[9] "BA, for example, felt increasingly disadvantaged in the transatlantic market because of the huge pool of passengers in the USA located away from international gateways. While its American competitors could draw these passengers into their hubs for onward flights across the Atlantic BA was not allowed to." Ibid., pp. 189–190.

[10] "Both had developed their main international airports as gateways to and from Europe and they wanted better access to foreign passenger markets. They also had the best developed national reform programs in the early 1980s." Ibid., p. 179.

though their transport ministries were formally opposed to any transfer of negotiating competence.[11] The position of British Airways, as expressed by its chairman, was also that the European air transport market should be liberalized first, and that the Community should then take over the negotiations with the United States: "We need the Community to begin to make use of its negotiating strength against the strong countries outside."[12] On grounds of sovereignty principles, however, the British government opposed the Commission's proposal to take over aviation negotiations. Britain was supported by several small member states, which had liberalizing preferences regarding air travel deregulation and feared that the takeover of external negotiating competence by the Community would exert a protectionist pressure.

In 1990 the Commission proposed to the Council (composed of transportation ministers) to become the exclusive negotiator of open skies agreements on behalf of the member states. In its communication entitled "Community Relations with Third Countries in Aviation Matters,"[13] the Commission claimed that article 113, governing the Common Commercial Policy, gave it the authority to negotiate international air services with third countries, as it did any other external trade agreement. This was the first time that the Commission used the argument that the external commercial aspects of transport were included in the Common Commercial Policy. In the past, the Commission's position had been that member states retained their competence to conclude aviation agreements with third countries, except in specific situations.[14] Under the impulse of its president, Jacques Delors, the Commission claimed that it was now time for the Community to take over the external negotiating responsibilities in air transport.[15] Since the Commission's services were not technically and administratively ready to assume such a role, however, the communication suggested that member states could conclude bilateral open skies agreements with third countries until December 31, 1992, provided that such negotiations had been authorized by the Council. After this date, the Commission would be granted full negotiating competence.

The transportation ministries refused to let go of their traditional competence to negotiate air transport agreements. The member states unanimously rejected the Commission's second proposal in 1992 and settled temporarily the internal conflict by preventing the Community from taking over external negotiating competences in this field. Member states

[11] Interview with EU Commission official, December 1997.
[12] Lord King's remarks to the Royal Aeronautical Society, May 16, 1991, text courtesy of BA, quoted in Dobson (1995: 190).
[13] COM(90) 17 final, Brussels, February 23, 1990.
[14] For a detailed analysis of the Commission's communication, see Close (1990).
[15] Interview with Jacques Delors, December 1997.

therefore embarked on the renegotiation of (or refusal to renegotiate) their bilateral Air Service Agreements with the United States on their own, hoping to obtain a better deal for themselves individually.[16]

Bilateral Agreements as an Effective "Divide and Rule" Strategy

As a result of the big member states' opposition to the U.S. policy challenge, the small states of the European Community became the focus of the EC-U.S. open skies dispute and of the internal EC feud. This American strategy of picking off one country at a time had a domino effect, leading to member states changing their position on the open skies issue one after the other and preventing the Community from exercising its potential bargaining power.

Focus on Small States

The successive U.S. administrations paid close attention to the legal wrangling in the EC regarding the issue of external competence. Under President George H. W. Bush, U.S. transportation officials genuinely believed that having a single Community interlocutor was more in their interest than a multitude of European voices. They judged the liberalizing efforts coming from Brussels to be more in line with U.S. economic and ideological objectives than the policies emanating from the majority of European member states.[17]

In July 1991 the Commission presented its proposals for the completion of the single aviation market, which covered issues such as route and airline licensing, ownership regulations, and the fare regime.[18] The EC-led deregulation did not go as far as the U.S. model. It did not cover crucial items such as the allocation of airport gateway slots and still left the door open to government financial assistance to bail out national airlines, leading the British and Dutch governments to criticize the proposals for not being adventurous enough. Yet the Commission's proposals were still several steps ahead of what the majority of EC member states were willing to accept.

The Clinton administration publicly encouraged the supranational takeover of aviation policy. U.S. aviation officials visited Brussels to express support for the Commission's attempts to secure external compe-

---

[16] Interview with Commission official, December 1997.

[17] Ibid.

[18] Dobson (1995: 222).

tence.[19] When it became clear that the Commission could not obtain an external negotiating mandate from the member states, however, the U.S. administration changed its strategy on the issue.[20]

In the absence of Community negotiating authority, the United States was legally allowed to enter into bilateral agreements with individual member states. The strategy it adopted was to "pick off one country at a time."[21] Federico Peña, the U.S. secretary of transportation, made publicly clear that the administration had adopted a deliberately discriminatory and divisive strategy—the "divide and rule" type.[22] Peña's aim was to pick off some countries in order to "put competitive pressure on neighboring countries to follow suit."[23] In particular, American negotiators hoped that bilateral agreements with the smaller EC countries would pressure the big countries to conclude similar deals.[24]

Airlines in small EC countries—such as Sabena in Belgium and KLM in the Netherlands—were particularly interested in the international liberalization offered by the United States because they were not providing domestic service and therefore needed to compete aggressively on international routes. Moreover, as Staniland points out, they already had experience and interests in international aviation markets: "Ex-imperial countries, such as Belgium and the Netherlands, have inherited large stakes in the long-distance market, sustained by the commercial and cultural networks that empire leaves behind."[25]

A Commission official warned the member states of the "very real danger that our trading partners will pick off one country against another, and make a mockery of our single market" if the practice of individual bilateral negotiations continued.[26] Yet this threat was not sufficient to tilt the member states in favor of a common negotiating framework.

The Domino Effect

The Commission's attempt to take over the competence to negotiate external trade agreements was seriously undermined in 1992 by the conclusion of the first open skies pact between the United States and an EC

[19] Mark Odell, "The Great Divide," *Airline Business*, July 1993.
[20] The administration returned to the "divide and conquer" strategy that the United States used during the Carter administration.
[21] "Standing Firm for Open Skies," *New York Times*, December 24, 1992.
[22] As Secretary Kahn had done in the late 1970s.
[23] Quoted by Neil Kinnock, EC transport commissioner, in a speech to the Association of European Airlines, Luxembourg, April 18, 1995.
[24] Staniland (1996: 4).
[25] Ibid., p. 15.
[26] Jonathan Faull, head of travel and tourism at the EC competition directorate. Quoted in Odell, "The Great Divide."

member state. This prompted a multitude of other member states to subsequently conclude their own individual open skies agreements with the United States.

In September 1992 the Netherlands and the United States signed the first of the open skies agreements. It gave KLM Royal Dutch Airlines virtually unrestricted access into the U.S. market. To observers at the time, the "treaty looked oddly one-sided: it gave U.S. carriers access to a post-age-stamp-size country, while giving the Dutch access to the U.S. But the Administration's rationale emerged later when KLM, the Dutch carrier, took advantage of the treaty to seek approval for a plan to link up with Northwest Airlines."[27]

The Commission, once again, warned the member states that the United States was attempting to "divide and conquer EC aviation."[28] On the one hand, aviation officials at the Commission argued that the bilateral deals gave U.S. carriers much more favorable access to the Community market than they would have obtained had the EC negotiated as a single bloc. The greater market leverage that the EC could have derived from negotiating as a whole could have earned EC carriers the right to carry passengers between U.S. airports.[29] On the other hand, they believed that the unilateral Dutch action would undermine future negotiations should the Community take over.[30]

Other EC member states were fearful of the consequences of the Dutch-U.S. open skies agreement. They believed it would increase competition, offer greater capacity, and lower transatlantic fares. Feeling threatened by the privileged access enjoyed by KLM to the U.S. market, airline carriers from other European countries started to link up with U.S. partners. To do so, however, they needed their governments to sign open skies treaties with the U.S. government.[31]

The United States approached each of the member states in turn, hoping to obtain the liberalization of air transport in fragmented European markets until all of them would be covered by bilateral open skies agreements. As predicted by EC officials, this strategy was successful: like a row of

[27] "Standing Firm for Open Skies." Of course one needs to look at KLM's international routes as well to explain the attractiveness of this small country for the United States.
[28] Bruce Barnard, "EC Weighs Pooling of Aviation Accord," *Journal of Commerce*, March 15, 1993.
[29] Ibid.
[30] "Especially under the Carter and Clinton administrations, the U.S. has openly adopted such a 'divide-and-rule' tactic in dealing with the EU. The tactic has failed to break down the resistance of the more obdurate Member States, but it has (in association with a policy of encouraging alliances between U.S. and European carriers) been highly successful in diverting trade toward more cooperative countries such as the Netherlands." Staniland (1996: 4–5).
[31] "Standing Firm for Open Skies."

dominoes, bilateral open skies agreements with individual member states were concluded with the United States one after the other. In the absence of Community competence, several member states started negotiating their own bilateral open skies pacts with the United States in order to reap some of the benefits of air travel liberalization for themselves. As a result, between 1992 and 1995 nine European countries, including six EU member states (Belgium, Luxembourg, Finland, Austria, Sweden, and Denmark) concluded individual agreements with the United States, which removed restrictions on capacity, frequency of flights, and destinations.[32] They did so in spite of the Commission's explicit request for them not to sign.

In February 1995 Neil Kinnock, the EC transport commissioner, wrote to the governments of six small EC states—Austria, Belgium, Denmark, Finland, Sweden, and Luxembourg—to ask them not to sign their planned open skies agreements with the United States. Kinnock argued that such arrangements would benefit the United States at Europe's expense. The Commission's view was that the open skies pacts offered by the United States "would perpetuate the current imbalance characterizing the international air transport system which, for historical reasons, discriminates in favor of American companies." If, instead, the EC negotiated as one, it would have the clout to get a better bargain. Moreover, Kinnock warned that the "cumulative effect" of open skies pacts with the United States and American competition within the EU market could "undermine and ultimately destroy" EU policy on air transport.[33] The Commission argued that the bilateral accords would undermine its own attempts to reach a wider EU air pact with the United States, come the day that external negotiating competence was transferred to the supranational level.[34] The ultimate goal of the Commission was to obtain total freedom of access to the U.S. air transport market, including the cabotage rights to carry passengers on domestic American routes, even within one state, and to embark passengers in the United States and fly them to a foreign destination. Individual member states negotiating on their own with the United States did not, and could never, obtain such rights.

Yet the U.S. lure of immediate rewards proved more convincing to those member states who had negotiated bilateral open skies deals than the EC promise of greater rewards in the future, should they negotiate as one. Part of the U.S. strategy to "divide and conquer" EC aviation was the announcement, at the very outset of the open skies negotiations, that the bilateral accords would be confirmed only if all nine countries approached

[32] The other three European states were Iceland, Norway, and Switzerland.
[33] "EU/United States: Commission Proposes Talks on Airline Agreements," *Transport Europe*, May 24, 1995.
[34] "US Signs 'Open Skies' Air Pact with Belgium," *Reuters*, September 6, 1995.

signed.[35] This tactic put additional pressure on France, the United Kingdom, and especially Germany, since its traffic could easily be diverted to the Netherlands if it did not sign an open skies pact of its own.

Toward Supranational Competence in Aviation

The Dutch-U.S. agreement had prompted the Commission to attempt again to assert its negotiating authority in the field of international aviation to "prevent discriminatory rights being gained by individual states at the cost of fellow members."[36] Yet apart from Spain and, to some extent, Germany, the member states staunchly refused until 1996 to transfer the external negotiating competence to the EU level.[37] It took the success of the U.S. "divide and rule" strategy, as well as a changing legal framework in the EU, to trigger some move on the external competence front. Yet the four years during which the Commission was not allowed to negotiate open skies agreements on behalf of the EU as a whole fundamentally altered the set of possible concessions that it could later obtain from the United States.

A Changing Legal Framework

The issue of external negotiating competence in international aviation was not formally settled in the EU for several years because the member states were not willing to abdicate their sovereignty in a field that, unlike other areas of trade policy, had not been "communitarized" from the early days of European integration. The concern over sovereignty was particularly salient given the monopolistic and symbolic nature of most national airlines, and the historical connection between aviation and national security.

On one hand, the member states used a practical argument, which the Netherlands voiced publicly to justify its 1992 deal with the United States, against Community competence: the Commission was not bureaucratically equipped to deal with international aviation negotiations. Its understaffing and inexperience in the matter would certainly be handicaps vis-à-vis U.S. negotiators.[38] On the other hand, the member states could just

[35] "Air Transport: Commission Ready to Go to Court over Agreements with the US," *European Report*, March 3, 1995.
[36] Dobson (1995: 225).
[37] "Aviation: Transport Ministers Agree on Allocating Slots at Airports," *European Intelligence*, December 20, 1992.
[38] Ibid.

not agree on the desirable negotiating position to adopt. Some countries, such as France and Greece, feared that the Commission would be too liberal. Other member states, such as the United Kingdom, suspected that the EU negotiators would be too conservative in their demands and concessions and probably biased in their allocation of routes. Each member state felt that it would obtain a deal more satisfactory for its own interests if its national administration negotiated on its behalf.

Institutional paralysis meant that the status quo prevailed, thereby opening the door for the domino succession of bilateral U.S.-European open skies agreements. The legal framework of EU aviation policy, however, started changing around 1993–1994, opening up new debates and possibilities for a Community takeover of external negotiating competences in air transport.

On January 1, 1993, the third and final package of measures laying down the foundations of deregulation of European civil aviation entered into force. They completed the process of gradual market liberalization initiated with the 1987 and 1990 packages. This "third package" consisted mainly of three complementary sets of regulations, which largely replaced the bilateral agreements existing between member states.[39] First, it established common rules for the granting of licenses to European carriers: air carriers could be licensed in the EU only if they were majority owned and effectively controlled by member states or nationals of member states. Second, air carriers licensed in the EU would mostly enjoy free access to all intra-Community routes. Finally, EU carriers would be free to set their fares and rates for services within the internal market, with government intervention on pricing limited to exceptional circumstances only.

The implementation of the third package extended the competence of the Commission over aviation policy by expanding the number of air transport issues to be decided and managed at the collective EU level. While it did not directly address the Commission's external negotiating competence, indirectly the third package severely restricted the content of international agreements that member states could negotiate on their own without implications for the internal European air transport market.

Another major legal development in the EU to affect directly the dispute over external negotiating competences in aviation was the opinion on article 113 delivered by the European Court of Justice in November 1994.[40] The legal issue concerning the future of trade negotiating author-

---

[39] On the third package, see Niejahr and Abbamonte (1996). See also "Air Transport: Total Liberalization of European Skies on April 1," *European Report*, March 19, 1997.

[40] For a detailed analysis of the Court's Opinion 1/94, see Meunier and Nicolaïdis (1997). See also chapter 1 of this book.

ity in the Community emerged at the outset of the Uruguay Round in 1986. Who, of the Commission or the member states, was responsible for negotiating the "new issues" (services and intellectual property) not explicitly covered in the Treaty of Rome? The judges confirmed that the Community had sole competence to conclude international agreements on trade of goods. In the most controversial aspect of the ruling, however, the Court held that the member states and the Community shared competence in dealing with nongoods trade.[41] On the particular issue of air transport, the judges ruled that international agreements on transportation did not fall under the Community's trade policy competence because they were covered by separate articles in the EU treaty.

By ruling in favor of the institutional status quo, this judgment can be interpreted as a setback for the unity of external representation in the EU and, more generally, for the process of European integration. Nevertheless, this judgment also had a positive impact on the Commission's quest for collective authority in open skies negotiations. By clarifying, even restrictively, the legal definition of the scope of article 113, the Court's opinion forced the Commission to explore other legal avenues for obtaining the right to negotiate external aviation agreements on behalf of the EU as a whole.

In March 1995 the Commission announced that it would use legal recourse to obtain the right to negotiate open skies agreements on behalf of the EU. In June the Commission declared that it would take Great Britain to the European Court of Justice and that it was preparing similar action against the member states who had signed open skies agreements with the United States.[42] Despite threats that the Commission would challenge open skies pacts signed by individual member states at the Court of Justice, the bilateral agreements between the United States and EU member states went ahead as scheduled.[43] Since the Court's January 1994 opinion had confirmed that international transport fell outside of the scope of the Common Commercial Policy, member states felt that their bilateral agreements were legally safe.

On the other hand, the Commission selected the option of approaching the competence issue from a different legal angle, based on previous case law according to which the Commission is responsible for any foreign negotiations that affect internal EU regulations ("*in foro externo, in foro*

---

[41] Court of Justice of the European Communities, *Opinion 1/94*, November 15, 1994, I-123.

[42] Barry James, "EU Seeks to Block Open Skies Deals," *International Herald Tribune,* June 13, 1995. See also "Of Airlines and Airwaves," *The Economist,* March 18, 1995.

[43] "EU Nations Sign Open Skies Pact with US in spite of Commission's Threats," *Aviation Europe,* March 9, 1995.

interno").[44] If, by examining the proposed accords, "we can prove that they will impact on existing Community legislation, then they fall within the Community's mandate," said a Commission spokesperson.[45] The liberalization of the EU's internal air transport market, resulting from the entering into force of the third package in 1993, had changed the Commission's bargaining leverage vis-à-vis the member states. If the Commission could prove that the new bilateral open skies agreements negotiated between the United States and individual EU member states had a direct effect on the single market, then it was legally allowed to contest the legality of such agreements in Court.[46] The Commission was all the more entitled to pursue such a legal recourse if it could prove that the individual agreements would have an adverse economic effect on the single aviation market.

One legal avenue that the Commission chose to explore in particular was the exclusive competence that it possessed under competition policy. Commission officials complained that the United States had been using its antitrust powers as a lever to force open transatlantic markets on its own terms.[47] For instance, the granting of antitrust immunity to shield the KLM/Northwest alliance from the rigors of American competition law weighed heavily in the Netherlands' acceptance of an open skies agreement with the United States. The United States had subsequently bestowed similar immunity on the SAS/United alliance, the tripartite SAS/United/Lufthansa alliance, and the Delta/Sabena/Austrian partnership. The Commission realized that the combination of new authority, as a result of the liberalization of the EU's internal aviation market, with its exclusive powers over competition policy could be used as leverage to obtain from the member states the external competence for negotiating international aviation agreements.

Restricted Supranational Competence

In the spring of 1995, the member states started talking about ensuring the coherence of their positions in the open skies negotiations with the United States. British Transport Minister Brian Mawhinney argued that

---

[44] The Commission was following the "AETR jurisprudence," according to which the EU has the exclusive powers to conclude agreements that affect internal EU regulations.

[45] "EU Nations Sign Open Skies Pact."

[46] Ibid.

[47] Ron Katz, "Trust in US Multinational Airline Alliances Make Harmonized Competition Rules between US and European Union Indispensable," *Airline Business*, February 1996.

there was no urgency in defining a common attitude because it is "hard to see how smaller nations signing bilateral air agreements with the United States would plunge European aviation into a crisis."[48] The French government, by contrast, believed that all ongoing bilateral talks with the United States should be frozen until the EU received the negotiating competence.

A Limited Negotiating Mandate

In June 1995 Neil Kinnock, the transport commissioner, made a proposal to the Council mandating the European Commission to open negotiations with the United States in the field of civil aviation. He argued that such a common mandate would be

> a positive response to the US effort which they frankly admit [is]—to divide Europe in setting the ground rules for relations in the field of civil aviation and to impose pressure on the other member states that are not considering the "open skies" proposal. . . . These are the advances that can best be achieved when Europe acts together in civil aviation as it has in other areas of international commerce. That is surely one of the central purposes of being a Union. Sovereignty is about the ability to exercise power and in this case the member states are at their most powerful acting together.[49]

Yet the member states once again rejected the Commission's plea for the right to negotiate external aviation agreements. In September the United States announced the signing of an open skies agreement with Belgium, completing a goal of reaching six individual accords with EU nations.

The U.S. "divide and rule" strategy came closer to full success when Germany, in a fundamental reversal of position, agreed to sign an open skies agreement with the United States in February 1996 (the agreement was formally signed in May). The bilateral deal was accompanied by an antitrust exemption granted by the U.S. government to the Lufthansa/ United alliance. Until then, Germany (on behalf of Lufthansa) had been one of the fiercest opponents of the bilateral accords and one of the only voices mildly sympathetic to the Commission's call for negotiating competence. Once Germany was in the "bilaterals" camp, it gave, in the words of one analyst, a "sense of inevitability about the future of remaining U.S.-Europe bilaterals."[50]

[48] "Transport Ministers, Facing Open Skies, Call for Consistency 'Wherever Needed,' " *Aviation Europe,* March 16, 1995.
[49] "Commission Approves EU-US Air Accord Mandate," *Reuters,* April 26, 1995.
[50] Leonard Hill, "Bilateral Ballistics," *Air Transport World,* February 1997.

The German change of heart regarding the open skies issue put the Commission in a delicate situation. On the one hand, the Commission vowed to take Germany to court if it signed an open skies accord with the United States. Washington had indeed made the open skies agreement a precondition of the granting of antitrust immunity to the Lufthansa/United alliance. On the other hand, the Commission needed the support of the German government in its institutional battle to gain some external negotiating competence away from the member states.[51]

The succession of bilateral open skies deals between the United States and individual member states, coupled with the recent legal changes regarding the internal aviation market, contributed to a partial delegation of negotiating competences to the EU level in June 1996. Seven out of fifteen member states had already concluded transatlantic agreements. Through their individual actions, they had put market pressures on their European partners, forcing them to initiate their own transatlantic arrangements. At the same time, their opposition to a Commission takeover of negotiating competences diminished as they had already secured their individual deals. As long as negotiations led by the Commission did not endanger the advantages they had already won individually, they appeared favorable to such a transfer of competences.[52] Of course, under these conditions, there was not much left for the Commission to negotiate.

Some of the member states were also worried about the decision by the Commission to use its powers under competition policy to unravel the individual deals they had signed with the United States. A precondition to most deals had been the granting of antitrust immunity to transatlantic airline alliances by the U.S. administration. Yet none of these deals had been exempted from antitrust violations by the EU. The Commission's threat to examine minutely each of these deals for antitrust violations and to take each of them to court was no bluff. In early June Transport Commissioner Neil Kinnock and Competition Commissioner Karel van Miert sent shock waves throughout the Community by placing the proposed alliance between British Airways and American Airlines under investigation, and announcing that they would simultaneously investigate the five existing transatlantic alliances: Lufthansa/United, SAS/United, Sabena/Austrian Airlines/Delta, KLM/Northwest, and BA/US Air.[53] Part of the explanation for why the member states, after so many years of opposition, eventually agreed to give the EU some negotiating authority in the

[51] Bruce Barnard and Lisa Burgess, "Germany Faces EU Suit if It Signs US Air Pact," *Journal of Commerce*, February 16, 1996.

[52] "European Union Still Split over Air Transport Talks with US," *Agence France Presse*, March 11, 1996.

[53] Mark Odell, Lois Jones, Mead Jennings, "Antitrust Is Key in Open Skies Talks," *Airline Business*, August 1996.

field of international aviation was the promise by the Commission to withdraw the legal action it had already engaged.[54] The antitrust investigation of the deals, however, continued.

By June 1996, when the Council once again formally addressed the issue of EU competence, only Great Britain remained staunchly opposed to some delegation of authority to the supranational level. The British transatlantic market represented 30 percent of the European market for the United States, and the British government believed as a matter of principle that its interests would be best served if taken care of by British negotiators. The position of the British government, however, seemed at odds with the views of British Airways, whose chief executive, Bob Ayling, expressed himself in support of the common EU voice on open skies agreements.[55]

The French government favored a partial takeover by the Commission but insisted that its negotiating mandate should exclude air traffic rights between the EU and the United States.[56] Therefore, despite formal opposition from Great Britain, the June 1996 Transport Council finally granted the Commission some authority to negotiate a multilateral aviation agreement with the United States in a 14 to 1 vote—majority voting applied on the issue.

The mandate, however, was extremely limited. Member states authorized the Commission to talk only about secondary aviation issues (such as access to computer reservation systems, code-sharing, and ownership restrictions). To be able to discuss the central issue of traffic rights with their American counterparts, EU negotiators would have to come back to the Council for a new mandate.[57] Moreover, the mandate was accompanied by a commitment from the Commission not to roll back the liberalization that had already been achieved in bilateral agreements.[58]

Bilateral talks between senior U.S. and EU aviation officials were to start in October 1996, with the goal of allowing American carriers to fly anywhere in the EU and offer European airlines access to every U.S. city. An overall EU-U.S. agreement would replace all the existing bilateral agreements between the United States and EU member states, as well as the commercial alliances between United Airlines and Lufthansa, Northwest Airlines and KLM, and Delta Airlines and Sabena and Austrian Airlines.

[54] Interview with Commission official, December 1997. See also Odell, Jones, and Jennings, "Antitrust Is Key in Open Skies Talks."

[55] Odell, Jones, and Jennings, "Antitrust Is Key in Open Skies Talks."

[56] "European Union Still Split over Air Transport Talks with US."

[57] "Elections Ground Talks on 'Open Skies,' *European Voice*, June 12–18, 1997.

[58] Neil Kinnock, "The Liberalization of the European Aviation Industry," *European Business Journal*, 1996.

The U.S. administration publicly expressed its skepticism over the two-stage mandate granted to the EU negotiators, with the "soft issues" such as state aid and antitrust policy being negotiated first, before approaching the more contentious issues such as traffic rights.[59] American officials even said that they would not negotiate aviation pacts with the EU until its negotiators had full authority to discuss issues that would move the market toward completely free competition.[60] Charles Hunnicut, U.S. assistant secretary for aviation, therefore claimed that he expected the October talks to be primarily "a listening session" on the U.S. part, since the Clinton administration was unwilling to negotiate until the EU had complete authority to discuss core issues. In the meantime, U.S. negotiators would continue to seek bilateral deals with European countries and would concentrate their efforts on reaching agreements with Great Britain, France, Italy, and Spain.[61]

The 2002 "Open Skies" Ruling and the Future of EU Competence

The Commission has always argued that it was seeking to gain full negotiating competence in external aviation agreements not for political "virility" but on economic grounds. EU aviation officials have long claimed that the open skies agreements proposed by Washington were "unfair and grossly unbalanced against Europe."[62] In general, "America, because it is home to the world's biggest domestic air-travel market, gets the upper hand. European governments accept this because it helps their national airlines obtain at least some valuable landing rights in America."[63] The Commission maintained that these bilateral deals gave U.S. carriers unrestricted rights to operate to and from European countries without giving EU airlines equivalent access to the internal U.S. market, beyond a limited number of gateways. These deals, argued the Commission, would circumvent EU regulations on fair trading and consumer protection.[64] Faced with the United States, therefore, it is better in terms of bargaining power to negotiate as a collective entity.

[59] Leonard Hill, "Bilateral Ballistics," *Air Transport World*, February 1997.
[60] Michele Kayal, "Clinton Puts Conditions on Aviation Talks with EU," *Journal of Commerce*, October 1, 1996.
[61] Bruce Barnard, "EU Launches Probe of Airline Alliances," *Journal of Commerce*, October 3, 1996.
[62] Barry James, "Gingerly, EU and US Move toward Open Skies." *International Herald Tribune*, September 2, 1996.
[63] "A Victory for Brussels, Sort of," *The Economist*, November 5, 2002.
[64] James, "Gingerly, EU and US Move toward Open Skies."

The Commission's case for full competence was strengthened by the final stage of airline deregulation in Europe. April 1, 1997, marked the entry into force of the complete liberalization of the EU's internal aviation market. Among the most important measures included in this final deregulation package was the introduction of unrestricted cabotage—meaning that a European airline will be able to use the national routes of any member state.[65]

Nevertheless, frustrated with only a partial mandate that did not allow the EU to negotiate a comprehensive arrangement, the European Commission finally took the open skies competence dispute to court in October 1998. The Commission referred the bilateral agreements signed by Austria, Belgium, Denmark, Finland, Germany, Luxembourg, Sweden, and the United Kingdom to the European Court of Justice (ECJ).

The Commission's case was based on the argument that because in 1992 the member states agreed to create a single market in air transport, bilateral open skies agreements between the United States and an EU member affect the way the Single Market operates and give airlines from one member state unfair competitive advantage over airlines from other member states. The Commission claimed that, by negotiating separately, the EU states that concluded bilateral agreements with the United States have given American airlines considerable access to the domestic European market without gaining rights of equivalent value for the European airlines in the United States. The Commission believed that pooling the negotiating leverage of all EU member states together would be the only way to achieve a more balanced outcome with the United States. The Commission argued that bilateral agreements denied passengers the full benefits of airline deregulation, and that a single voice in aviation agreements would lead instead to much needed consolidation and lower prices for consumers. It would allow any European airline to operate a transatlantic service from any European airport and give American carriers the same right—provided European ones could fly to any American airport of their choice.

Between the time the Commission brought the cases to court and the ECJ ruling, four additional open skies agreements were concluded with the United States, by France, Portugal, the Netherlands, and Italy.

On November 5, 2002, in a long-awaited judgment, the European Court of Justice delivered its ruling on open skies. In what looked like a judgment of Solomon, the Court made three key findings. First, the judges held that some provisions of the U.S. agreements with European countries

---

[65] For more information on the deregulation of the EU's air transport, see "Air Transport: Total Liberalization of European Skies on April 1," *European Report*, March 19, 1997.

were in violation of EU law: specifically, the establishment of fares on intra-EU routes and rules governing the operation of computer reservation systems. In these two areas, the Court ruled that the EU has exclusive competence to negotiate with third parties.

Second, the Court held that exclusive nationality provisions contained in the existing bilateral agreements infringe the fundamental principle of European law that there should be no discrimination on grounds of nationality. Most bilateral agreements state that only carriers that are majority-owned in the state that is granting the rights can operate on the routes in question.

Third, however, the Court rejected the Commission's claims that the EU has exclusive competence to negotiate aviation agreements with third countries. Instead, the judges ruled that member states remain free to conclude air service agreements with the United States and other third countries, provided they do not contain provisions on computer reservations and intra-EU pricing, or a nationality clause that excludes airline ownership by nationals of other EU countries.

In February 2003 the Commission announced a plan to negotiate a new EU-wide agreement with the United States. The old bilateral deals would remain in place until the conclusion of the new agreement.[66] In March 2003 EU transport ministers accepted the principle of an EU mandate for the negotiation of a Euro-wide deal with the United States. The United Kingdom agreed with the Commission that Brussels should have the competence to negotiate international deals.[67] France and Germany insisted, however, that the EU does not have competence over bilateral agreements with countries other than the United States (such as Russia and Japan).[68] The competence dispute is still unfolding.

Conclusion: Horatii, Curiatii, and the EU-U.S. Open Skies Agreements

The agreement to delegate some negotiating competence to the supranational level eventually came, but it may have come too late for the EU to be able to exercise the potential bargaining leverage that it had claimed to possess all along. The absence of a prior common EU front on the issue of international aviation undoubtedly affected the current European

[66] Paul Meller, "Europeans Propose to End Open Skies Deals," *New York Times*, February 26, 2003.

[67] Russell Hotten, "Lords Back EU over Open Skies Deals," *The Times*, May 10, 2003.

[68] Colin Baker, "Timetable for EC Mandate Slips Back," *Airline Business*, May 1, 2003.

bargaining position and will therefore have consequences for the content of the final agreement eventually reached with the United States.

By concluding bilateral agreements with several member states before the negotiating authority was transferred to the Community level, the United States managed to change the bargaining conditions for the upcoming negotiations in its favor. Given the initial opposition of the three biggest member states to the U.S. open skies initiative, it would have been much more difficult for the U.S. administration to secure a favorable deal for its international airline carriers if the EU had negotiated as a whole with decisions taken under the unanimity rule because the big member states would have captured the European negotiating position. Even under majority rule, the small member states would not have carried enough voting weight to push the whole Community into as liberalizing a transatlantic deal as the individual deals they achieved for themselves.

Instead, unable to agree on their preferred policy orientation and therefore unwilling to transfer the negotiating responsibility to the collective level, the member states chose to take the matter into their own hands. First the Dutch-U.S. deal, and then the succession of bilateral deals between the United States and individual EU member states, presented the rest of the EU with a fait accompli.

Like the lone remaining Horatius fighting to rule and not be ruled, the United States benefited from the absence of Community solidarity in its contest for favorable open international skies.[69] Instead of fighting them as a bloc and probably incurring more severe damage, the United States had to wait for the single member states to separate and distance themselves from each other in their race to reach individual open skies agreements. Like the three Curatii, the member states, starting with the Netherlands, rushed to conclude deals with the United States, but they did so at different speeds. In lieu of stabbing them, as in the Roman legend, all the U.S. administration had to do was to conclude reasonable individual agreements with each of them—all of which seemed beneficial enough for both parties, but none of which could obtain major rights that only the lure of a unified market equivalent in size to that of the United States could have conferred.

The open skies dispute is a clear case where the absence of a unitary bargaining position played to the benefit of the EU's negotiating opponent, and where a different institutional framework would have produced extremely different outcomes. Moreover, the separate open-skies accords that the United States had initially reached with eight European countries

[69] I am thankful to former EC Commission President Jacques Delors for suggesting this analogy to me, presented in the epigraph to this chapter.

tilted the cards for the remainder of the U.S.-EU open skies discussions. Now that about 40 percent of U.S.-Europe traffic flies under open skies, the EU will never be able to deliver the collective gains that it claimed it would be able to achieve better than the collection of individual member states. Whether the partisans or opponents of supranational competence in trade matters will use this unique case of member state autonomy in trade negotiations remains to be seen.

7

Trading Voices: Efficiency vs. Legitimacy

> We often find, at least in practice, an opaque system and unclear lines
> of authority between the Commission and the member states, which
> slows decision-making and appears to make it difficult for the Com-
> mission to change policies—whether to comply with WTO rulings,
> or to take advantage of newly emerging opportunities.
>
> — Charlene Barshefsky, January 17, 2001
>
> Contrary to what some believe, legitimacy does not come at the cost
> of efficiency, it increases the efficiency: if my opponents in a negotia-
> tion know that I have the full backing of the directly-elected represen-
> tatives of 350 and soon 450 million inhabitants, that reinforces my
> position and the weight of what I say and ask.
>
> — Pascal Lamy, February 5, 2002

"UNITED WE STAND, divided we fall" is a phrase often used by Pascal
Lamy, the former trade commissioner of the European Union, to justify
a larger delegation of trade competence by the member states to the supranational union. It implies that institutional rules that allow the twenty-
five countries to make decisions more quickly and the Commission to
represent them internationally in a unified manner give the collective entity an edge in international bargaining. As this book has shown, however,
the international bargaining power of the EU is not a linear function of
its degree of integration. The case studies provided empirical evidence
supporting the central hypothesis: the EU's complex pooling of external
representation has an important, sometimes decisive, impact on international trade negotiations—but a different one from what is commonly
believed. Most claim that the EU has little influence or that it strengthens
the European voice in such disputes; I maintain that the requirement to
present a common front in international trade negotiations can strengthen
or weaken the EU's bargaining leverage, predictably so, depending on the
type of voting rules employed and the specifics of the issue. Specifically, I
find that unanimity voting strengthens the hand of EU negotiators to resist
demands for policy changes but weakens their ability to advocate policy
changes—willingly or not.

This final chapter assesses the strength of the institutionalist hypothesis
in accounting for the outcomes observed in the four case studies. It ex-

plores the theoretical and policy implications of the focus on institutional rules as a determinant of international bargaining leverage. And it analyzes the theoretical and empirical links, as well as supposed trade-offs, between efficiency and legitimacy in trade policy.

Preferences, Power, and Institutions in EU-U.S. Trade Negotiations

International trade negotiations are necessarily overdetermined by virtue of their complex nature. In each of the cases studied, the nature of the negotiating context and the degree to which member states were willing to let go of their sovereignty, through both the voting rules and the delegation of negotiating competence to supranational negotiators, affected the final trade agreement reached with the United States. Yet could the observed outcomes in each of these cases conceivably be attributed to other variables, such as those based on power, preferences, and ad hoc explanations?

Power

Power is often analyzed as an essential determinant of external bargaining leverage. The stronger one country's structural position, whether in security or market terms, the more likely it is to get its way in international negotiations.

POWER BASED ON SECURITY ENVIRONMENT

The evolution of the international security environment and the primacy of security concerns have provided policy analysts with the most common explanation for the discrepancies in European and American bargaining power in trade negotiations since the 1960s. As several scholars have argued, from the 1950s to the 1970s the preference system instituted between EC countries and their former colonies was mostly sufficient to ensure economic growth in Europe.[1] The EC was not too dependent on the results of GATT multilateral negotiations and could therefore hold a strong stance against the United States, even at the cost of failure of the round.[2] By contrast, the United States needed access to the European mar-

[1] For instance, see Thierry de Montbrial, "Aménager le protectionnisme," *Le Figaro*, October 20, 1993. See also Messerlin (1993).

[2] See "Common Market Is Cool to Concessions for US," in *New York Times*, May 12, 1962, which shows that the EEC was in a good bargaining position because "the US market

ket since neither Asia nor Latin America was providing enough outlets for American production. The United States was therefore in a situation of *demandeur*, thereby providing the EC with a bargaining asset, which could explain its victory in the Kennedy Round agricultural negotiations.

At the time of the Uruguay Round negotiations, the situation was reversed. For the first time the United States had other channels of negotiations outside GATT, while the EC could not expect major gains from further regionalization: the countries of the European Free Trade Association were already closely associated with the EC internal market, and neither Eastern Europe nor the developing countries seemed at the time able to trigger the expansion of the Western European economies in the near future. By opposition, the United States could then count on Asia and on the North American Free Trade agreement (NAFTA) with Canada and Mexico. During the course of the Uruguay Round negotiations, the United States entered into a series of cooperation arrangements and free trade agreements with non-European countries, showing the EC that outside options were available. The NAFTA negotiations were completed in August 1992, and the treaty was formally signed on December 17, 1992.[3]

During the same year, President George H. W. Bush declared the U.S. intent of entering into a free trade agreement with Chile and implemented the Andean Trade Preferences Act with Bolivia and Colombia. Also, most countries in the Caribbean Basin benefited from preferential tariffs and quota treatment under the U.S. Caribbean Basin Economic Recovery Act. Indeed, "the proportion of total U.S. imports from countries benefiting from such preferences reached an all-time high of 16 percent in 1992."[4] As the result of these outside options, the U.S. administration, conscious of this new situation, could tough it out when bargaining with the EC. Thus, when Clayton Yeutter, the U.S. trade representative, declared in September 1986 that the United States would walk away from the negotiations if its demands (including the complete ending of farm subsidies) were not met, the threat appeared credible.[5]

The "outside option" argument could also be used to explain the case of open skies. One could argue that since the EC was not presenting a common front in the aviation negotiations, the U.S. "outside option" was indeed inside the Community. The United States was not fighting for access to any particular market, except possibly for London's Heathrow

---

is less important for the Common Market members than the European market is for the United States."

[3] For an exhaustive report of U.S. agreements with third countries, see US International Trade Commission, *The Year in Trade, 1992: Operation of the Trade Agreements Program*, 44th Report, USITC 2640, July 1993.

[4] Ibid., p. xii.

[5] See Robert Trautman, "US to Walk Out of Trade Talks if Demands Are Not Met," *Reuters*, September 8, 1986.

Airport, but for a foothold inside the Community, through which connecting traffic could be directed. Hence, the Dutch-U.S. open skies deal could be interpreted as an alternative option for the United States to the signing of a bilateral deal with Germany, for instance.

In the public procurement case, however, the EC had no outside option available that could compensate for the failure to access American procurement markets. Even the prospect of the opening up of Central and Eastern Europe was no match for the potential of U.S. procurement, were the Buy American restrictions lifted. Yet in spite of the absence of an outside option, the EC succeeded in obtaining concessions from the United States. One of the shortcomings of this explanation of international negotiation outcomes is that it is problematic for a country to use the outside-option card when it is the one initiating the reform of the other's policy status quo. The defending country in a negotiation can always claim to have outside options in case the negotiation fails since it did not want the agreement in the first place. But for the challenger, the lure of the opening up of the defendant's market is by definition more attractive than any alternative option—otherwise the challenger would have concentrated its efforts on the other option in the first place.

Another shortcoming of this analysis of international negotiations is that even when it exists, an outside option is rarely of equal value to the first option pursued. Most often, both the negotiating challenger and the negotiating defendant know that this outside option is only a second choice. The Clinton administration inaugurated Asian Pacific Economic Cooperation with great fanfare in 1993 to signal to the Europeans that were the Uruguay Round to fail, the United States would still have a backup position, but the argument that a GATT agreement was no more valuable than Pacific economic cooperation was not credible. Moreover, outside options are often a complement to, not a substitute for, the negotiation initially pursued. The structure of U.S. trade with Mexico is significantly different from the structure of U.S. trade with the EC. Therefore NAFTA is not a substitute for transatlantic free trade, but a complement. As a result, the outside-option variable, although clearly a contributor to a country's bargaining leverage, carries only limited power to explain international negotiating outcomes.

POWER BASED ON MARKET ENVIRONMENT

According to the power explanation, it could also be the strength of the EU's internal market that explains the outcomes observed in the cases. Indeed, the market hypothesis convincingly explains the long-term evolution of the EU as an international actor able increasingly to shape the world political economy in its favor. It predicts that the EU should become both more offensive and more able to resist challenges as the integration of its internal market progresses. Indeed, the EU now increasingly initiates international policy changes in international trade. It is undoubtedly the completion of its internal market in many sectors of the economy that has enabled the EU to set the agenda in key areas of the international economy.

The market hypothesis, however, fails to explain particular international trade negotiations. It predicts that the EU's external bargaining strength should be positively correlated with its level of internal economic integration. Therefore it cannot explain the process and outcomes of the Kennedy and Uruguay Round negotiations on agriculture since it cannot account for why the EU is able to hold out concessions from its negotiating challenger in areas where the European internal market is barely integrated. Moreover, it cannot account for variation or reversal of the EU's bargaining strength within the same negotiation, while the internal market is held constant or integrates even further. Therefore it cannot explain the conclusion of the Blair House agreement nor predict its renegotiation. Neither can the market hypothesis account for variation across issues at a given time, despite a similar degree of internal market integration. It could therefore not predict that the EU would obtain a favorable outcome in the public procurement negotiations, while having internal and external difficulties with agricultural negotiations.

Overall, power-based variables cannot explain variance in outcomes of simultaneous cases. Security and market explanations are based on slow-moving changes in the state of the system and can thus explain only long-trend evolutions. Yet two different negotiations held simultaneously between the same actors can result in divergent outcomes, such as the agricultural negotiations in the Uruguay Round and the public procurement negotiations conducted in parallel.

Preferences

An alternative determinant of the distributional outcomes of international trade negotiations is the configuration of preferences of the bargaining parties. In this view, the willingness of states to make concessions in a negotiation depends on the nature and relative intensity of the actors' preferences—and so does the bargaining outcome.

SECURITY PREFERENCES

According to this argument, security imperatives outweighed economic interests in the determination of U.S. trade policy in the Kennedy Round era. Since it was crucial for U.S. security to maintain Western Europe under the American defense umbrella, the EEC could use the Gaullist

threat of building a European "third force" or of initiating a rapproche-
ment with Eastern Europe as leverage to obtain what it wanted from the
trade negotiations. Indeed, according to Shonfield, "in the folklore, the
reason for the failure [of the Kennedy Round] is simple: the United States
was too tender with its clever and ruthless allies."[6] In the bipolar world
of the 1960s, American negotiators were cautious not to antagonize the
members of the EEC, which served as a protective bulwark against the
spread of communism.[7]

By contrast, the time when economic interests had to be subordinated
to foreign policy imperatives and when security commitments in effect
burdened the U.S. economy is gone. With the end of the Cold War, coin-
ciding with the middle of the Uruguay Round negotiations, the European
bargaining assets based on security imperatives faded. Therefore Mickey
Kantor, at the time the Clinton administration's trade representative, declared that since the cohesion of the Western bloc against the East was no
longer a primary necessity, there was no reason for the United States to
continue granting economic sacrifices to its allies. Thus, as a result of
transformation in the international distribution of power, the EC lost one
of its main bargaining assets.[8]

Although it is true that trade policy decisions are not made without
taking into account the general context of the relationship between one
country and its negotiating opponent, the security leverage argument falls
short on three grounds. First, there is no historical evidence that the
United States acted in the Kennedy Round on the assumption that security
imperatives prevailed over economic interests. On the contrary, hundreds
of pages of internal U.S. documents at the Kennedy Presidential Library
recount discussions of the U.S. strategy in the Kennedy Round negotiations without ever mentioning security arguments. When they did, it
was instead to suggest that although security had overshadowed trade
imperatives in the immediate postwar period, the context had changed
and therefore economic interests should no longer be held hostage to security interests.[9]

[6] Shonfield (1976: 31).
[7] Care should be taken, however, not to overemphasize the political objectives of the
round and the subordination of economic to political imperatives. Answering the question,
"Are we prepared to make economic concessions to secure in return certain political objectives?" Robert McNeill, deputy assistant secretary for trade policy in the Department of
Commerce, declared: "We are prepared to make only those economic—well, we are prepared to conclude a trade agreement that is truly reciprocal in the economic sense. We are
not prepared in the executive branch to conclude an agreement that will be underbalanced
insofar as our economic interests are concerned, in order to achieve a political objective"
(1966 Hearings: 55).
[8] For instance, see Ludlow (1993); Oye (1992).
[9] Special Trade Representative Christian Herter makes this very clear in the following
excerpt from an internal 1964 memorandum: "Perhaps I was the first to do this in stating

Second, the end of the Cold War did not put an end to the U.S. need for European allies. Many threats to U.S. security replaced the former Communist threat. The uncertainties surrounding the fall of the Berlin Wall, the collapse of the Soviet Union, and the disintegration of Yugoslavia intensified the need for coalition building in a multipolar world. As was demonstrated by the Gulf War, which took place during the Uruguay Round, the United States needed allies with whom to face these new dangers, both as geographical beachheads from which to launch attacks (for instance, Saudi Arabia during the Gulf War, or Europe if the United States were to intervene in the Balkans), and to secure votes in the United Nations to obtain a mandate to act (especially in the Security Council). Therefore, given the uncertain security context in which the Uruguay Round took place, the security argument would predict that the United States could not have attempted to engage in any economic bargaining that could have alienated its European allies.

Third, the security leverage argument could be interpreted as going in the opposite direction. We can argue that it is the United States that had political leverage back in the 1960s thanks to its commitment to European security, and it is the United States that today has lost this main bargaining leverage. This is indeed the interpretation many U.S. policymakers used in the 1960s. In the early days of the Kennedy Round, President Kennedy threatened to cut back the level of U.S. troops overseas if American agricultural exporters could not be guaranteed access to European markets.[10] The threat that should the EEC block GATT trade liber-

---

my opinion that the negotiations should be pursued with the utmost determination through whatever crises may arise and without fear that such determination might lead to the disruption of the Common Market. However, Under Secretary Ball made clear that the State Department was fully in accord with this position and was only concerned that our negotiating strategy and tactics be as little disruptive as possible. As he noted, the Common Market will not fall apart because of US insistence on a fair and reasonable trade bargain." Christian Herter, Memorandum to Hon. Orville Freeman and Hon. George W. Ball, Box 5, Agricultural Policy 1/30/64–7/1/64, February 6, 1964.

[10] See Special Message to the Congress on Agriculture, January 31, 1963, *Public Papers*, 1963, p. 118. Cited in Zeiler (1992: 172). George Ball, under secretary of state, in 1963 discussed "the use of political leverage" as part of his proposed strategy for the Kennedy Round and, most importantly, addressed the shortcomings of the use of political leverage for detailed economic issues: "Quite clearly the limits of our commercial bargaining position are such that we could hardly hope to bring about the drastic liberalization of world trade at which we are aiming without the employment of political leverage. We hold the paramount position in the Atlantic Alliance and most of our negotiating partners are committed to our fundamental political strategy of Atlantic partnership. Moreover, they all have reason to fear our reactions should such a basic and far-reaching American initiative as the TEA be allowed to fail. But at the same time we must be aware of the limits of political pressure. In sensitive sectors—such as agriculture and coal—these limits are narrow. Our experience with poultry demonstrated that clearly. It also demonstrated another important

EFFICIENCY VERSUS LEGITIMACY   **173**

alization, the United States would pull its troops out of Europe was often made indirectly clear by subsequent U.S. administrations. As the Soviet threat was progressively waning throughout the 1980s, however, several European leaders, led by the French, suggested that if the United States wanted to withdraw its troops from Europe, it was welcome to do so. This created a perception that a U.S. bargaining asset was disappearing. But in practice the EC never took seriously this threat of a linkage between troops and trade concessions. Moreover, with the end of the Cold War, the threat has become more credible. On balance, therefore, changes in the international security environment have somewhat decreased the bargaining leverage of the EC in trade negotiations, but not clearly enough to explain the paradoxical results of the case studies.

DOMESTIC PREFERENCES

The particular stance adopted by an actor in an international trade negotiation can also be analyzed as deriving from the configuration of its domestic economic interests. Because different actors often have conflicting interests, preferences are a function of domestic politics. According to this view, both the international negotiating position and the bargaining strength of a country can be directly traced to the domestic power of certain pressure groups. The relative influence of one pressure group over another may explain cross-sectional differences in bargaining outcomes of two simultaneous international negotiations. This is in marked contrast to the power variables, which could offer an explanation only for time-series differences in negotiations.

   Following in the Olsonian tradition of pressure group analysis, one could expect groups representing protectionist-oriented sectors to mobilize their political resources in a conservative negotiation, while a reformist negotiation would not yield similar mobilization by the more diffuse interests served by the opening of international trade borders. Even if the particular interests of those hoping to benefit from international liberalization were concentrated, such as those representing large European banks or construction companies, one can expect the fight put up by sectors and individuals set to lose well-known advantages to be fiercer than the one led by those hoping to derive as yet unknown benefits in international trade negotiations.

   The pressure group model could therefore explain the case studies by arguing that the Community obtained better results in agriculture in the

principle—that political leverage has limited value when applied to questions of detail." "Components of a Strategy for the Kennedy Round," preliminary draft, December 10, 1963, Box 7 George Ball.

1960s than in the 1990s because the agricultural pressure groups in the member states were more politically powerful at the time, mostly for demographic reasons. Moreover, France eventually kept a low profile in the last leg of the Uruguay Round negotiations because its agricultural lobby had been assuaged by significant financial compensation as a result of the arrangements related to the reformed CAP in the fall of 1993.[11] Side-payments can therefore tame the protectionist power of special interests. With respect to the conservative/reformist dichotomy, the pressure group model seems to predict that the EC would be firmer in its defense of existing interests than in the offensive pursuit of new benefits. Therefore, one should observe better success of the EC in defending internationally its agricultural status quo during the Uruguay Round than in pushing to change the American status quo in public procurement during the same period, since the firms and industries that expected to benefit from a relaxation of the Buy American legislation had more diffuse interests than the farmers' groups fighting to preserve their subsidies.

Change in governmental coalitions or in party ideology may also affect the degree of protectionism acceptable to domestic political forces. One could argue that when the Democratic Party was the herald of free trade, starting in the mid-1930s and all the way throughout the Kennedy Round negotiations, the United States was more willing to settle any trade agreement—even an unbalanced one—with the European Community since any agreement was better than no agreement for the promotion of the free trade ideology. By contrast, a U.S. president elected on a platform of "managed trade," like Clinton, might have been more likely to accept a certain dose of protectionism and thus to refuse making unilateral trade concessions to reluctant European negotiators.

Electoral cycles in the United States and the various EU member states can affect trade negotiations. The proximity of a crucial national election can paralyze international negotiations because the incumbent government chooses to halt temporarily the negotiating process to avoid making a stake of the international issue in the domestic political debate. On the contrary, a candidate may wish to present to his or her domestic audience an image of international firmness and may therefore use international negotiations for domestic posturing in an electoral period. For instance, Carla Hills publicly announced the retaliatory sanctions against the EC in the oilseeds case in the week preceding the American presidential election of November 1992. Furthermore, the controversy about the Blair House agreement and the firm determination of the French socialist government to immediately demand its renegotiation can be directly attributed to the crucial parliamentary election of March 1993, in which the incumbents had to fend off their right-wing adversaries' virulent criti-

---

[11] See Devuyst (1997).

cisms that the interests of French farmers had been sold off at Blair House. One could similarly argue that the end of the "empty chair" crisis and the resumption of the Kennedy Round negotiations in early 1966 resulted from the French presidential election of December 1965, in which the strong electoral support for the Common Market, especially by farm groups, was partly responsible for de Gaulle's failure to win a majority vote in the first round of balloting.[12] The French attitude toward its European partners became more conciliatory in between the two electoral rounds, and de Gaulle ended the crisis soon after his short victory on December 19.

Several criticisms can be made of this analysis. First, it fails to explain the outcomes of negotiations on issues of lesser public political salience. While the public in France and Ireland was well aware of agricultural negotiations over suppressing farm subsidies during the Uruguay Round, the public procurement talks never made it either to the headlines or to the debates during national electoral campaigns. Yet public procurement represents 11 percent of the European Union's GNP. Second, the electoral cycle argument can play in the opposite direction if the incumbent government chooses to time negotiating concessions sooner, rather than closer to the election date. Third, negotiating deadlines are often independent of national electoral cycles, especially in multilateral settings like the GATT negotiations, where it would be too complex to accommodate each major participant's domestic electoral schedule. Finally, on major issues, the fracture lines in public opinion may not fall along party lines. In the United States, as in most European countries, free trade is favored by the center and abhorred by the extremes. It may be divisive inside each major party and each major government coalition (e.g., both the Democratic and Republican parties in the United States have pro– and anti–free trade factions). As a result, it might not be in the interest of any big party to make liberalizing international trade agreements a partisan issue in electoral times.

These domestic variables clearly have to be taken into account while analyzing international negotiations. They all contribute to explaining a country's bargaining position by building a theory of preference formation. Nevertheless, these analyses do not answer the central question of this book because they do not explain how preferences are translated into bargaining leverage. By contrast, the institutionalist analysis takes preferences as given and illuminates the link between negotiating preferences and negotiating leverage by focusing on the determinants of bargaining leverage. In that sense, explanations based on preferences and institutionalist analysis are complementary in the study of international negotiations.

[12] Preeg (1970: 120).

Ad hoc Explanations

The last category of arguments often advanced to explain differences in bargaining outcomes is based on ad hoc factors, such as the nature of the issue at stake or the personality of the negotiators.

In this view, outcomes can always be explained with reference to the "specificity" of the issue area addressed in the negotiation. In other words, it is not possible to compare apples with oranges—or agriculture with aviation or public procurement. Even for two negotiations in the same sector (such as the Kennedy Round and Uruguay Round negotiations on agriculture), it might be impossible to undertake a comparison because the nature of the specific issues being negotiated is different. Indeed, if emphasis was placed in both the Kennedy and Uruguay rounds on agriculture, the nature of the proposed agricultural reform differed. The main instrument through which market access in agriculture would be guaranteed according to the Kennedy Round's initial objective was the control of world prices of agricultural commodities. It was more a price-fixing exercise than a liberal endeavor. The Uruguay Round, by contrast, aimed at eliminating trade distortions in world agricultural trade by focusing on national agricultural policies. Second, the Uruguay Round was the eighth round of multilateral negotiations undertaken under the aegis of the GATT. Each round resulted in a significant reduction in tariffs, measures having equivalent effect, and even nontariff barriers. As a result, there were less "easy" issues upon which to bargain. The Uruguay Round tackled either new issues never negotiated before, such as services or cultural goods, or issues addressed but unresolved in previous negotiations, such as agriculture. As a result of the inherent difficulty of the issues in discussion, it could have been expected that the bargaining strength of the EC would be impaired as the negotiations became tougher.

Therefore, according to this ad hoc argument, no explanation is necessary for the variations in the outcomes of the case studies since, in the absence of possible comparison between the bargaining outcomes in different negotiations, there is no paradox at all. Yet, can the focus on the nature of the issues being negotiated be an encompassing explanation of international trade negotiations? It is not sufficient to say that the specificity of the issues drives the differences in bargaining outcomes. The real challenge is to explain what determines this specificity—for instance, by examining pressures by domestic interest groups or the relative weight of the issue in question in the national economy of the parties to the negotiation.

Another variable that recurs in historical accounts of all negotiations as well as in negotiation theory is the personality of the negotiators. According to this view, the process and outcomes of negotiations can be explained, at least partly, by the skills, personal experience, values, and ideology of individual negotiators and decision makers.[13]

In external settings, the EU derives some of its autonomy from the multilevel nature of the international negotiating process, which requires agreements to be reached at the domestic, Community, and international levels. The two-level game highlighted by Robert Putnam implies that chief negotiators are able to increase their influence on the final outcome of a negotiation by using their relay position to manipulate both their domestic constituency and negotiating opponents.[14] Applied to the three levels of bargaining faced by EU representatives when they engage in international negotiations, this argument suggests that the external bargaining impact of the Community is determined by the ambitions of its institutional agents. As a result of their partial autonomy and ability to manipulate their various constituencies, the supranational negotiators can exert a definite impact on the final international agreement, which is likely to be tilted in favor of their own pro-integrationist (or proliberalizing) views. In practice, however, EU negotiators are often forced to defend internationally a Community position that goes against their own preferences. Neither Hijzen in the Kennedy Round nor Brittan in the Uruguay Round favored particularly the negotiating instructions that they had been assigned by the Council. And yet they concluded the agreements for which they had been mandated. When EU negotiators did try to overstep their instructions to reach an international agreement more in line with their own preferences, such as MacSharry in November 1992, the agreement was later contested.

In a related argument, many commentators have attributed the display of European force and antagonism toward the United States during the Kennedy Round to de Gaulle himself. His strong personality led the United States to believe his threats of sabotaging any deal not favorable to French interests and sacrificing the Common Market, and even the Atlantic Alliance, to do so. The EC negotiators were no match to de Gaulle in their dealings with the United States. Therefore, the United States conceded in the agricultural negotiations. By opposition, no vocal European personality aiming at reducing American hegemony governed one of the EC member states during the Uruguay Round. Moreover, the EC negotiators during Blair House, Frans Andriessen and Ray MacSharry, were biased in favor of agricultural liberalization and ready to interpret loosely their negotiating instructions in order to devise creative solu-

---

[13] Not surprisingly, the various individuals whom I interviewed for this book all emphasized the crucial role played by individual negotiators in striking deals and concluding negotiations.

[14] Putnam (1988); Evans, Jacobson, and Putnam (1993).

tions to solve the agricultural impasse. As a result, the United States was able to conclude with the EC the favorable Blair House agreement. The replacement of the two EC commissioners who negotiated the agreement with two other personalities, Leon Brittan and René Steichen, in January 1993 may explain its eventual renegotiation.

Similarly, references have been made to the personalities of the various American trade negotiators. Christian Herter, the first U.S. special trade representative, was an Atlanticist. Born in Paris, he was a key member of Congress in the passage of the Marshall Plan in 1947 and served as secretary of state in 1959.[15] Associated with the pro-European clique of Jean Monnet's friends in the American government, he was not prone to a conflictual style of negotiating with the Common Market, which may have contributed to the eventual failure of the United States in the agricultural part of the Kennedy Round. Herter's personality was highly different from that of Carla Hills, the U.S. trade representative in the Uruguay Round, who vowed to bring down European and Japanese trade barriers with a "crowbar." The combination of weaker European leadership and stronger American antagonism may partly explain why the United States ultimately made more concessions in the Kennedy than in the Uruguay Round.

While the personal skills and values of individual negotiators may indeed play some role in the negotiating process, they can explain only marginal outcomes.[16] There is only so much a negotiator can do when he or she is constrained in each move by strict negotiating instructions emanating from the home government. The firmness, friendliness, and creativity that individual negotiators might display at the international table are allowed to exist only within the limits set by their principals. The variable focusing on the delegation of negotiating competence, which constitutes part of my central argument, is more valuable—and more generalizable—in explaining international bargaining outcomes than a strict emphasis on the negotiators themselves.

Central Findings and Implications

The main approach of this book to understanding the EU's external bargaining impact has centered on the institutional framework at the supranational level. The argument is that the institutions through which preferences are aggregated influence outcomes. An institutionalist model of the

---

[15] For a history of Herter's tenure as special trade representative, see Dryden (1990: 15–16).

[16] See Moravcsik (1999) for a detailed critique of this argument.

bargaining power of the European Union in international trade negotiations was developed. Differentiating between conservative and reformist negotiating contexts, I argued that the EU's effectiveness as an international trade negotiator is determined partly by two distinct, but correlated, institutional mechanisms: the de facto voting rules used by the Council and the negotiating competence delegated to Commission representatives. The case studies of EU-U.S. trade negotiations on agriculture, public procurement, and open skies illustrated these propositions.

Going back to some of the initial questions that motivated my inquiry, I am now able to offer the following answers—with the caveat that four case studies can go only so far in providing support for the hypotheses.

Effect of the EU on International Agreements

Whether it is a deliberate strategy on the part of some member states or an inescapable constraint, the EU does exert an independent causal effect on international agreements. Both the theoretical model and the case studies of EU-U.S. trade negotiations in agriculture, public procurement, and open skies confirmed that, given exogenous member states' preferences, the institutional mechanisms through which member states transfer their sovereignty impact international trade agreements. This finding contradicts the standard realist view that the existence of the EU is inconsequential since it serves only the purposes of a forum where member states make deals and a messenger, relaying positions from the collective to the international levels. The central question that this book attempted to address was, therefore, not only whether the EU matters, but how it matters.

An exclusive focus on states' relative capabilities cannot provide an accurate explanation of the outcomes of international negotiations. Because it ignores the fact that beyond mediating preferences, institutions indeed produce a collective bargaining position distinct from the mean of member state preferences and have some bargaining effects of their own, realism is ill-equipped to analyze the international bargaining leverage of a "divided but united" collection of states like the European Union. Instead, the supranational institutionalist argument has shown that a state with relatively large capabilities can be constrained by prior institutional rules into lending its power internationally to defend a bargaining position that it dislikes—and as a result see its international voice diluted. Conversely, a state with relatively small capabilities can see its voice amplified internationally because the supranational institutions constrain its European partners to accommodate its power of blockage. The realization that small states may exert a disproportionate influence on world affairs through the institutional design of the Community should be seriously considered in light of the recent enlargement of the European Union to Central and Eastern European states—small states in their majority.

Furthermore, this supranational institutionalist argument has a contribution to make to current literatures on domestic factors in international relations. As Helen Milner deplored, "although the importance of domestic politics to international relations has been noted frequently, a theory of domestic factors is not available. No counterpart exists to Waltz's *Theory of International Politics* for the role of domestic factors."[17] Scholars interested in highlighting the importance of domestic, particularly institutional, factors in determining international outcomes could consider, as I did in this book, the nonneutral role of institutions in the aggregation of individual preferences at a collective level.

The Effect of a "Single Voice" on the Likelihood and Content of International Agreements

The obligation of the EU member states to unite their bargaining positions into a single voice has varied effects, depending on the case. By combining the two key variables of supranational competence (voting rules and delegation) and negotiating context, I was able to highlight four ideal scenarios about the strategic effects of the EU's institutional structure on international trade negotiations.

RESTRICTED SUPRANATIONAL COMPETENCE AND CONSERVATIVE NEGOTIATION

When Commission negotiators act in a conservative case with no autonomy following a unanimous decision by the member states, the agenda is set by the most conservative state, and the hands of EU negotiators are tied. The challenging opponent is therefore forced into making concessions or keeping the status quo. The conclusion of an international agreement is less likely, but if signed, the final agreement reflects an enhanced EU bargaining strength. The EU collective bargaining power is high, but the extremist state is the main beneficiary.

EXTENSIVE SUPRANATIONAL COMPETENCE AND CONSERVATIVE NEGOTIATION

When member states choose their collective negotiating position according to majority rule and Commission negotiators have some bar-

---

[17] Milner (1997: 233).

gaining latitude in a conservative case, median states set the bargaining agenda, and the conclusion of an international agreement is more likely. From the opponent's point of view, the EU is not a tough bargainer. The majority of member states gain, but the most conservative members, whose voice has been attenuated, lose from being forced to negotiate as a whole.

RESTRICTED SUPRANATIONAL COMPETENCE AND
  REFORMIST NEGOTIATION

When Commission negotiators act in a reformist case with no autonomy following a unanimous decision by the member states, the most conservative state, possibly co-opted by the defending opponent as a "Trojan Horse," can set the agenda and cut short the offense. Therefore most reformist cases do not materialize into actual negotiations. The opponent is protected from policy change; thus the EU bargaining power is low. Most member states lose by being subjected to the amplified preferences of the extremist country.

EXTENSIVE SUPRANATIONAL COMPETENCE AND
  REFORMIST NEGOTIATION

When a majority of member states suffices to launch a reformist action, it is harder for the defending opponent to play divisive tactics inside the EU, and therefore offensives become more frequent. Median states set the agenda. The conclusion of an international agreement is more likely and will probably be tilted in favor of the EU's position. The voice of the extreme state is attenuated, but the majority of member states gain from negotiating as a single bloc.

EU Effectiveness in International Trade Negotiations

Has the EU become increasingly effective in trade negotiations as it has integrated and consolidated internally? Contrary to the conventional assumption that the EU's cumbersome decision-making procedures have negative effects on its external bargaining potential, I argued that in specific cases the EU could use its institutional constraints strategically to reach its negotiating objectives. This is where being divided but united can give the EU an edge in international bargaining. More often than not, however, the EU's institutional peculiarities are more constraints than strategic advantage—even if the outcome is the same for the negotiating opponent.

As for member states, they do not benefit equally from being forced to share their external trade powers with others. States with conservative preferences can improve their bargaining power over acting on their own on the international scene by negotiating with a single voice while retaining their power to veto the deal and control the negotiators' moves. Member states with median preferences, especially if they are small, are better off inside a Community where sovereignty is pooled through majority rule. Of course the alignment of member states' preferences varies by issue, but member states cannot opt in and out of the EU on an issue-by-issue basis.

Refining the Argument

There are several possible extensions of the present study that I did not explore systematically in this book but constitute an agenda for future research—in particular, the credibility of institutional constraints in a repeated game, and the analysis of the negotiating opponent's own institutional constraints.

THE CREDIBILITY OF INSTITUTIONAL CONSTRAINTS
   IN A REPEATED GAME

Institutional constraints can play to the EU's international bargaining advantage in certain circumstances, but does the repetition of negotiations over time affect the negotiating opponent's strategy in dealing with the EU? The issue of iteration is indeed central to game theory research. Axelrod, for instance, has shown that iteration could foster cooperation in games that had noncooperative solutions when played only once.[18] I believe that the linked issues of iteration and credibility are important for predicting the process and outcomes of international trade negotiations. It is likely that the tools and tricks used in one negotiation, such as the "empty chair" policy, cannot be duplicated in a subsequent negotiation. When negotiations are repeated, the parties learn about each other's constraints and attempt to adjust accordingly, for instance by transforming their own institutions to mirror their opponent's constraints, or by ceasing to give in to the opponent's institutional blackmail. Indeed, constraining domestic institutions that can force an agreement reached internationally to be renegotiated damage, in the long run, the reputation of negotiators as well as institutions. The study of how one learns to cooper-

---

[18] Axelrod (1984).

ate with a complex party and how some institutional assets get transformed into handicaps over time could be a logical extension of this book.

The whole Blair House renegotiation debate triggered questions about
the EU's external legitimacy, leading some of its negotiating partners to
question its credibility if it "cannot deliver on the outcome of a negotiation."[19] Since then, there have been other instances of deals that were
negotiated with a single voice by the Commission on behalf of the whole
EU, only to be reneged upon later by the member states.[20] Because negotiations are an iterated game, the growing uncertainty that the concluded
deal will hold may weaken the long-term credibility of the Commission
and render its negotiating task more difficult in the future.[21] The EU will
be hampered in its more frequent reformist endeavors by the constant
threat of having one of its numerous member states break from its ranks.
U.S. trade negotiators should increasingly try to play the "divide and rule"
strategy of seeking bilateral deals with "friendly" member states when
the EU negotiating authority is contested, as they did in the open skies
case. Indeed, U.S. negotiators have already started to exploit the EU's
institutional uncertainties as bargaining leverage in their favor, for instance by contesting the legality of the negotiators' competence when the
proposals do not favor the United States.[22]

TAKING THE NEGOTIATING OPPONENT INTO ACCOUNT

Throughout this study I held the institutional structure of the EU's negotiating opponent constant and treated the opponent as a black box. This
is why I often spoke of "potential" bargaining leverage and not actual
bargaining power. Another logical extension of this study could be to
relax the assumption that the opponent's institutions are constant and
inconsequential. Instead, one could take into account the institutional
structure of the opponent, examine the constraints that it imposes on the
international negotiation, and see how the institutional constraints interact on both sides of the bargaining table. Comparing and contrasting the
EU and U.S. trade policymaking processes could prove particularly interesting since the European Union and the United States share many similar-
ities and, given their place as the world's two foremost trading entities,

[19] Peter Cook, Australian trade minister, quoted in "US Position on Uruguay Round Talks
Needs to Be Less Rigid, French Official Says," *Bureau of National Affairs*, October 21,
1993.
[20] In 1997 the Council attacked deals with Mexico and Jordan. "Trade Deal Debacles
Bring Criticism of Union Mandate," *European Voice*, July 10–16, 1997.
[21] This problem is not unique to the EU. This is one of the main rationales for the fast-
track procedure in the United States.
[22] Interview with DGI official, April 1997.

have the potential to learn from each other with every negotiation. Another research project could then be to study the bargaining effects of a variety of institutional systems and examine their interactions.[23]

Policy Implications

The realization that the institutional structure of the EU affects the nature of international trade agreements also has important policy implications. Three of these policy issues stand out as particularly important in my view: the existence of an optimal institutional design, the liberalizing or protectionist effect of the EU on the world political economy, and the role of EU institutions in trade as a template for other policy sectors and other state groupings in formation.

OPTIMAL INSTITUTIONAL DESIGN

Policymakers may seek to derive lessons from this analysis for designing the optimal institutions, in a similar way to the questions asked by Milner and Rosendorff about the optimal design of international trade institutions.[24] My short answer to the question of whether there is an optimal institutional design is that it depends on the cases—as was summarized by the four ideal scenarios. My longer answer raises two additional issues.

First, when talking about "optimal" design, one has to ask: optimal for whom? For a state with typically protectionist preferences, the better institutional arrangement is one in which tight control can be exerted on the process of trade policymaking (through the requirement of unanimity) and trade negotiating (through strict constraints placed on the negotiators). For a state with typically liberalizing preferences, the reverse is true. The real-world problem is that states have different preferences on different issues. A state can be, generally, protectionist, but at the forefront of liberalization in a specific sector of the economy. Conversely, a state can be, generally, liberal, but held up by powerful protectionist interests on a specific issue. Is it possible to make up institutional arrangements regarding trade policy on an ad hoc basis? Only a system similar to the American fast track, or the Amsterdam decision by the member states to state the institutional arrangements at the beginning of each new negotiation, can solve this problem. They can do so only to a limited extent, however, since modern negotiations are often addressing a variety of issues simultaneously, and it would be impractical to bargain endlessly on which rules to use for which particular topic before the beginning of each negotiation.

---

[23] See Tarar (2001) for a negotiating model where the two parties face two-level games.
[24] Rosendorff and Milner (2001).

Second, the question of optimal design raises an issue of fairness. The current political equilibrium in the EU is that the interests of a country can be subordinated to the national interests that another country deems vital. Most national policymakers seem to recognize that they could be in the shoes of the others and are therefore satisfied with keeping the veto power. This explains partly the current drive by a majority of member states to expand the rule of unanimity decision making in the new areas of trade policy. From a democratic perspective, however, one can question the fairness of an arrangement according to which the blocking minority always gets its way. A different equilibrium could be one in which the decision is always made by majority vote and therefore imposed upon the states for which it causes a vital problem. Since the voting weights of member states necessary to cast a majority vote are only remotely proportional to the countries' population, thereby favoring smaller states, the democratic aspect of this arrangement can also be subject to scrutiny. Both solutions, therefore, lead to problems of democratic deficit, which in turn can damage the political legitimacy of the EU in the European member states, as will be discussed later in this chapter.

THE EU AS LIBERALIZING OR PROTECTIONIST FORCE ON THE WORLD POLITICAL ECONOMY

Another direct policy implication of this study lies in the determination of the EU's liberalizing or protectionist impact on the world's political economy. My institutionalist model suggests that the EU's capacity to set the agenda in key areas of the international economy depends heavily on the EU's own institutional features. In its initial decades of existence, the EU was a passive actor in international negotiations, more preoccupied in building its own internal policies and defending them against assaults by the outside world than in initiating international policy changes. As a result, it exerted a more protectionist pressure on the world political economy, especially given the definition of the Community's bargaining position at the lowest common denominator of its members. Since the early 1990s, however, the EU has been initiating international policy changes rather than reacting to them. If the international negotiations on telecommunications and information technology, where internal policy developments in the EU led the rest of the world into their path, are any indication, one could expect the Community to be increasingly at the forefront of liberalization of the world economy.[25] The NGOs have

[25] Using a different argument, Messerlin (2001) also expects that the EU will become a more liberalizing force in international trade because of its own experience in dealing with the mutual recognition of standards and regulatory competition.

understood this quite well, which is why since 2000 many counterglobal-ization organizations have focused their attacks against an institutional reform of the common commercial policy: if the EU is blocked by the unanimity requirement, so will the WTO. What institutional arrangement regarding trade policy the member states can agree on (if the EU constitu-tion is ratified for instance) will determine whether the EU will indeed be able to materialize into this liberalizing force for the rest of the world.

Finally, the process of "trading voices," which can make the EU a stronger bargainer and thus stronger actor on the world stage, could potentially serve as a template for other sectoral and regional endeavors. First, the approach developed in this book should be useful for explaining the effec-tiveness of the EU as an external actor in other policy areas. A similar analysis could be fruitfully applied to the study of the EU's role in interna-tional environmental negotiations, where the institutional structure of the Community, as in trade policy, has exhibited some variance across cases.[26] This framework could also be used to analyze the external impact of Euro-pean Monetary Union, whereby monetary decisions in the majority of EU countries are now made by a single entity and eventually may be carried through internationally with a single voice.[27] Finally, if the EU is ever to take on an international role in foreign policy matters, the impact of its single voice in shaping world affairs will need to be studied. I hope that the present argument can provide some analytical elements for this task.

Second, European integration could also be a template for other at-tempts at regional integration in the world. The European Union was originally a unique experience designed to transcend the old rivalries of the Western European nation states. It was conceived neither as a simple free trade area nor as a fusion of previously sovereign states into a federal entity. The initial institutional design of the EU attempted a delicate bal-ance between ripping off the economic benefits of a large internal market while retaining some degree of national sovereignty. Increasingly, the exis-tence of the Community seems to be influencing the behavior of other actors in the international political economy. Above all, the Community is a model for other regional integration efforts. In Asia, North America, and Latin America, countries are trying to imitate the apparent successes

[26] Borrowing from this theoretical framework, Jupille (2000) has developed a bargaining model of the impact of various institutional arrangements in the EU on its bargaining power, and that of the individual member states, in environmental negotiations. Sbragia (1997) has also addressed similar issues in global environmental politics.

[27] On the single EU voice in monetary and financial affairs, see McNamara and Meunier (2002).

of the EU in the commercial sphere.[28] Unlike the founding members of the Common Market, however, they have the benefit of hindsight and can look back to the successes and failures of the EU's unique institutions. What they can learn about the optimal institutional design to enhance their external effectiveness might crucially influence their decision to emulate or reject the Community's original approach to sovereignty sharing.

Trade policy in the European Union will likely come under strain in the next few years from at least three different angles. First, as was seen during the European Convention in charge of drafting a constitution for Europe, many voices are now heard that demand a greater role for the European Parliament in trade policy. Second, the 2004 enlargement either will render the practice of unanimity unpractical or, if used, will make the EU a strongly protectionist force in the world, as predicted by the model developed in this book. Third, many serious conflicts are threatening the already uneasy EU-U.S. trade relationship. State intervention and protectionism have made a comeback, in the United States and elsewhere, as evidenced in the disputes over agriculture and steel. The United States has launched a major complaint against the EU in the WTO on the issue of genetically modified foods, while the WTO has allowed the EU to impose sanctions worth four billion dollars against the United States in the Foreign Sales Corporation case. In this context of increased transatlantic acrimony, it is useful, both for the Europeans and for their American opponents, to be aware of the constraints and opportunities provided by the EU's original institutional structure.

Efficiency vs. Legitimacy in Trade Policy

Even though this book has focused primarily on the implications of certain institutional rules in terms of bargaining power, let us remember that efficiency is not the only concern when politicians design and alter the rules for making trade policy.[29] Increasingly, political leaders are struggling to find a politically acceptable balance between efficiency and legitimacy. Trade policy has a long history of engendering protests, usually fomented by the "losers" from trade—interest groups adversely affected by liberalization. Recently, however, a new form of trade protests has emerged, in which demonstrators oppose trade liberalization not only because of its contents, but also because of the process through which it is made. Activists worldwide have denounced the "democraticidal" nature of international economic institutions and have called for a revision

---

[28] See "Introduction" in Rhodes (1998).
[29] This section is based on Meunier (2003).

of their governance structure to make them more politically legitimate. The grievances regarding the undemocratic nature of trade policy have the potential to be particularly acute in the European Union, where the democratic deficit has been a mainstay complaint for more than a decade. Therefore, the issue of political legitimacy of trade policymaking institutions can no longer be taken lightly.

The Legitimacy Debate in Trade Policy

For almost four decades, trade policy was the matter of complex, technical deals between obscure negotiators and as such raised little media and public interest. But today, the legitimacy of trade policy has become a political issue. As evidence of this newfound scrutiny over the arcane makings of EU trade policy, it is interesting to contrast the 1997 Amsterdam negotiations with the 2000 Nice negotiations.[30] Striking is how little attention EU trade policy received in the past. The Amsterdam fight over whether the Community or the member states were ultimately responsible for negotiating trade agreements in the area of services took place in complete public indifference. By contrast, several civil society organizations mobilized ahead of the Nice summit, in which the same, unresolved issue was going to be revisited, and publicized their actions in the media, especially a widely circulated document entitled "Red Alert on the 133."[31]

The new political spotlight put on the linkage between trade and legitimacy can be explained by the potentially explosive combination of the perceived "democratic deficit in the EU"; the traditional distorted interest representation in trade policymaking and therefore the subsequent insulation of the trade policymaking process; and the Pandora's box of democratic legitimacy complaints opened up in Seattle. All are transforming the environment for making trade policy efficiently.

Before being applied to trade policy, the expression "democratic deficit" had been widely used since the 1990s to describe, and often overemphasize, the presumed gaps in democracy characterizing the workings of the EU. An abundant literature has disseminated the term, which is used in general to explain popular resistance to integration.[32] Above all is the impression of the undemocratic structure of European institutions, whose

---

[30] See Meunier and Nicolaïdis (1999); Nicolaïdis and Meunier (2002).

[31] For the text of this document, see, for instance, http://attac.org/fra/list/doc/georgeen.htm.

[32] On the controversial issue of the "democratic deficit," see, among others, Williams (1991); Wallace (1993); Majone (1996); Weiler (1997); Banchoff and Smith (1999); Scharpf (1999); Cederman (2000); Schmitter (2000); Moravcsik (2001); Siedentop (2001).

creation has been historically driven by elites, not popular vote.[33] More-over, the European Parliament—the only body directly elected in the EU's complex institutional apparatus—has limited powers and is perceived to be too weak to provide effective democratic representation. Furthermore, the institutions of the EU are often referred to as undemocratic because of the lack of transparency of the policymaking process and the extreme complexity of decision-making procedures, which allegedly makes EU in-stitutions impossible to understand for the average citizen. Critics deplore the lack of a real cross-national debate on grand societal questions, as well as the nonexistence of Europe-wide political parties. Finally, because Europe is composed of a multitude of peoples, each with their own sense of national identity and belonging, it is difficult for its citizens to develop attachment to the EU. Therefore, as Siedentop has argued, the EU often appears as an "alien government of strangers" imposed from a remote capital.[34]

Not everyone, however, agrees that the EU actually suffers from a dem-ocratic deficit. The EU is not a nation-state, and its member states and supranational institutions coexist side by side; therefore the EU should not be held to the same democratic standards.[35] As Moravcsik has argued, the true pillars of the European Union—economic welfare, human rights, liberal democracy, and the rule of law—appeal to Europeans regardless of national or political identity. Moreover, the EU is not out of line with the widespread and legitimate practices of Western democracies; it is not contributing to an *overall* system biased against social welfare and regula-tion—i.e., a "race to the bottom"; and it is not dealing with issues that would lend themselves to deliberative ("strong") democracy, even if the political structures were there.[36] Furthermore, the EU has created many mechanisms through which citizens can now participate in the process and, in doing so, has opened up a lot of democratic space. For instance, because of the EU's fragmented authority, an interest group can now put an issue on the agenda in any of the member states, as well as in Brussels. Therefore, the EU has multiplied the number of avenues for civic partici-pation. Nevertheless, the fact is that even if those who talk about a demo-cratic deficit are mistaken, what matters is that these perceptions are wide-spread. In trade policy, the resentment is getting even bigger as citizens become increasingly aware that a growing number of decisions affecting their daily lives are being taken at EU level, while they feel excluded from the process.

[33] See, for instance, Banchoff and Smith (1999).
[34] See Siedentop (2001).
[35] See, for instance, Banchoff and Smith (1999); Moravcsik (2002).
[36] Moravcsik (2001).

Trade is also a policy area that can arouse suspicions of illegitimacy because of its traditional reliance on delegation, executive authority, and technicality. As was discussed in the introduction to this book, trade policymaking has often given the impression of shutting off, by design, popular input from the process. In part because of collective action problems, there is a chronic imbalance between those who benefit from trade protection and those who pay the costs. Those who benefit from trade liberalization are diffuse, and their gains are small, whereas those who lose from trade are concentrated and organized. The trade policymaking process can thus be easily captured by protectionist interests (such as farmers, manufacturers, and labor unions). Therefore, the authority for making trade policy is often delegated to the executive, in order to bypass these protectionist pressures.[37] This insulation-by-design has paved the way for criticisms of democratic illegitimacy, based on lack of popular participation and lack of transparency.

Finally, legitimacy concerns have started to focus on trade policy because of the changing nature of trade. When trade liberalization was primarily about tariffs and quotas on certain types of goods, trade politics revolved essentially around economic arguments about jobs and prices. Trade policy could be manipulated to protect special interests, and when governments decided to open up certain economic sectors to international competition, these special interests could be compensated. With each round of multilateral trade negotiations under the General Agreement on Tariffs and Trade, however, traditional trade barriers have been further reduced and new types of nontariff barriers tackled. The new areas falling under trade policy raise new concerns about legitimacy, since trade now touches on domestically sensitive sectors (such as education, health care, and culture) and therefore impinges on national prerogatives and affects definitions of national identity. Conversely, trade is also becoming an extension of the range of very contentious domestic policies, by extending domestic conflicts into the international arena.

Institutional Rules and Trade Policy Legitimacy

Trade policy is often presented as involving a fundamental trade-off between efficiency and legitimacy. Every movement in the direction of swifter negotiations, which ultimately become internationally adopted agreements, would entail some loss of legitimacy because actors have less opportunity to influence the process. Conversely, every movement in the direction of increased legitimacy would supposedly reduce the margin of

---

[37] See, for instance, O'Halloran (1994); Destler (1996).

maneuver of negotiators and impede their ability to conclude complex international agreements. Upon closer scrutiny, is it true that efficiency and legitimacy are always antagonistic? Can we find institutional and political conditions under which efficiency and legitimacy can actually complement each other?

The public debate over the democratic deficit in the European Union usually assumes a definition of legitimacy based on process.[38] Critics of EU trade policy complain about the lack of influence of "civil society" on the process through which decisions are made. The majority of scholars studying the democratic deficit have focused on the design of EU institutions and on concrete steps to adapt the European Parliament, the decision-making process in the Council and the Commission, and the European party system in order to increase democratic accountability.[39] By comparison, there has been very little debate in the literature on what institutional rules produce more legitimate outcomes than others.[40] Yet both "process" and "outcome" are essential components of political legitimacy. They are intimately linked because the quality of the process may influence the quality of the outcome.

Can EU trade policy be considered legitimate in both its process and outcome dimensions? As was presented in chapter 1, trade policy in the EU involves two levels of delegation—one from the individual member states to the collective entity, and a second one from the Council of Ministers to the Commission. The legitimacy of EU trade policy in cases of exclusive competence is questionable from a "process" perspective. With respect to the first level of delegation, national parliaments have abdicated their control over the making of trade policy, at both the negotiating and the ratification stages. Yet at least until the EU Constitution is ratified and implemented, the European Parliament is absent from the process, with neither prior nor final say. The legitimacy traditionally conferred by proper democratic procedures may therefore seem lacking. Some "deliberative" legitimacy coming from civil society applies to trade policy, however. Many interest groups have a way of being heard, through either formal consultation or informal lobbying. Moreover, trade policy is made by the Council of Ministers, which then gives a mandate to Commission negotiators. Therefore, one could expect the Council, made up of national ministers, presumably chosen in the wake of competitive elections, to be perceived as just as legitimate as a parliament, unlike the reproach that can be made to the unelected panels of judges in Geneva adjudicating WTO disputes. From an "outcome" perspective, this delegation of competence to the suprana-

---

[38] On process vs. outcome legitimacy, see Scharpf (1999); Meunier (2003).
[39] See, for instance, Hix (1998).
[40] With the exception, for instance, of McKay (2000).

tional level means that special interests have less opportunity to impact or disrupt the conclusion of complex multilateral trade agreements that may be, overall, beneficial to society at large. It also means, however, that entire groups may suffer negatively from the economic consequences of such agreements without having been able to influence them.

The second level of delegation in EU trade policy is the practical transfer of competence from the Council of Ministers to the European Commission. As was discussed in this book, the "majoritarian" and "consensual" models of decision making often coexist in the EU with respect to trade. Court jurisprudence and treaty articles spell out the cases in which policy decisions are made according to majority or unanimity—for instance, majority for trade in manufactured goods, but unanimity for trade in cultural services. From the process perspective, both rules seem to have the same effect on participation and transparency. But from the outcome perspective, the effects of majority and unanimity voting seem to differ. The answer to the question of which institutional rule produces more legitimate outcomes depends on whose interests are taken into account, since the benefits from trade liberalization or protection are distributed unevenly. A useful dichotomy is the one distinguishing between the collective interests of the state and the individual interests of citizens or special social groups. Another useful distinction is whether the benchmark by which a trade policy is judged successful is a fair repartition of resources or the provision of special welfare to some elements of society.

QUALIFIED MAJORITY

One quasi-universally accepted way of ensuring a democratic government is in recognizing, according to Tocqueville, "the absolute sovereignty of the majority." The majoritarian model of democracy is straightforward because the best way to come up with a common rule for all individuals intuitively seems to be go with the wish of the majority. Can this majoritarian model designed for individuals within a state be easily transposed to individual, but sovereign, states within a supranational polity? From the process perspective, majority (especially when qualified by voting weights) seems, on the face of it, a fair rule for aggregating the diverse interests of the EU member states into a coherent common position for trade negotiations, since it gives every member a say in the process. From the outcome perspective, majority also seems a fair rule. Because the opening of trade barriers has a redistributive effect, creating winners and losers, there will inevitably be conflict over such redistribution. Majority voting seems equipped for resolving such conflict in a legitimate manner.

Why, then, did the counterglobalization activists, who demonstrated loud and clear during the preparation of the December 2000 Nice summit, whose agenda included the reform of trade policymaking institutions in the EU, demand the opposite? They claimed that majority was not legitimate because, from the outcome perspective, it tends to produce more liberal, less protectionist policies. In the eyes of many critics, majority is illegitimate at the supranational level because it enables member states to override the interests and preferences of another sovereign member state. This is why, for instance, NGOs were so insistent in Nice that France did not give up unanimity on trade in cultural goods but instead enshrine in the treaty the clause known as cultural exception. Antiglobalization protesters were thus put in the difficult position of denouncing the voting rule traditionally accepted as the most democratic.

If Tocqueville talked about the "sovereignty of the majority," however, he also warned about the "tyranny of the majority." The majoritarian process may be legitimate, but the outcome may not be necessarily so. Even a proper majority, which follows proper democratic procedures, may produce decisions that affect a minority so negatively that the outcome may seem illegitimate. In the supranational EU, majority voting is particularly contested in those areas where decisions may negatively impact the interests not of a specific social group but of the entire country at large—as would be the case in the field of cultural policy versus agriculture, for instance. This is why, even though most of trade policy in the EU is now made according to qualified majority rule, battles over the preservation of a veto right have been so salient.

UNANIMITY/CONSENSUS

The main alternative to the majoritarian model for ensuring democracy while aggregating diverse preferences is the "consensus model."[41] In this model, particular policies are chosen when they can muster broad agreement, mostly by inclusiveness, bargaining, and compromise. In the EU, many decisions are made according to consensus, even when the formal rules as laid out in the treaties state otherwise. In trade policy, even though the default voting rule is majority, most decisions on agriculture, for instance, have been made on a consensual basis.

From the process perspective, the unanimity/consensus rule does not seem less legitimate than majority rule, especially since the actors whose preferences may be passed over in a majoritarian setting are entire states, each representing millions of individuals. In plural societies, where homogeneity and a common sense of purpose are absent, the majority rule can be undemocratic and dangerous in the long run "because minorities that are continually denied access to power will feel excluded and discrimi-

---

[41] Lijphart (1999).

nated against and may lose their allegiance to the regime."[42] To the contrary, the consensual model of democracy ensures that no large groups are left out of the possibility to control and influence the policy process. From the outcome perspective, unanimity/consensus may seem one obvious remedy to the legitimacy shortcomings of majority voting because it is less exclusive and protects the rights of minorities. Dahl's remarks on the possibility of democracy in international organizations could apply to the EU as well: "Given huge differences in the magnitude of the populations in different countries, no system of representation could give equal weight to the vote of each citizen and yet prevent small countries from being steadily outvoted by large countries; thus all solutions acceptable to the smaller democracies will deny political equality among the members of a larger demos."[43] All these arguments suggest that consensual policymaking would make EU trade policy more legitimate.

On the other hand, one can also make the argument that a majority of member states should not be held hostage to the preferences of a single state, just for the sake of being inclusive. In trade, a policy with redistributive effects, the need to achieve consensus may lead to unfair results. Why would it be more legitimate for France to be dictating the course of Europe's protectionist position on agricultural negotiations than for the majoritarian advocates of liberalization to do so? As the EU enlarges to more countries, unanimity might pose even more problems in terms of political legitimacy since the divergence in member states' preferences can be expected to widen as new countries join the club. In the areas where trade policy continues to be made according to the practice of consensus (e.g., agriculture) or the rule of unanimity (e.g., cultural services), a consensus will be harder to find with the increase in the number of potential vetoes resulting from enlargement. When qualified majority voting is used, the interests of the new members will transform the current balance of interests, thereby infuriating some domestic interest groups.

The EU's Response to the Efficiency vs. Legitimacy Debate

The perceived lack of legitimacy of EU trade policy is not leaving "Eurocrats" indifferent. To the contrary, they realize that their very survival depends on their ability to reduce the gap between perception and reality, and the Commission has therefore engaged in a massive PR effort to convey the message that "civil society" has been heard and has from now on been included in the process. This attempt to develop a legitimate,

[42] Ibid., p. 33.
[43] Dahl (1998: 116).

democratic rule at the supranational level has no exact historical precedent. Europe is facing a moment of historical innovation, which shares some resemblance, but also dissimilarities, with past efforts at building federal states.[44] The EU is different from typical international institutions, but it is not a federal state either. Even though the EU polity has many peculiarities and idiosyncrasies, the current European attempts at addressing concerns of political legitimacy while continuing to ensure efficiency of policymaking in the field of trade could perhaps serve as a blueprint for issues surrounding the governance of international economic institutions.

Not surprisingly, EU efforts to close the perceived democratic gap have focused mostly on process legitimacy, since it is the most apparent and the most discussed publicly. In particular, the Commission has actively tried to include civil society in the policymaking process. The involvement of nongovernmental actors in the making of trade policy is nothing new. Trade unions, industry associations, and business groups have long had a place for lobbying on trade policy, at both the national and the supranational levels. NGOs claiming to represent "civil society" complain, however, about the closer links and privileged consultation methods between the makers of EU trade policy and groups representing European business—as illustrated, for instance, by the formally organized consultations within the framework of the Transatlantic Business Dialogue.[45]

Yet the role of civil society in trade policy has changed in recent years, both because of the evolving nature of trade and because of technological developments, such as the Internet, which have "made the market for political ideas contestable."[46] As a result of the new ease of access to information, NGOs have seen their means of oversight and influence increase considerably. To rein in some of these critics and address its perceived lack of political legitimacy, the Commission has engaged in an ambitious program of consultation with civil society in the specific area of trade. Launched in 1998 at the initiative of its Trade Directorate General, in the wake of the public mobilization around the Multilateral Agreement on Investment, the "trade dialogue with civil society" was designed to associate representatives of civic organizations more closely with the trade policymaking process.[47] This dialogue has consisted of a number of "general meetings" (where the trade commissioner informs representatives about the state of WTO negotiations, presents the EU position for upcoming

[44] Nicolaïdis and Howse (2001).

[45] Cowles (2001).

[46] Lamy (2002).

[47] In 1999 Trade Commissioner Pascal Lamy took along with the EU delegation to Seattle an advisory group of civil society representatives drawn from organizations representing social, consumer, development, environmental, and business interests, among others.

trade negotiations, and gives them a chance to voice concerns and ask questions), as well as "issue groups" (thematic meetings where representatives of civil society present to the Commission proposals of their own).[48]

This move on the part of the Commission was designed to quench the complaints of many civil society groups, who have organized, in recent years, to investigate and participate in the making of trade policy in Europe. In particular, they have put under scrutiny the links existing among trade, environment, and labor standards. The legitimacy of such groups, however, is itself questionable. From a process perspective, NGOs want participation and transparency. But governments are elected, whereas they are not. They are self-appointed spokespersons for a cause and as such would pass neither the "representative" nor the "accountable" test. Often, their only legitimacy is the one they have created for themselves. Yet these unelected activists have taken on an increasingly preeminent role in shaping the agenda for trade policy in recent years. From an outcome perspective, it is not clear that "civil society" passes the legitimacy test either. In several instances, "first world" NGOs denounce injustices in third world countries (such as child labor), but those on behalf of whom they claim to be speaking may believe conversely that the erection of new trade barriers is not the best solution to lift them out of poverty and dismal social conditions.

Concluding Remarks

Clearly, the EU is a unique beast, and we are therefore tempted to study it *sui generis*. With its multilayered levels of governance, coexistence of supranationalism and national sovereignty, and idiosyncratic institutions, it is neither a federal state nor an international institution. Globalization—that is, the creation of a global marketplace thanks to freer and more rapid flows of transportation and information—also erodes the borders around nations, and therefore the boundaries separating the citizens of those nations, although in a less systematic, organized way than European integration. Globalization has put new constraints on states: it has limited their margins of maneuver and consequently eroded their sovereignty. Many issues have become global, transnational issues that can no longer be addressed and solved uniquely at the national level.[49] As

---

[48] Of course, involving civil society in the preparatory phase of decision making is not the same as inviting it to participate directly in the decision. As long as representatives of various groups are only making suggestions and voicing their concerns but there is no obligation to integrate their input into the final decision, this involvement of civil society may be seen as more window-dressing than real legitimation.

[49] See, for instance, Florini and Simmons (2000).

a result, globalization has also highlighted some need for international governance.

Even though the EU is unique and is hardly a template for a legitimate institution, the world at large can still learn valuable lessons from its institutional experiment in the field of trade policymaking. One such lesson would be to explore whether the concept of "multilevel governance" could be useful at the international level. As a growing number of EU scholars have shown, there is not necessarily a binary opposition between national and European institutions and identities. Instead, European polities are characterized by a constellation of institutions embedded in a dense network of informal interactions bringing together supranational, national, and subnational actors. Indeed, individuals in Europe now feel multiple allegiances. On some occasions, the EU level of governance can be even more responsive to some societal interests than the national level. For example, organized producer interests, which are relatively entrenched in domestic politics, may lose their advantage over broader "civic" interests, such as consumers and environmentalists, in the European arena.[50] This coexistence of multiple levels of identity (to a region, to a country, to a social group, etc.) may be used in some settings to legitimize governance at the international level as well.

Another lesson from the EU experience with legitimacy in trade might be to extend some of these debates to other regional trading arrangements, such as APEC and Mercosur, as well as to some sovereign countries. In particular, the EU is dealing with many issues similar to the ones involved in the U.S. debate on the delegation of trade negotiating authority—once known as "fast-track" and now as "trade promotion authority." Chief among these common concerns is how to balance democracy (the process legitimacy) and efficiency (the outcome legitimacy). The fact that individual states fear exclusion from the trade policymaking process in Washington when authority is delegated to the executive has long blocked the renewal of the granting of fast-track in the United States. Actually, the EU process for participating in international trade negotiations is quite similar to the U.S. fast-track procedure, with states (individual in the United States, sovereign nation-states in the EU) delegating the authority (through the "fast-track" vote in the United States, through a negotiating mandate in the EU) to the most centralized level of government (the Office of the Trade Representative, directly dependent on the White House, in the United States, the Directorate General for trade and the external trade commissioner in the EU). The debates surrounding the delegation of trade authority in both settings could usefully inform one another.

[50] Majone (1996).

It may be more difficult to extend the lessons learned from the EU experience to other international governance structures, such as the Group of Eight, the International Monetary Fund, or the WTO. Even though antiglobalization supporters have often lumped the EU together with these international organizations in their criticisms of neoliberal free trade, they are of a quite different nature. The EU is a supranational polity, whereas the WTO and the IMF, for instance, are not. One of the unique characteristics of the EU, by which it resembles more a federal structure than an international organization, is the supremacy of European over domestic law. The decisions of the EU are ultimately binding, whereas WTO decisions are not. As long as it remains the case, this means that EU decisions will be more legitimate than those of the WTO, since the peoples of Europe have willfully transferred some sovereignty to the supranational level.

Also, as several scholars of federalism and European integration have noted, the EU distinguishes itself from other international organizations in that it can achieve both negative and positive integration.[51] Most attacks on the supposed illegitimacy of international economic institutions are triggered by negative integration—mostly when a court strikes down a national regulation as illegal and, as a result, lowers regulatory standards. Such critics flare, for instance, whenever WTO judges deem national regulations to be trade barriers (e.g., a ban on hormone-treated beef). International organizations are ill-equipped to counter these accusations because they can only introduce new regulations to replace the ones stricken down by opening up whole new international negotiations. By contrast, the EU has the capacity to undertake positive actions and legislate to create common standards. Therefore, the supranational EU is better positioned to claim back its legitimacy because it can respond to its critics by reregulating. In that respect, the EU resembles more a federal entity than an international organization.

Finally, the level of democratization of other polities is a major obstacle to the direct applicability of the complex EU trade policymaking system. It seems uncertain, to say the least, that institutional rules designed for mature economies and democracies (liberal societies with democratic politics, active social groups, and private business sectors) are also desirable and transposable to other types of countries. The EU is made up of advanced industrialized democracies—indeed, democracy is a prerequisite for membership. Other international economic organizations do not share such a prerequisite. Therefore, one cannot expect to hold the organization collectively to a higher standard of political legitimacy than each of its members individually.

[51] See, for instance, Scharpf (1999); Kelemen (2002).

Trade and legitimacy are now inextricably linked. The question is whether they are antithetical or can coexist. Efficiency and legitimacy are often opposed, as if representing two contradictory pulls on trade policy. As this chapter has shown, however, they are indeed two sides of the same coin. Most of the public protest and criticism in the social science literature against existing trade institutions emphasize procedural aspects—the representativity, accountability, and transparency of the trade policymaking process. When one judges EU trade policy according to the traditional liberal democratic criteria of legitimacy, critiques of the democratic deficit abound. These criteria, however, may not be directly applicable to the institutions of the EU, whose supranational polity cannot be held to the same standards of legitimacy as sovereign states. By breaking down the analysis of political legitimacy into its process and outcome components, this chapter has shown that the infamous democratic deficit may not be as important as is commonly perceived, and that the remedies put forth by protesters may not be as legitimate as they claim—especially when criticizing the process serves as an easy pretext to denounce unwanted policy outcomes.

National governments have a large part of responsibility in propagating perceptions of the EU's democratic deficit. More often than once have European politicians blamed unpopular decisions on the EU, thereby fueling the misperception that Brussels can dictate its will and act forcefully against the interests of some of its sovereign member states. Indeed, the EU has become a scapegoat for justifying unpopular measures that national leaders do not have the political courage to put forth. The spectacular gains by extreme right and Euroskeptical protest parties in several recent elections throughout Europe showed that voters did not favor giving more power to Brussels; to the contrary, they blamed Europe as the source of their society's ills.

Politicians, however, are not the only ones to blame for this perceived illegitimacy of the European Union. Voters have some responsibility too. In the traditional democratic framework, legitimacy rests on political parties and elections. Yet how could the EU ever be considered legitimate when nearly half of the European voters abstain from casting their ballot in the European elections every five years? By not using their own political right to vote, and thereby failing to influence the direction and evolution of European integration, European citizens also contribute to creating the illegitimacy to which representatives of "civil society" are so quick to point.

Overall, this general political scapegoating has only reinforced the impression of a democratic deficit in the European Union. As a result, it has become commonplace, and commonly accepted, to lump together criticism of the EU and criticism of the various institutions of international economic governance—the IMF, the WTO, and the G8, to cite a few. Yet the amalgamation of the so-called democratic deficit in the EU and the problems of governance in international economic institutions can go only so far. The EU is not solely a precursor and a miniature version of globalization, with all its neoliberal excesses. Paradoxically, it is also a tool against globalization, a bulwark against deregulation and lower standards. If European politicians had the courage to advertise this to the public, then suddenly the EU might seem very legitimate.

One can wonder whether any institutional fix could ever assuage the critics. The EU often seems to be targeted on grounds of legitimacy more because it is an easy target than because of its real nature. The disgruntled tend to turn their anger against those institutions that are easy targets, thanks to the constant political scapegoating and the fact that it is difficult to change the course of international organizations. Yet with twenty-five members, the EU can now exert a formidable counterweight to the power of the United States in international trade negotiations. Paradoxically, it may be its efficiency which, in the end, lends legitimacy to the EU.

Bibliography

Ahearn, Raymond J. 2002. "Trade Policymaking in the European Union: Institutional Framework," CRS Report for Congress, RS21185, March 27.

Alter, Karen. 1998. "Who Are the Masters of the Treaty? European Governments and the European Court of Justice." *International Organization* 52(1): 121–147.

———. 2002. *Establishing the Supremacy of European Law: The Making of an International Rule of Law in Europe.* New York: Oxford University Press.

Alter, Karen, and Sophie Meunier. 1994. "Judicial Politics in the European Community: European Integration and the Pathbreaking Cassis de Dijon Decision." *Comparative Political Studies* 26(4): 535–561.

Anderson, Christopher. 1995. "Economic Benefits and Support for Membership in the EU: A Cross-national Analysis." *Journal of Public Policy* 15:231–249.

Arnull, Anthony. 1996. "The Scope of the Common Commercial Policy: A Coda on Opinion 1/94." In *The European Union and World Trade Law*, edited by Nicholas Emiliou and David O'Keeffe. Chichester: John Wiley and Sons.

Aspinwall, Mark, and Gerald Schneider. 2001. *The Rules of Integration: Institutionalist Approaches to the Study of Europe.* Manchester: Manchester University Press.

Avery, William P. ed. 1993. *World Agriculture and the GATT.* Boulder: Lynne Rienner.

Axelrod, Robert. 1984. *The Evolution of Cooperation.* New York: Basic Books.

Bailey, Michael A., Judith Goldstein, and Barry R. Weingast. 1997. "The Institutional Roots of American Trade Policy: Politics, Coalitions, and International Trade." *World Politics* 49(3) (April): 309–338.

Baldwin, Robert E. 1984. "The Changing Nature of US Trade Policy since World War II." In *The Structure and Evolution of Recent U.S. Trade Policy*, edited by Robert E. Baldwin and Anne O. Kruger. Chicago: University of Chicago Press.

Banchoff, Thomas, and Mitchell P. Smith, eds. 1999. *Legitimacy and the European Union: The Contested Polity.* New York: Routledge.

Bauer, Raymond, Ithiel De Sola Pool, and Lewis Anthony Dexter. 1963. *American Business and Public Policy: The Politics of Foreign Trade.* Chicago: Aldine-Atherton.

Bayard, Thomas, and Kimberly Ann Elliott. 1994. *Reciprocity and Retaliation in U.S. Trade Policy.* Washington, DC: Institute for International Economics.

Beetham, D. and C. Lord. 1998. *Legitimacy and the European Union*, London: Addison Wesley Longman.

Berman, Sheri, and Kathleen McNamara. 1999. "Bank on Democracy—Why Central Banks Need Public Oversight." *Foreign Affairs* 78(2) (March/April): 1–7.

Bourgeois, Jacques H. J. 1995. "The EC in the WTO and Advisory Opinion 1/94: An Echternach Procession." *Common Market Law Review* 32: 763–787.

Brinkley, Douglas, and Clifford Hackett, eds. 1991. *Jean Monnet, the Path to European Unity*. New York: St. Martin's Press.

Burley, Anne-Marie, and Walter Mattli. 1993. "Europe before the Court: A Political Theory of Legal Integration." *International Organization* 47(1): 41–76.

Calingaert, Michael. 1994. "High Stakes in U.S.-EU Public Procurement Negotiations." *EuroWatch* 6, 1 (April 4).

Cameron, Fraser. 1998. "The European Union as a Global Actor." In *The European Union in the World Community*, edited by Carolyn Rhodes. Boulder: Lynne Rienner.

Caporaso, James A., and John T. S. Keeler. 1995. "The European Union and Regional Integration Theory." In *The State of the European Union*. Vol. 3: *Building a European Polity?*, edited by Carolyn Rhodes and Sonia Mazey. Boulder: Lynne Rienner.

Casadio, Gian Paolo. 1973. *Transatlantic Trade: USA-EEC Confrontation in the GATT Negotiations*. Westmead, England: Saxon House.

Cecchini, Paolo. 1988. *The European Challenge 1992: The Benefits of a Single Market*. Aldershot, England: Gower/Commission of the EC.

Cederman, Lars Erik. 2000. "Nationalism and Bounded Integration: What It Would Take to Construct a European Demos." Robert Schuman Centre for Advanced Studies Working Paper no. 2000/34.

Checkel, Jeffrey T. 2003. " 'Going Native' in Europe? Theorizing Social Interaction in European Institutions." *Comparative Political Studies* 36(1–2): 209–231.

Clark, William, and Erick Duchesne. 1997. "A Formal Model of the Canada-U.S. Free Trade Agreement." Paper presented at the annual conference of the Canadian Political Science Association.

Clark, William, Erick Duchesne, and Sophie Meunier. 2000. "Domestic and International Asymmetries in US-EU Trade Negotiations." *International Negotiation Journal* 5(1): 69–95.

Close, George. 1990. "External Relations in the Air Transport Sector: Air Transport Policy or the Common Commercial Policy?" *Common Market Law Review* 27: 107–127.

Coglianese, Cary, and Kalypso Nicolaïdis. 2001. "Securing Subsidiarity: Mechanisms for Allocating Authority in Tiered Regimes." In *The Federal Vision*, edited by Kalypso Nicolaïdis and Robert Howse. New York: Oxford University Press.

Collinson, Sarah. 1999. "Issue-Systems, Multi-level Games, and the Analysis of the EU's External Commercial and Associated Policies: A Research Agenda." *Journal of European Public Policy* 6(2): 206–224.

Commission of the European Communities. 2001. *European Governance: A White Paper*. Brussels, 25.7.2001 COM(2001) 428 final.

Conybeare, John. 1987. *Trade Wars: The Theory and Practice of International Commercial Rivalry*. New York: Columbia University Press.

Costa Tavares, Samia. 2003. Setting the Common Customs Tariff: Does the EU act as a country or a group of countries? Working Paper, Department of Economics, Rochester Institute of Technology.

Cowles, Maria Green. 2001. "The Transatlantic Business Dialogue: Transforming the New Transatlantic Dialogue." In *Transatlantic Governance in a Global*

Economy, edited by Mark Pollack and Gregory Shaffer. Lanham, MD: Rowman and Littlefield.

Cowles, Maria Green, James Caporaso, and Thomas Risse. 2001. *Transforming Europe: Europeanization and Domestic Change*. Ithaca: Cornell University Press.

Curtis, Thomas B., and John Robert Vastine. 1971. *The Kennedy Round and the Future of American Trade*. New York: Praeger.

Dahl, Robert. 1998. *On Democracy*. New Haven: Yale University Press.

Davis, Christina L. 2003. *Food fights over Free Trade: How International Institutions Promote Agricultural Trade Liberalization*. Princeton: Princeton University Press.

Dehousse, Renaud, and Giandomenico Majone. (1999) "Reforming European Governance: Options for the New Commission." Working paper, Centre Européen de Sciences Po.

Denza, Eileen. 1996. "The Community as a Member of International Organizations." In *The European Union and World Trade Law*, edited by Nicholas Emiliou and David O'Keeffe. Chichester: John Wiley and Sons.

Destler, I. M. 1996. *American Trade Politics*. Washington, DC: Institute for International Economics.

Deutsch, Karl, et al. 1957. *Political Community and the North Atlantic Area*. Princeton: Princeton University Press.

Devuyst, Youri. 1992. "The EC's Common Commercial Policy and the Treaty on European Union: An Overview of the Negotiations." *World Competition* 16(2): 67–80.

———. 1995. "The European Community and the Conclusion of the Uruguay Round." In *The State of the European Union*. Vol. 3: *Building a European Polity?*, edited by Carolyn Rhodes and Sonia Mazey. Boulder: Lynne Rienner.

———. 1998. "European Unity in Transatlantic Commercial Diplomacy." In *Policy-Making and Decision-Making in Transatlantic Relations*, edited by Eric Philippart and Pascaline Winand. Manchester: Manchester University Press.

Dinan, Desmond. 1994. *Ever Closer Union? An Introduction to the European Community*. Boulder: Lynne Rienner.

Dobson, Alan P. 1995. *Flying in the Face of Competition:The Policies and Diplomacy of Airline Regulatory Reform in Britain, the USA and the European Community 1968–94*. Aldershot, England: Avebury Aviation, Ashgate Publishing.

Donahue, John, and Mark Pollack. 2001. "Centralization and Its Discontents: The Rhythms of Federalism in the United States and the European Union." In *The Federal Vision*, edited by Kalypso Nicolaïdis and Robert Howse. New York: Oxford University Press.

Dowding, Keith. 2000. Institutionalist Research on the European Union: A Critical Review. *European Union Politics* 1: 125–144.

Dryden, Steve. 1990. "Trade Warriors." *Europe* (May).

Duchesne, Erick. 1997. "International Bilateral Trade and Investment Negotiations: Theory, Formal Model, and Empirical Evidence." Ph.D. dissertation, Michigan State University.

Emiliou, Nicholas, and David O'Keeffe. 1996. *The European Union and World Trade Law*. Chichester: John Wiley and Sons.

Evans, John W. 1971. *The Kennedy Round in American Trade Policy: The Twilight of GATT?* Cambridge: Harvard University Press.

Evans, Peter, Harold Jacobson, and Robert Putnam, eds. 1993. *Double-Edged Diplomacy: International Bargaining and Domestic Politics.* Berkeley: University of California Press.

Florini, Ann M., and P. J. Simmons. 2000. "What the World Needs Now?" In *The Third Force: The Rise of Transnational Civil Society*, edited by A. M. Florini. Washington, DC: Carnegie Endowment for Peace.

Franchino, Fabio. 2001. "Delegation and Constraints in the National Execution of the EC Policies: A Longitudinal and Qualitative Analysis." *West European Politics* 24(4): 169–192.

Franklin, Mark, Michael Marsh, and Lauren McLaren. 1994. "Uncorking the Bottle: Popular Opposition to European Integration in the Wake of Maastricht." *Journal of Common Market Studies* 32(4): 455–472.

Garrett, Geoffrey. 1992. "International Cooperation and Institutional Choice." *International Organization* 46 (Spring): 533–560.

———. 1995. "From the Luxembourg Compromise to Co-Decision: Decision-Making in the European Union. *Electoral Studies* 14(3): 289–308.

Garrett, Geoffrey, and George Tsebelis. 1996. "An Institutional Critique of Intergovernmentalism." *International Organization* 50 (Spring): 269–300.

Gilligan, Michael J. 1997. *Empowering Exporters: Reciprocity, Delegation and Collective Action in American Trade Policy.* Ann Arbor: University of Michigan Press.

Gilpin, Robert. 1981. *War and Change in World Politics.* Cambridge: Cambridge University Press.

Goldstein, Judith. 1993. *Ideas, Interests, and American Trade Policy.* Ithaca: Cornell University Press.

Golt, Sidney. 1988. *The GATT Negotiations 1986–1990: Origins, Issues and Prospects.* London: British-North American Committee.

Gordon, Philip, and Sophie Meunier. 2001. *The French Challenge: Adapting to Globalization.* Washington, DC: Brookings Institution Press.

Gourevitch, Peter. 1986. *The Politics of Hard Times.* Ithaca: Cornell University Press.

Graham, Edward M. 2000. *Fighting the Wrong Enemy.* Washington, DC: Institute for International Economics.

Greven, Michael. 2000. "Can the European Union Finally Become a Democracy?" In *Democracy beyond the State?*, edited by M. Greven and L. Pauly. Lanham, MD: Rowman and Littlefield.

Greven, Michael, and Louis Pauly, eds. 2000. *Democracy beyond the State? The European Dilemma and the Emerging Global Order.* Lanham, MD: Rowman and Littlefield.

Grieco, Joseph M. 1990. *Cooperation among Nations: Europe, America, and Non-Tariff Barriers to Trade.* Ithaca: Cornell University Press.

Haas, Ernst B. 1958. *The Uniting of Europe.* Stanford: Stanford University Press.

Habeeb, William Mark. 1988. *Power and Tactics in International Negotiation: How Weak Nations Bargain with Strong Nations.* Baltimore: Johns Hopkins University Press.

Hall, Peter, and Rosemary C. R. Taylor. 1996. "Political Science and the Three New Institutionalisms." *Political Studies* 44: 936–957.

Hampson, Fen Osler, with Michael Hart. 1995. *Multilateral Negotiations: Lessons from Arms Control, Trade, and the Environment*. Baltimore: Johns Hopkins University Press.

Harrison, Glennon, ed. 1993. *Europe and the United States: Competition and Cooperation in the 1990s*. Armonk, NY: M. E. Sharpe.

Hayes, John Philip. 1993. *Making Trade Policy in the European Community*. New York: St. Martin's Press.

Hayes-Renshaw, Fiona, and Helen Wallace. 1997. *The Council of Ministers*. New York: St. Martin's Press.

Henderson, David. 1999. *The MAI Affair: A Story and Its Lessons*, London: The Royal Institute of International Affairs.

Hilf, Meinhard. 1995. "The ECJ's Opinion 1/94 on the WTO—No Surprise, but Wise?" *European Journal of International Law* 6: 245–259.

Hirschman, Albert. 1945. *National Power and the Structure of Foreign Trade*. Berkeley: University of California Press.

Hiscox, Michael. 2001. *International Trade and Political Conflict: Commerce, Coalitions, and Mobility*. Princeton: Princeton University Press.

Hix, Simon. 1998. "Elections, Parties and Institutional Design: A Comparative Perspective on European Union Democracy." *West European Politics* 21: 19–52.

Hocking, Brian, and Michael Smith. 1997. *Beyond Foreign Economic Policy: The United States, the Single European Market and the Changing World Economy*. London: Pinter.

Hosli, Madeleine. 1996. "Coalitions and Power: Effects of Qualified Majority Voting on the Council of the European Union." *Journal of Common Market Studies* 34: 255–275.

Hufbauer, Gary Clyde, ed. 1990. *Europe 1992: An American Perspective*. Washington, DC: The Brookings Institution.

Hug, Simon, and Thomas Konig. 2002. "In View of Ratification." *International Organization* 56: 447–476.

Iklé, Fred C. 1965. *How Nations Negotiate*. New York: Praeger.

Jackson, John H. 1992. "The European Community and World Trade: The Commercial Policy Dimension." In *Singular Europe: Economy and Polity of the European Community after 1992*, edited by William James Adams. Ann Arbor: University of Michigan Press.

Johnson, M. 1998. *European Community Trade Policy and the Article 113 Committee*. London: The Royal Institute of International Affairs.

Jupille, J. 1999. "The European Union and International Outcomes." *International Organization* 53(2): 409–425.

Jupille, J., and J. A. Caporaso. 1999. *Annual Review of Political Science* 2: 429–444.

Keeler, John T. S. 1996. "Agricultural Power in the European Community: Explaining the Fate of the CAP and GATT Negotiations." *Comparative Politics* 28 (January): 127–149.

Kelemen, R. Daniel. 2001. "The Limits of Judicial Power: Trade-Environment Disputes in the GATT/WTO and the EU." *Comparative Political Studies* 34(6): 622–650.

Kelemen, R. Daniel. 2002. "Globalization, Federalism and Regulation." In *The Regulations of Nations: The Impact of Globalization*, edited by David Vogel and Robert Kagan. Berkeley: University of California Press.

Kennedy, John F. 1962. *Special Message to the Congress on Foreign Trade Policy, January 25, 1962*. Public Papers of the President.

Kennedy, Paul. 1987. *The Rise and Fall of Great Powers*. Random House.

Keohane, Robert O. 1971. "The Big Influence of Small Allies." *Foreign Policy* 2:161–182.

———. 1984. *After Hegemony: Cooperation and Discord in the World Political Economy*. Princeton: Princeton University Press.

Keohane, Robert O., and Lisa Martin. 1999. "Institutional Theory, Endogeneity and Delegation." Paper prepared for Conference on Progress in International Relations Theory: A Collaborative Assessment and Application of Imke Lakatos's Methodology of Scientific Research Programs, January 15–16, Scottsdale, AZ.

Kerremans, Bart. 2003. "Who Cares about Modalities? The European Commission and the EU Member States as Interdependent Actors in the WTO Negotiating Process." Paper presented at the EUSA Conference, Nashville, March 27–30.

Kindleberger, Charles P. 1973. *The World in Depression, 1929–1939*. Berkeley: University of California Press.

Kissinger, Henry A. 1969. "Domestic Structure and Foreign Policy." In *International Politics and Foreign Policy*, edited by James N. Rosenau. New York: Free Press.

Krause, Lawrence B. 1968. *European Economic Integration and the United States*. Washington, DC: The Brookings Institution.

Kuilwijk, Kees Jan. 1996. *The European Court of Justice and the GATT Dilemma: Public Interest vs. Individual Rights?* Beuningen: Nexed Editions.

Lamy, Pascal. 2002. "From Doha to Cancun." Speech at the 25th Anniversary of the Foreign Trade Association, Brussels, June 5.

Laver, Michael, and John Underhill. 1994. "The Bargaining Advantages of Combining with Others." *British Journal of Political Science* 12 (July): 27–42.

Legras, Guy. 1993. "L'Uruguay Round et la réforme de la PAC." *Politique Etrangère* (Summer): 325–331.

Lewis, Jeffrey. 1998. "Is the 'Hard Bargaining' Image of the Council Misleading?" *Journal of Common Market Studies* 36(4): 479–504.

Libby, Ronald. 1992. *Protecting Markets: US Policy and the World Grain Trade*. Ithaca: Cornell University Press.

Lijphart, Arend. 1999. *Patterns of Democracy: Government Forms and Performance in Thirty-Six Countries*. New Haven: Yale University Press.

Lindberg, Leon. 1971. "Political Integration as a Multidimensional Phenomenon Requiring Multivariate Measurement." In *Regional Integration: Theory and Research*, edited by Leon Lindberg and Stuart Scheingold. Cambridge: Harvard University Press.

Lindberg, Leon, and Stuart Scheingold. 1970. *Europe's Would-Be Polity: Patterns of Change in the European Community*. Englewood Cliffs, NJ: Prentice-Hall.

———. 1971. *Regional Integration: Theory and Research.* Cambridge: Harvard University Press.

Livius, Titus, ed. 1899. *Roman History.* Translated by John Henry Freese, Alfred John Church, and William Jackson Brodribb. New York: D. Appleton and Company.

Ludlow, Peter. 1993. *EC-US Relations: Priorities for the Next Four Years.* Brussels: CEPS.

Magee, Stephen P., William A. Brock, and Leslie Young. 1989. *Black Hole Tariffs and Endogenous Policy Theory.* New York: Cambridge University Press.

Majone, Giandomenico. 1996. "Regulatory Legitimacy." In *Regulating Europe,* edited by Giandomenico Majone. London: Routledge.

March, James, and Johan Olsen. 1984. "The New Institutionalism: Organizational Factors in Political Life." *American Political Science Review* 78(3) (September): 734–749.

Maresceau, Marc. 1993. *The European Community's Commercial Policy after 1992: The Legal Dimension.* Dordrecht: Martinus Nijhoff Publishers.

Martin, Lisa L. 1992. *Coercive Cooperation: Explaining Multilateral Economic Sanctions.* Princeton: Princeton University Press.

Mayer, Frederick W. 1992. "Managing Domestic Differences in International Negotiations: The Strategic Use of Internal Side-Payments." *International Organization* 46(4) (Autumn): 793–818.

Mayhew, David. 1974. *Congress: The Electoral Connection.* New Haven: Yale University Press.

McCubbins, Mathew, and Terry Sullivan. 1987. *Congress: Structure and Policy.* New York: Cambridge University Press.

McKay, David. 2000. "Political Legitimacy and Institutional Design: Comparative Lessons for the European Union." *Journal of Common Market Studies* 38(1): 25–44.

McNamara, Kathleen R., and Sophie Meunier. 2002. "Between National Sovereignty and International Power: What External Voice for the Euro?" *International Affairs* 78(4).

de Melo, Jaime, and Arvind Panagariya. 1993. *New Dimensions in Regional Integration.* Cambridge: Cambridge University Press.

Mercer, Jonathan. 1995. "Anarchy and Identity." *International Organization* 49: 229–252.

Messerlin, Patrick. 1993. "Le Rôle du GATT et les enjeux de l'Uruguay Round." *Politique Etrangère* (Summer): 255–276.

———. 2001. *Measuring the Costs of Protection in Europe: European Commercial Policy in the 2000s.* Washington, DC: Institute for International Economics.

Meunier, Sophie. 2000a. "What Single Voice? European Institutions and EU-US Trade Negotiations." *International Organization* 54(1): 103–135.

———. 2000b. "The French Exception." *Foreign Affairs* 79(4): 104–116.

———. 2003. "Trade Policy and Political Legitimacy." *Comparative European Politics* 1(1): 67–90.

Meunier, Sophie, and Kalypso Nicolaïdis. 1999. "Who Speaks for Europe? The Delegation of Trade Authority in the European Union." *Journal of Common Market Studies* 37(3): 477–501.

Milner, Helen V. 1997. *Interests, Institutions, and Information: Domestic Politics and International Relations*. Princeton: Princeton University Press.

Milner, Helen V., and Peter Rosendorff. 1997. "Democratic Politics and International Trade Negotiations: Elections and Divided Government as Constraints on Trade Liberalization." *Journal of Conflict Resolution* 41: 117–146.

Milward, Alan. 1984. *The Reconstruction of Western Europe 1945–1951*. London: Methuen.

Mo, Jongryn. 1994. "The Logic of Two-Level Games with Endogenous Domestic Coalitions." *Journal of Conflict Resolution* 38: 402–422.

Moe, Terry. 1984. "The New Economics of Organization." *American Journal of Political Science* 28(4) (November): 739–777.

Monnet, Jean. 1978. *Memoirs*. Garden City, NY: Doubleday.

Moravcsik, Andrew. 1991. "Negotiating the Single European Act." In *The New European Community*, edited by Robert Keohane and Stanley Hoffmann. Boulder: Westview.

———.1998.*The Choice for Europe: Social Purpose and State Power from Messina to Maastricht*. Ithaca: Cornell University Press.

———. 1999. "A New Statecraft? Supranational Entrepreneurs and International Cooperation." *International Organization* 53(2): 267–306.

———. 2001. "Despotism in Brussels? Misreading the European Union." *Foreign Affairs* 80(3): 114–122.

———. 2002. "In Defence of the 'Democratic Deficit': Reassessing Legitimacy in the European Union." *Journal of Common Market Studies* 40(4): 603–624.

Moravcsik, Andrew, and Kalypso Nicolaïdis. 1998. "Federal Ideals and Constitutional Realities in the Amsterdam Treaty." *Journal of Common Market Studies*, Annual Review.

Moravcsik, Andrew, and Andrea Sangiovanni. (N.d.) "On Democracy and the Public Interest in the European Union." Manuscript.

Murphy, Anna. 1990. *The European Community and the International Trading System*. Brussels: Centre for European Policy Studies.

Newhouse, John. 1967. *Collision in Brussels: The Common Market Crisis of 30 June 1965*. New York: W. W. Norton.

Neyer, Jürgen. 2004. "Weak States in the WTO." Paper presented at the 6th ECSA-Canada Biennial Conference, Montreal, Canada.

Nicolaïdis, Kalypso. 1997. "Negotiating Mutual Recognition Agreements: A Comparative Analysis." Paper presented at the annual meeting of the American Political Science Association, Washington, DC, August 28–31.

———. 1999. "Minimizing Agency Costs in Two-Level Games: Lessons from the Trade Authority Controversies in the United States and the European Union." In *Negotiating on Behalf of Others*, edited by R. H. Mnookin et al. Thousand Oaks, CA: Sage Publications.

Nicolaïdis, Kalypso, and Robert Howse, eds. 2001. *The Federal Vision: Legitimacy and Levels of Governance in the United States and the European Union*. New York: Oxford University Press.

Nicolaïdis, Kalypso, and Sophie Meunier. 2002. "Revisiting Trade Competence in the European Union: Amsterdam, Nice and Beyond." In *Institutional Challenges in the European Union*, edited by M. Hosli and A. van Deemen. New York: Routledge.

Niejahr, Michael, and Giuseppe Abbamonte. 1996. "Liberalization Policy and State Aid in the Air Transport Sector." *EC Competition Policy Newsletter* 2(2) (Summer).

North, Douglass C. 1990. *Institutions, Institutional Change and Economic Performance*. Cambridge: Cambridge University Press.

Nye, Joseph. 1968. "Comparative Regional Integration: Concept and Measurement." *International Organization* 22(4) (Autumn): 855–880.

———. 1971. "Comparing Common Markets: A Revised Neo-Functionalist Model." In *Regional Integration: Theory and Research*, edited by Leon Lindberg and Stuart Scheingold. Cambridge: Harvard University Press.

Odell, John. 1993. "International Threats and International Politics: Brazil, the European Community, and the United States, 1985–1987." In *Double-Edged Diplomacy: International Bargaining and Domestic Politics*, edited by Peter Evans, Harold Jacobson and Robert Putnam. Berkeley: University of California Press.

O'Halloran, Sharyn. 1994. *Politics, Process, and American Trade Policy*. Ann Arbor: University of Michigan Press.

Olson, Mancur. 1965. *The Logic of Collective Action*. Cambridge: Harvard University Press.

———. 1982. *The Rise and Decline of Nations: Economic Growth, Stagflation, and Social Rigidities*. New Haven: Yale University Press.

Oye, Kenneth, ed. 1992. *Eagle in a New World: American Grand Strategy in the Post–Cold War Era*. New York: HarperCollins.

Paarlberg, Robert. 1993. "Why Agriculture Blocked the Uruguay Round: Evolving Strategies in a Two-Level Game." In *World Agriculture and the GATT*, edited by William Avery. Boulder: Lynne Riener.

Paemen, Hugo, and Alexandra Bensch. 1995. *From the GATT to the WTO: The European Community in the Uruguay Round*. Leuven, Belgium: Leuven University Press.

Pahre, Robert. 1997. "Endogenous Domestic Institutions in Two-Level Games and Parliamentary Oversight of the European Union." *Journal of Conflict Resolution* 41: 147–174.

Patterson, Lee-Ann. 1997. "Agricultural Policy Reform in the European Community: A Three-level Game Analysis." *International Organization* 51(1).

Paul, T.V. 1994. *Asymmetric Conflicts: War Initiation by Weaker Powers*. New York: Cambridge University Press.

Peterson, John and Maria Green Cowles. 1998. "Clinton, Europe and Economic Diplomacy: What Makes the EU Different?" *Governance* 11(3): 251–271.

Petersmann, Ernst-Ulrich. 1991. *Constitutional Functions and Constitutional Problems of International Economic Law: International and Domestic Foreign Trade Law and Foreign Trade Policy in the United States, the European Community and Switzerland*. Boulder: Westview Press.

Peyrefitte, Alain. 1997. *C'était de Gaulle*. Vol. 2. Paris: Editions de Fallois/Fayard.

Pierson, Paul. 1996. "The Path to European Integration: A Historical Institution-alist Analysis." *Comparative Political Studies* 29(2) (April): 123–163.

Pierson, Paul. 2000. "Increasing Returns, Path Dependence, and the Study of Poli-tics." *American Political Science Review* 94(2): 251–267.

Pollack, Mark. 1996. "The Engines of Integration? Supranational Autonomy and Influence in the European Community." Center for German and European Studies Working Paper 2.41, University of California, Berkeley.

———. 1997. "Delegation, Agency and Agenda-setting in the European Commu-nity." *International Organization* 51: 99–134.

———. 2003. *The Engines of European Integration: Delegation, Agency, and Agenda Setting in the EU.* Oxford: Oxford University Press.

Pollack, Mark, and Gregory Shaffer, eds. 2001. *Transatlantic Governance in the Global Economy.* Lanham, MD: Rowman and Littlefield.

Pratt, John W., and Richard Zeckhauser. 1991. *Principals and Agents.* Boston: Harvard Business School Press.

Preeg, Ernest H. 1970. *Traders and Diplomats: An Analysis of the Kennedy Round of Negotiations under the General Agreement on Tariffs and Trade.* Washington, DC: The Brookings Institution.

Putnam, Robert D. 1988. "Diplomacy and Domestic Politics: The Logic of Two-Level Games." *International Organization* 42: 427–460.

Rasmussen, Hjte. 1986. *On the Law and Policy in the European Court of Justice, A Comparative Study in Judicial Policy Making.* Dordrecht: Martinus Nijhoff Publishers.

Riker, William. 1980. "Implications from the Disequilibrium of Majority Rule for the Study of Institutions." *American Political Science Review* 75: 432–447.

Rogowski, Ronald. 1987. "Political Cleavages and Changing Exposure to Trade." *American Political Science Review* 81: 1121–1137.

Rosendorff, B. Peter, and Helen V. Milner. 2001. "The Optimal Design of Interna-tional Trade Institutions." *International Organization* 55(4): 829–857.

Sandholtz, Wayne, and John Zysman. 1989. "1992: Recasting the European Bar-gain." *World Politics* 42(1): 95–128.

Sbragia, Alberta M. 1997. "Institution-Building from Below and from Above: The European Community in Global Environmental Politics." Paper presented at the Fifth Biennial Meeting of the European Community Studies Association, Seattle, May 29–June 1.

Scharpf, Fritz. 1988. "The Joint-Decision Trap: Lessons from German Federalism and European Integration." *Public Administration* 66 (Autumn): 239–278.

———. 1999. *Governing in Europe: Effective and Democratic?* New York: Ox-ford University Press.

———. 2001. "European Governance: Common Concerns vs. the Challenge of Diversity." In *Symposium: Responses to the European Commission's White Paper on Governance,* edited by C. Joerges, Y. Meny and J.H.H. Weiler. Flor-ence: European University Institute.

Schelling, Thomas. 1960. *The Strategy of Conflict.* Cambridge: Harvard Univer-sity Press.

Schmitter, Philippe. 1969. "Three Neo-Functional Hypotheses about Interna-tional Integration." *International Organization* 23(1) (Winter): 161–166.

———. 2000. *How to Democratize the European Union . . . And Why Bother?* Lanham, MD: Rowman and Littlefield.

Schnattschneider, E. E. 1935. *Politics, Pressure, and the Tariff: A Study of Free Private Enterprise in Pressure Politics as Shown in the 1929–1930 Revision of the Tariff.* Hamden, CT: Archon Books.

Schott, Jeffrey. 1994. *The Uruguay Round: An Assessment.* Washington, DC: Institute for International Economics.

Shepsle, Kenneth A. 1989. "Studying Institutions: Some Lessons from the Rational Choice Approach." *Journal of Theoretical Politics* 1: 131–147.

Shonfield, Andrew. 1976. "International Economic Relations of the Western World: An Overall View." In *International Economic Relations of the Western World 1959–1971*, edited by Andrew Shonfield. London: RIIA, Oxford University Press.

Siedentop, Larry. 2001. *Democracy in Europe.* New York: Columbia University Press.

Smith, Michael. 1994. "The Commission and External Relations." In *The European Commission*, edited by G. Edwards and D. Spence. London: Longman.

Snyder, Glenn, and Paul Diesing. 1977. *Conflict among Nations: Bargaining, Decision Making, and System Structure in International Crises.* Princeton: Princeton University Press.

Staniland, Martin. 1996. "Open Skies—Fewer Planes? Public Policy and Corporate Strategy in EU-US Aviation Relations." Center for West European Studies Policy Paper no. 3, University of Pittsburgh.

Stein, Eric. 1991. "External Relations of the European Community: Structure and Process." In *Collected Courses of the Academy of European Law*, edited by Academy of European Law. Vol. 1, Book 1. Dordrecht: Kluwer Law International.

Steinmo, Sven, et al. 1992. *Structuring Politics: Historical Institutionalism in Comparative Analysis.* New York: Cambridge University Press.

Stiglitz, Joseph. 2000. "What I Learned at the World Economic Crisis." *The New Republic*, April 17.

———. 2002. *Globalization and Its Discontents.* New York: W.W. Norton.

Talbot, Ross B. 1978. *The Chicken War.* Ames: Iowa University Press.

Tarar, Ahmer. 2001. "International Bargaining with Two-Sided Domestic Constraints." *Journal of Conflict Resolution* 45(3): 320–340.

Thelen, K. 1999. "Historical Institutionalism in Comparative Politics." *Annual Review of Political Science* 2: 369–404.

Tocqueville, Alexis de. 2001 (1835). *Democracy in America.* New York: Signet Classic.

Tsebelis, George. 1994. "The Power of the European Parliament as a Conditional Agenda-Setter." *American Political Science Review* 88: 128–142.

United States General Accounting Office. 1994. "International Trade: Observations on the Uruguay Round Agreement." *Testimony before the Subcommittee on Trade, Committee on Ways and Means, House of Representatives*, February 22.

United States International Trade Commission. 1989. *The Effects of Greater Economic Integration within the European Community on the United States: Fourth Follow-up Report*. USITC 2204, July.

———. 1993. *1992: The Effects of Greater Economic Integration within the European Community on the United States: Fifth Follow-Up Report*. USITC 2628, April.

Viner, Jacob. 1950. *The Customs Union Issue*. New York: Carnegie Endowment for International Peace.

Vogel, David. 1995. *Trading Up: Consumer and Environmental Regulation in a Global Economy*. Cambridge: Harvard University Press.

Wallace, Helen. 1993. "Deepening and Widening: Problems of Legitimacy for the EC." in *European Identity and the Search for Legitimacy*, edited by S. Garcia. London: Pinter.

Walton, Richard, and Robert McKersie. 1965. *A Behavioral Theory of Labor Negotiations: An Analysis of a Social Interaction System*. New York: McGraw-Hill.

Waltz, Kenneth N. 1959. *Man, the State, and War: A Theoretical Analysis*. New York: Columbia University Press.

Warley, T. K. 1976. "Western Trade in Agricultural Products." In *International Economic Relations of the Western World 1959–1971*, edited by Andrew Shonfield. London: RIIA, Oxford University Press.

Weber, Max. 1978. *Economy and Society: An Outline of Interpretative Sociology*. Berkeley: University of California Press.

Weiler, Joseph. 1991. "The Transformation of Europe." *Yale Law Journal* 100: 2403–2483.

———. 1997. "Legitimacy and Democracy of Union Governance." in *The Politics of European Treaty Reform: The 1996 Intergovernmental Conference and Beyond*, edited by G. Edwards and A. Pijpers. London: Pinter.

Weingast, Barry, and William Marshall. 1988. "The Industrial Organization of Congress." *Journal of Political Economy* 96(1): 132–163.

Wendt, Alexander. 1994. "Collective Identity Formation and the International State." *American Political Science Review* 88: 384–396.

———. 1999. *Social Theory of International Politics*. Cambridge: Cambridge University Press.

Williams, Shirley. 1991. "Sovereignty and Accountability in the European Community." In *The New European Community: Decisionmaking and Institutional Change*, edited by R. O. Keohane and S. Hoffmann. Boulder: Westview.

Winham, Gilbert. 1979. "Practitioners' Views of International Negotiation." *World Politics* 32 (October): 111–135.

———. 1986. *International Trade and the Tokyo Round Negotiation*. Princeton: Princeton University Press.

Woolcock, Stephen. 1992. *Trading Partners or Trading Blows? Market Access Issues in EC-US Relations*. London: The Royal Institute of International Affairs.

———. 1993. "Trade Diplomacy and the European Community." In *The New Europe: Politics, Government and Economy since 1945*, edited by Jonathan Story. Oxford: Blackwell.

———. 1996. "Europe's International Trade Policy: The Policy Process under Strain." In *Policy-Making in the European Union*, edited by Helen Wallace and William Wallace. Oxford: Oxford University Press.

Woolcock, Stephen, and Michael Hodges. 1996. "EU Policy in the Uruguay Round." In *Policy-Making in the European Union*, edited by Helen Wallace and William Wallace. Oxford: Oxford University Press.

Wriggins, Howard. 1987. "Up for Auction." In *The 50% Solution: How to Bargain Successfully with Hijackers, Strikers, Bosses, Oil Magnates, Arabs, Russians, and Other Worthy Opponents in the Modern World*, edited by William Zartman. New Haven: Yale University Press.

Young, Alasdair R. 2000. "The Adaptation of European Foreign Economic Policy: From Rome to Seattle." *Journal of Common Market Studies* 38(1): 93–116.

Zartman, William. 1987. *The 50% Solution: How to Bargain Successfully with Hijackers, Strikers, Bosses, Oil Magnates, Arabs, Russians, and Other Worthy Opponents in the Modern World*. New Haven: Yale University Press.

Zeiler, Thomas W. 1992. *American Trade and Power in the 1960s*. New York: Columbia University Press.

Zürn, M. 2000. "Democratic Governance beyond the Nation-State." *Democracy Beyond the State? The European Dilemma and the Emerging Global Order*, edited by Michael Greven and Louis Pauly. Lanham, MD: Rowman and Littlefield.

Index

Page references followed by *t* indicate a table.

"Action Committee for the United States of Europe," 10

agricultural policy: Blair House agreement (1992), 112–22; diversity of EC Kennedy Round preferences on, 80–83; Franco-German disagreement over grains prices, 81–82; Kennedy Round agreements on, 87, 96–99; Kennedy Round "empty chair" crisis impact on, 35–36, 72, 87–91; Kennedy Round U.S. preferences on, 78–80; Luxembourg compromise (1996) on, 91–92; The Mansholt Plan (1964) proposal for, 85; Treaty of Rome on establishing common rules for, 76–77; U.S. poultry export issue ("Chicken War"), 77–78. *See also* CAP (Common Agricultural Policy); EU trade policy

Amsterdam summit (1997), 28–29, 37, 188

Andean Trade Preferences Act (U.S.-Bolivia-Colombia), 168

Andriessen, Frans, 112, 114, 177

article 29. *See* reciprocity clause (utilities directive)

article 113 (Treaty of Rome): Amsterdam compromise extending, 28–29, 37, 188; aviation negotiation authority claimed under, 149; competence as delegated by, 22–23; European Court of Justice opinion (1994) on, 155–56; requiring unanimous bargaining position, 87. *See also* Common Commercial Policy; Treaty of Rome (1957)

article XXIV (GATT), 6, 42

ASAs (Air Service Agreements): as "divide and rule" strategy, 150–54; European Court of Justice ruling (2002) on, 162–63; governing aviation sector, 147, 148; as threatening Commission's negotiating competence, 151–54. *See also* aviation sector; open skies agreements (1992–2003)

Austria: Amsterdam compromise position of, 29; EC request to not sign open skies agreement with U.S., 153

authority: defining negotiator, 58; dispute over negotiating aviation, 145–50; "fast-track" (now trade promotion authority), 197. *See also* efficiency vs. legitimacy issue; EU supranational trade competence

autonomy, 58, 59

aviation sector: absence of supranational competence in, 146–47; deregulation of U.S., UK, and Netherlands, 146–49; dispute over negotiating authority over, 145–50; legal rules governing, 145; moving toward supranational competence in, 154–57; "Nouvelles Frontières" ruling (1986) on competition in, 146, 147; U.S. antitrust immunity granted to international alliances in, 157. *See also* ASAs (Air Service Agreements)

Ayling, Bob, 160

Ball, George, 93

Bangemann, Martin, 130

bargaining leverage: defining, 40n.1; determinants of, 41–48, 49t; EU institutional structure and impact on, 63–70; using EU-U.S. negotiations as test cases for, 71–73; institutional integration and, 47–48; internal constraints/external strength and, 48–53; Schelling conjecture on, 50–53; taking negotiating opponent into account, 183–84; two-level games on, 51–53. *See also* EU trade policy

bargaining leverage determinants: ad hoc variables as, 46–47; institutions as, 47–48; power as, 41–44; preferences as, 44–46; summary of, 49t

bargaining parties: power of, 41–44; preferences of, 44–46; skills of individual negotiators of, 47

under, 149; international trade negotiation efficiency focus of, 23; as Kennedy
Round agricultural issue, 78–80. *See
also* article 113 (Treaty of Rome); CAP
(Common Agricultural Policy)
Common Market. *See* EEC (European Economic Community)
"Community Relations with Third
Countries in Aviation Matters" (Commission), 149
competence. *See* EU supranational trade
competence
"Components of a Strategy for the Kennedy Round" (Ball), 93
"consensus" decision making. *See* unanimity voting rule
conservative negotiating: extensive competence due to qualified majority voting,
65–66; extensive supranational competence and, 180–81; impact of EU voting
rules on, 64; Kennedy Round (1964–
1967) as example of, 18, 83; overview
of, 61–62, 63–64; restricted competence
due to unanimity voting rule, 64–65; restricted supranational competence and,
180; summary of EU's institutional structure and, 69*t*; Uruguay Round (1986–
1993) as example of, 102. *See also* negotiating context; reformist negotiating
Constitutional Convention (2002–2004), 13
constructivist approach to international relations, 45–46
COREPER (Committee of Permanent Representatives), 35
Council of Foreign Ministers, 35
Council of Ministers: internal decision-
making rules followed by, 54–57; limited
mandate for Commission aviation negotiation by, 158–61; national interests represented by, 33; proposed as open skies negotiator, 149; trade negotiating mandate
role of, 35–37; transfer of trade competence to Commission from, 22, 33–39,
191–92
Cresson, Edith, 130
customs union theory, 42

"decouplage" of negotiations (1964), 84,
86, 87, 97
de Gaulle, Charles, 11, 35, 72, 84, 88, 89,
91, 175, 177
delegation of competence, 57–59
Deloitte and Touche, 140

Delors, Jacques, 110, 111, 135, 149
Delta/Sabena/Austrian partnership, 157
"democratic deficit," 188–90
Denmark, 153
Deutsch, Karl, 46
DG Trade (Brussels), 34–35
Dillon Round (1960–1962), 75
"divide and rule" strategy: domino effect
of, 151–54; focus on small states as part
of, 150–51
Doha Development Round (2001), 4, 32–33
domestic preferences, 173–75
Dunkel, Arthur, 107
Dunkel Draft (1991), 107

EC (European Community): description of,
47–48n.17; "empty chair" crisis of, 35–
36, 72, 88–92; Kennedy Round objectives of, 80–84; Uruguay Round (1986–
1993) objectives during, 103–6; utilities
directive/reciprocity clause (1990)
adopted by, 63, 127, 130. *See also*
EU (European Union); Single European
Market
EC-U.S. agricultural negotiations. *See* Kennedy Round (1964–1967); Uruguay
Round agricultural negotiations (1986–
1993)
EC-U.S. public procurement negotiations.
See Government Procurement Agreement
(1994); Uruguay Round public procurement negotiations (1990–1994)
EEC (European Economic Community): Atlantic Common Market as proposed alternative to, 91; Common Commercial
Policy of, 6, 23; French veto of UK entry
into, 76; Kennedy Round and U.S. reaction to, 75–76; legality under GATT
rule, 5, 6; pooling international representation by, 5; "third force" dangers associated with creation of, 12; U.S. policy to
prevent expansion of, 76
efficiency vs. legitimacy issue: EU's response to the, 194–96; examining trade
policy, 187–88; institutional rules and
trade policy, 190–94; legitimacy debate
in trade policy, 188–90; lesson learned
from EU's, 196–200. *See also* authority
electoral cycles, 174–75
"empty chair" crisis: background of, 87–
88; impact on Kennedy Round, 89–91;
Luxembourg compromise ending, 91–
92; origins of, 35–36, 88–89; U.S.